MW01613397

THE MARCH OF FOLLY
IN AFGHANISTAN
1978–2001

The March of Folly in Afghanistan
1978–2001

JAGAT S. MEHTA

MANOHAR
2002

First published 2002

© Jagat S. Mehta, 2002

ISBN 81-7304-461-9

Published by
Ajay Kumar Jain for
Manohar Publishers & Distributors
4753/23 Ansari Road, Daryaganj
New Delhi 110 002

Typeset at
Digigrafics
New Delhi 110 049

Printed at
Lordson Publishers Pvt. Ltd.
Delhi 110 007

With gratitude to
Vijay, Vikram, Ajay and Uday
for their indulgence and affection
to a single parent since 1978

Contents

Preface and Acknowledgements

I confess to a sense of exceptional good fortune at the privileged
opportunities which came my way as a member of the Foreign
Service of India. By happenstance from the first day after the transfer
of power in 1947 and through more than three subsequent decades,
I found myself frequently in close proximity to policy making on
critical developments which beset our external relations. For
example as Foreign Secretary, I was with Prime Minister Mrs Indira
Gandhi and later with Atal Behari Vajpayee when he was Foreign
Minister during their visits to Kabul just before and after the Saur
Revolution. Although my insights on Afghanistan began in the South
Block, as this compilation will show, my anxious concern at the
developments continued for the next two decades after my
retirement. In 1981 as an Associate at the Harvard Centre for
International Affairs, I expressed my fears at the prospect of the
remilitarization of the subcontinent in the *New York Times*. It
was as a Fellow at the Woodrow Wilson Centre for Scholars in
Washington in 1982 that I made a detailed study and urged a
'Solution in Afghanistan: From Swedenization to Finlandization'. In
the customary fashion of the Centre, the paper was discussed at a
lunchtime seminar and was adopted and circulated by the Kennan
Institute of Advanced Russian Studies. Charles Maynes, the then
editor of *Foreign Policy*, who was one of the regular visitors to the
centre, urged me to write a shortened version which was published
in the Summer issue of 1982. I continued with my anxious interest in
Afghanistan when I was Professor at the LBJ School of Public Affairs
at the University of Texas in Austin. The Centres of European,
Middle Eastern and Asian Studies jointly asked me to organize a
conference on the Lesson and Legacy of Afghanistan in 1989.
However, the table of contents will show that only half the papers
were written in the United States; the others were put together in
India.

The intellectual inspiration, indeed the title of this book, borrows
unashamedly from Barbara Tuchman's *The March of Folly*. Soon
after its publication in 1984, it was on the bestseller list of non-

fiction books in the *New York Times*. Those familiar with the book will recall that her theme was, that throughout history, regardless of place or period, there was no field of human activity which showed a greater propensity of erroneous judgements as governmental decision-making. Folly, she defined, was when less damaging alternatives were known and available, but countries acted contrary to their own self-interest. She illustrated the thesis by four detailed studies: The first was how, after months of siege, when the Greeks having failed to rescue Helen, Troy was tricked into dragging the monstrously large wooden horse (with armed soldiers inside) into the walled city and this eventually led to the defeat of the Trojans. The second is a description of the myopic perspectives of the Renaissance Popes in not foreseeing that their rivalry and factionalism would destroy the universality of the Catholic church. In the third case, she describes how in the eighteenth century, a succession of coercive instead of conciliatory measures by London led to the loss of Britain's North American colonies. In the last case, she details how, in the 1960s, overlooking reason and experience, the United States betrayed itself by impetuous involvement and suffered defeat in Vietnam. When I was teaching a course to graduate students at the LBJ School on Misperception in Diplomacy, although I varied the choice of subjects every year, the *March of Folly* was always high on recommended reading list.

I was with the government in 1978 when the Saur Revolution erupted. Being concerned at the potentially serious damage to India's interests and the then subsisting regional harmony, I took some prophylactic steps, which are described for the first time, in the introduction. The purpose was to forestall the possible militirazation of the subcontinent. At the end of 1979 I was no more in the decision-making hierarchy; however it was obvious to me that the Soviet intervention and the alarm of the United States in President Carter's White House and the subsequent reinforcing the containment of the Evil Empire when Reagen assumed office in 1981 were wholly misconceived; the reactions in India and Pakistan at the Soviet invasions were also based on misreading the situation. The destruction of Afghanistan, the present stand-off between India–Pakistan can be traced back, step by step, to the compounding misjudgements by USSR, USA, India and Pakistan. One cannot help noticing that all these countries are now inclined to selective amnesia about their own share of guilt at the tragic developments, which eventually culminated in many catastrophes including Kargil and

9/11. For example it is seldom recalled that the Islamic fundamentalists were brought trained and inducted by the CIA; the Talibans were recruited by Pakistan and India betrayed the Pathans by abstaining from condemning the invasion. The whole tragic story is a case study in Folly. It is here urged that the lesions of history should have been more carefully digested; enlightened approaches should have been adopted to the resolution of Afghanistan; even now India and Pakistan have a common interest in harmonizing their cooperation. The United States and the International Community must face terror imaginatively not simply or primarily as a military problem but as a new dimension to security and governance in the new century.

A further clarification about this collection of papers might be offered. It was never planned as a book. These articles were written over a period of nearly two decades under different circumstances as adhoc pieces. Each had its own context; inevitably there are repetitions of arguments, analysis and even phrases. What binds it together is the lively sense of hazard implicit in the ongoing strife in Afghanistan. In the essay for the *Foreign Policy Annual* written at the request of Professor Satish Kumar of Jawaharlal Nehru University in 1986, I find I had said, 'Afghanistan has been about the worst case of intellectual failures, false judgements and misperceptions on the part of all countries. India's failure has been particularly unfortunate and unnecessary.' The volume contains, in chronological order, 16 pieces written between 1981 and 1997. The outlines of the solution which I first recommended in the Kennan Institute paper were summarized for the *Indian Express* 1982 elaborated in the *Foreign Policy Annual* in 1986 and again in the keynote address for the conference held in Austin in 1989. The running purpose in all of them was to create conditions which would assuage Soviet apprehensions for its security and so enable the withdrawal of its forces and, permit Afghanistan to revert to its traditional introverted normalcy. I must have attended a score of conferences updating the variant of my recommendations. The present compilation will inevitably invite impatience at repetitions which could be rationally amalgamated. However, the broad thesis behind this volume is that contemporaneous misjudgements were avoidable. Though not foreseen in the shape they took, the blowback nemesis for the subcontinent and the ascendancy of terror as a world problem was the result of original misperceptions. To avoid the charge of hindsight wisdom, beyond editorial corrections, the papers and articles have been left to stand without any substantive changes. I do however, apologize for the infliction of tedious stagnant thoughts running through the essays.

There is one further underlying theme which I hope gives an element of running coherence to the compilation. Accurate anticipation is the key to professionalism in diplomacy. There is, of course, always risk, even in broad predictions, but if professionals shirk from the courage of bold analysis, diplomacy would have no better rationale than historians and invite the mockery of after-the-event wisdom from political as well as public opinion. We may not always prove right but that is no justification for hesitation in projection or yielding to prevailing populism at the counseling stage.

I want to use this preface to thank Shri Ramesh and Ajay Jain, the publishers and the Editor Shri B.N. Varma at Manohar. It was Rameshji who suggested I put together the articles, supplementing them only with an introduction and a winding up conclusion on the implications of 9/11 for the future. I have no doubt that the editorial refinements have eliminated many of my grammatical howlers and semantic errors: the flaws of substance are of course, my own.

This preface would not be complete if I did not acknowledge, with gratitude, the encouragement and help which I received from many in Udaipur. Molly Abraham of Seva Mandir was always willing and cheerful in giving secretarial assistance. For many years she suffered my illustrating one of Professor Kenneth Galbraith's aphorisms. 'It is only in the seventeenth draft that I get spontaneity'. This I know is not true of his voluminous writings but very much approximates to my plodding work style. During the last year, my efforts were also facilitated by Sultan Singhji Bolia. His old-fashioned work ethics are rare these days. Similarly it was by happenstance that I tumbled to the editorial skill of my niece Tushita Lodha, who carefully went through the first galley proofs even while she was doing house keeping and helping her husband with the management of his business. I cannot overlook mention of Aftab, aged 10, a computer buff from Vidya Bhawan, who is such an expert in Internet surfing that he located, within half an hour, any information, however obscure, sought by me.

Finally I wish to thank Nilima Khetan in Seva Mandir and Riaz Tehsin in Vidya Bhawan and through them the whole fellowship around both institutions who have been my 'backslappers' in encouraging my scribbling. There are, no doubt, handicaps of inadequate libraries and limited intellectual interaction in trying to attempt informed analysis from a medium sized township in Rajasthan, but it is more than compensated by affection and friendship and the support system one finds only in one's hometown. This enables one to combine a little intellectual hobby-horsing with modest social activism.

31 December 2001 J.S. MEHTA

1

Introduction

The Crisis Began in 1978

Photo opportunity has become a ritual feature of modern diplomacy; we flaunt having been in close proximity not just to national leaders but also international figures like Mao tse-Tung, Ho-Chi-Minh, Leonid Brezhnev, Jimmy Carter, etc., whose names are expected to leave an imprint on history. While to have been near moral icons like the Dalai Lama and Mother Teresa makes one feel truly privileged, there were also others like Idi Amin with whom one had to shake hands and negotiate as part of one's professional duties. The keeping of photographs of such people justify my calling the whole lot as 'the rogues gallery'! On the wall of my house, there was only one photo frame with three photographs in it, all taken in Kabul with successive Presidents of Afghanistan. The photograph on the left taken in 1976, when, as Foreign Secretary, I happen to be sitting with Mrs Indira Gandhi, who is facing Mohammed Daud, the then President of the country; the one in the middle is with Noor Mohammed Taraki and was taken in June 1978 when I had rushed to Kabul after the Saur Revolution and the Democratic Republic of Afghanistan had been proclaimed; in the third, taken some months later, I am sitting with Hafizullah Amin who had appropriated power and embarked on turning Afghanistan, overnight, into an imitation Leninist utopia. The reason why I put them in one frame is because, within just three years, each of these Presidents had died, not peacefully in bed but by bullets fired in anger by fellow Afghans. All three were players and victims in a compounding crisis, which enveloped a brave country, inhabited by a people with an unmatchable capacity of defiance and an unremitting code of vendetta and sacrifice. Afghanistan has been in turmoil ever since and the return to normalcy even almost a quarter century later remains uncertain. The tragedy is traceable only partly to the folly of these Afghan leaders; it was hugely complicated by the ebb and flow of interventions by 'foreign friends' bringing their subjective mindsets and false fears but leaving a trail of misery and devastation.

The crisis in Afghanistan began on my watch as Foreign Secretary. There were other stalemated problems involving difficult negoti-ations to which I was pitch-forked, but in this case, I was as it were, 'Present at the Creation' in 1978. I took some initiatives in pro-phylactic diplomacy (described later) but I was out of the loop of decision-making by November 1979. By the 1990s, after impetuous blundering involvement, the superpowers had withdrawn from Afghanistan and shifted the focus of their attention to developments in Europe, détente, the fallout of Tien-an-men Square in China and consequently the ongoing bloody civil strife inside Afghanistan disappeared off the international radar screen. The suicidal attack on the twin towers of World Trade Center in the New York and the Pentagon on 11 September 2001 put Afghanistan back at the centre stage of global concern. It jolted the United States and raised the question whether the scourge of terrorism would shatter the safety and security of all legitimately constituted governments: indeed whether the twenty-first century would pose a novel threat to the enmeshed modern civilization itself.

One can understand the anger and the agony of US public opinion at the innocent deaths of over 3,000 lives and the demand for an unforgiving hunt for Osama-bin-Laden, the arch culprit, and the launching of a search and smother operations against his Al-Queda associates. The US President has called it a 'war' and pledged to fight the menace of terrorism everywhere and persist, however, long it takes. The consequences of '9/11' (as it is now encapsulated) are going to be complex. I will address myself to the problem in the last chapter entitled 'Human Bombs Attack America: The World After 9/11'. This chapter and the last were written after the attacks of 11 September 2001. If India along with other well-motivated countries is to help restore Afghanistan to independent viability and exorcise terrorism from the world, we must acknowledge that in the past, all of us—notably USSR, USA, Pakistan, India—have contrib-uted to the horrific consequences. In this introduction, the purpose is to recount how I saw the problem when it first confronted me long before 11 September 2001. Being schooled in the old fashioned norms of Civil Service ethics, I have not publicized my role in the brief initial period when I had an official dog collar round my neck and had the right to squeak in the decision-making process but now, after a lapse of 20 years, the new international concern persuades me to recapitulate my experience and approach as it might have some useful insights in grasping the origin and the dimensions of the current crisis around Afghanistan and evolve a strategy to meet the enormity of the challenge.

The Unexpected Saur Revolution (1978) and Prophylactic Initiatives

As I had mentioned in the keynote paper for the conference at the University of Texas in 1989, the Soviet Ambassador, Yuri Voronstov, happened to be sitting with me in my room in the Ministry of External Affairs on 27 April 1978 when, on an internal telephone, I received the report that President Daud, his family and the entire cabinet, which was in session, had been gunned down that morning and that Noor Mohammed Taraki, the leader of the Khalq faction, along with some others from the Parcham, had assumed power in Kabul. I conveyed the gist of what I had heard to the Soviet Ambassador and watched his reactions. He looked surprised and, while not discounting his ability to conceal what he knew, at least I got convinced that the Saur Revolution had not been masterminded in the Kremlin. (My judgement remained unchanged, even after, not unexpectedly, many in the West thought it was proof of planned Communist expansionism.) In the previous decade and particularly since 1973 when King Zahir was deposed, Afghanistan had faced growing economic problems and political disaffection. Daud had oscillated for financial and functional support from Brezhnev's Russia, the Shah in Iran, Mrs Gandhi in India and Bhutto in Pakistan. The different intelligence agencies must have continued to be active 'doing their thing', at times stretching beyond the approved limits of their government's policy, but I was persuaded that neither America nor Russia nor any other neighbour expected the dramatic and brutal development which transpired on that April morning. In 1978 Afghanistan was not high on the international agenda but I feared there could be knee-jerk interpretations, which could damage the prevailing satisfactory India–Pakistan relations. It was under Mrs Gandhi's leadership in May 1976 that I had negotiated the most comprehensive normalization of relations with Pakistan restoring civil, air, road and rail links with a commitment to complete the entire process within 8 weeks. This had a positive welcoming impact on public opinions in both countries. It had been endorsed by the successor Janata government, giving it bipartisan legitimacy and strength. This had got further reinforced only two months earlier in the spectacular and unforeseen success of the visit of Foreign Minister A.B. Vajpayee to Islamabad and Lahore.

I must digress to affirm that it had long been my professional conviction that the optimization of India's enlightened interests and security hinged on combining defensive vigilance with positively purported diplomacy with our contiguous neighbours. Relations with the rest of the world, including the superpowers, could have their independent ups and downs in the context of particular developments, but they too were more likely to fall into place if relations with our neighbours were free of serious misunderstanding. Over the decades we have had experience of provocations and malevolence which deflected our efforts even when our motivations were transparently sincere but the big powers have certainly, even if unintentionally, contributed to exasperate our problems. My own conviction and vision has remained unsullied! Our diplomacy has not infrequently and at times too readily, degenerated into the habit of complaint and becoming content with public relations to gratify domestic political opinion. The developments in Afghanistan, I felt, were a challenge to try to insulate against the entrenched hypnosis traceable to the Cold War, which could lead to India–Pakistan problems being recoupled with the persisting mutual paranoia of the superpowers. With the approval of the Prime Minister and Foreign Minister I saw it as an opportunity to take initiatives at damage control through prophylactic diplomacy.

On 28 April 1978—the morning after the Saur Revolution, I called the Acting High Commissioner of Pakistan (Abdus Sattar, the High Commissioner was not in Delhi) and told him that India had recognized the new government in Afghanistan, as in our view, it appeared to be effectively in control but our position should not be misunderstood in Islamabad. While expressing flattering confidence in the judgement of the Pakistan Foreign Office and notably my old colleague and friend, Agha Shahi with objectivity, I said it was conceivable that some media analysts may speculate that, on the basis of Indo–Soviet Treaty, singly or jointly, India may take advantage of the assumption of power in Kabul by a government sympathetic to Soviet Union. I told the Acting High Commissioner that there should be no such apprehension. For emphasis I added that I would extend a unilateral assurance of a kind never before volunteered by India, that not a single company of troops would be added to the present deployment on India–Pakistan frontier. In due course in its own way, Pakistan should be able to confirm that this was not a deceptive assurance.

The following day I called Ambassador Goheen of the United States, and after informing him of our decision to recognize the new government in Kabul, cautioned him that US should not repeat the mistake made a quarter century ago, when in 1954 disregarding the local nature of problems and regional tensions, United States accepted Pakistan as a military ally in the Baghdad Pact (later CENTO) and SEATO in the pursuit of its policy of containment of Communism and started the process of military aid to the country. Eleven years later US recognized that the arms supplied were, in fact, abused—as we had always feared they would—against India. The arms aid to Pakistan was stopped but in the 1950s and 1960s, it had cast a shadow on India–US relations. The stoppage of military aid in 1965 had incidentally disappointed Pakistan as it thought it enjoyed full discretion in the use of the arms gifted to Pakistan. I told him of the assurance I had volunteered to Pakistan to allay any suspicions of Soviet Union and India planning a pincer to dismember Pakistan. I added that with American satellites circling the skies, the US could verify this voluntarily offered commitment.

Soon afterwards, in fact in May 1978 itself, Agha Shahi, the Foreign Minister of Pakistan did go to Washington and pleaded for the resumption of arms aid in view of the Leftist complexion of the new government in Kabul. Specifically, I believe he requested for A-7s—a sophisticated subsonic strike aircraft. The US government point blank turned down the request; in fact it declined to supply any military hardware to Pakistan. This may well be the only occasion when, figuratively and literally, a green flag (in this case of Afghanistan) had changed into red and even though the Cold War was still the currency of international politics, that the United States refused to respond to the argument of the danger of Communist expansionism. When subsequently I happened to be on a visit to Washington, I was informally told by Harold Saunders, who was then the Assistant Secretary for the Middle East and South Asia, that he had privately advised Agha Shahi to go to France and buy Mirages but for its part, the Carter administration had decided to keep aloof from the militarization of South Asia. It gave me satisfaction as a proof of positive intent in preempting the militarization of the subcontinent through sensitive anticipatory diplomacy. (Of course the credit must also go to Cyrus Vance, Harold Saunders, Ambassador Goheen and others.)

We, in the ministry, knew about this welcome development but departing from the usual pattern of leaking it to the press, I decided we must not crow about it. In the following months, I made it a practice of periodically meeting Abdus Sattar, the Pakistan High Commissioner, and exchanging with him information in our possession with theirs on the developments, including on the growing insurgency and factional rivalry in Afghanistan. This preserved mutual confidence and India–Pakistan relations did not deteriorate, at least not for the next year and half. A few months later at a meeting of the Foreign Ministers held in Belgrade, when Pakistan's request to join the Non-aligned fraternity came up, on behalf of India I raised no objection to Pakistan's admission. India won plaudits from Saudi Arabia, the Arab countries and other member nations, who were generally hesitant when called upon to take positions on India–Pakistan problems.

The United States, of course, kept a vigilant watch on developments in Afghanistan but even in the face of increasingly strident anti-American propaganda, the diplomatic relations were not broken nor was the ongoing aid programme interrupted. In February 1979, there was a setback when Adolphe Dubs, the Ambassador, was kidnapped by some fundamentalists and even in the face of cautionary advice by an American official, the Afghan constabulary impetuously stormed the hotel room and the Ambassador was killed. The rescue was, no doubt, bungled but the intentions of the authorities in Kabul were not questioned and US did not wholly cold shoulder the Democratic Republic of Afghanistan.

After the Saur Revolution, the USSR of course had started providing generously arms, economic aid and advisers to support the fledgling Socialist State but it was only in response to requests; the decisions were taken in Kabul not in Moscow. Through 1978 and till the Spring of 1979, there was steady Soviet support for the Afghan government led by Hafizullah Amin, in the hope, that notwithstanding some tribal disaffection which first erupted in distant Nuristan, the gratuitous extension of the Socialist Commonwealth will consolidate itself and the insurgency will be effectively managed. Moscow, however, got a shock in March 1979 when units of the Afghan army mutinied, joined the Mujahidin and killed many Soviet advisers in Herat. But even then Western manipulations were not suspected and Afghanistan did not cast a long shadow on international and regional politics.

Ill-conceived Soviet Invasion and
Misperceived Reactions

During this period the lessons of history, gleaned in the Great Game were not outraged. After the shameful defeats in the First (1839-42) and the Second (1878-80) Afghan Wars, both the British and Czarist Imperialism had come to recognize that 'strict neutrality and non-intervention was best in Afghanistan'. One notices there is a convenient analytical amnesia about this period of the 20 months in 1978-9 when restraint was wisely exercised by all countries. What followed in December 1979 and January 1980 was, however, striking in contrast; the sagacity and objectivity of the previous year evaporated and exaggerated alarm and misapprehensions took over.

I was removed from the post of Foreign Secretary on 19 November 1979 and so was out of the decision-making loop when the Soviet intervention took place on 25 December. Most Indian analysts accepted the official Soviet explanation that it was to pre-empt a CIA conspiracy which was being hatched by the United States. In the paper written at the Kennan Institute in 1981-2, I may have been the first to describe that the Soviet Union found itself on the horns of a terrible dilemma. The USSR found that the advent of socialism was alienating a people previously friendly to the Soviet Union: that the advance of ideology had actually jeopardized Soviet security. After months of moderating counsel had proved infructuous and a conspiracy was planned in Moscow with Taraki (when he was on his way back from Non-aligned Summit in Havana), in which the USSR decided to 'eliminate' the pro-Soviet ideologue, Hafizullah Amin. When that attempt failed, Soviet Union became concerned that a disenchanted and 'orphaned' Amin, still in control of the levers of power, could do a 'Sadat' and switch allegiance to the West. When Amin suddenly came to recognize that Soviets were disenchanted with him, he then donned born-again nationalist colours. He re-opened mosques, released imprisoned nationalists and withdrew or eased the enforcement of his earlier radical decrees. Forgetting his original plea for Pakhtunistan, Amin invited Agha Shahi, the Pakistan Foreign Minister to Kabul in December 1979. Agha Shahi's plane, however, could not land in Kabul because of bad weather. (Many years later when I met Agha Shahi with Shah Nawaz in

New York, he told me that he was really baffled when he received this surprising gesture from Amin and I told him of the failed coup in the middle of September which had disillusioned him and precipitated the effort to wrench himself free from faith in the friendship with the Soviet Union.) The Soviets certainly blundered in the massive invasion, grossly underestimating the damage to its own international political standing. It was only further compounded by the propaganda rationalization that Amin had always been an agent of the CIA. The point, however, is that even in contemporaneous judgement, it could be perceived that the Soviet invasion was defensive in intent and local in scope.

The American reaction was equally intemperate and misguided. One presumes the White House ignored the evidence, fairly well-known at the time in diplomatic circles in Kabul including to Archer Blood (whom I met in Delhi on his return from Kabul) that the Soviet action was in response to internal security perceptions only. The White House misjudgement was of course, partly explained by conditioned Cold War reflexes but it was also because of the coincidence with wholly extraneous developments in next-door Iran. In November 1979—only some weeks before the Soviet intervention—the American embassy in Tehran had been stormed and some 40 members of the mission taken hostage. This had unhinged the cool of the Carter administration, which as late as December 1977 had consecrated the Shah as the regional gendarme of vital American interests. In this nervous mood, Soviet Union was misperceived as aiming at realizing Peter the Great's seventeenth century ambition for a warm water port and of throttling the oil artery and so strategically emasculating the United States. The Soviet action was declared 'as the greatest threat to World peace since World War II'. As a knee jerk response, the Carter doctrine to defend the Gulf was promulgated; a Rapid Reaction Force was constituted, and progress towards SALT-II, the promised sale of food grain worth millions to the Soviet Union and participation in the Olympics were all summarily reversed.

It was similarly the coincidence of extraneous factors, this time domestic, which led to the serious misjudgement by India. During the campaign for the general election through November and December 1979, Mrs Gandhi had refuted the Janata government's claim of success in foreign policy: if re-elected, she said, she would restore good relations with the Soviet Union. (In fact they had not been diluted but such distortion was understandable in electioneering.) The election manifesto embodied a needless commitment to recognize the Vietnam dominated Heng Samrin government with pro-Soviet inclination which had been installed in Kampuchea. (This incidentally laid the seeds of India's alienation from the ASEAN, which took 15 years to repair.) Mrs Gandhi was declared elected on 3 January 1980 with a thumping majority. This was only nine days after the Soviet Union had invaded Afghanistan. Hoisted by her election pledges and some ill-considered advice, she authorized the modification of the approach suggested by India's permanent representative to the UN (Brajesh Mishra) and the delegation was instructed to abstain from condemning Soviet Union. In the process of demonstrating our fidelity 'to the time tested friendship' probably never explicitly solicited by the Soviet Union, we betrayed the fundamentals of Non-aligned principles. By our vote we found ourselves not only in a small minority in the international community but we estranged from ourselves the long-standing equation with the Pathans and the mainstream Afghan nationalists. Later diplomatically to Gromyko, the Soviet Foreign Minister, when he visited Delhi and publicly during her own visit to Saudi Arabia, Mrs Gandhi did urge that the Soviet Union should withdraw its forces from Afghanistan but the voting was over and for the next 10 years, the pattern of abstaining remained unchanged and so India never regained credibility with the Afghan people or the embarrassment of being isolated from the bulk of the international community.

India's voting and reaction was a fatal mistake, as it played straight into the hands of hostile elements and agencies in Pakistan, which were quick to capitalize on their own contrasting sympathy for the Afghans. In any case Pakistan had the advantage of a shared frontier and common Pashtun ethnicity. Pakistan went on to provide asylum and succor to the refugees who started streaming into Pakistan (and from which the future Talibans were going to be recruited). The expectation was cherished by Pakistan that Western aid will follow anti-Soviet sentiments. It only became a flood of arms and economic aid after Reagan came to power in 1981, but this time Pakistan felt confident that with Russians on the Khyber, it will not be summarily terminated. While the initial offer of aid of US $ 400 million by Carter was dismissed as peanuts, the sanctions were immediately lifted and the policy of ostracizing Pakistan was reversed.

Attempt at Damage Control following the
Quadrilateral of Misperceptions

It was a quadrilateral of misperceptions with each misjudgement compounding the adverse consequences for Afghanistan. The Soviet impetuosity, the false American alarm, the unprincipled Indian defection from Non-alignment and Pakistan clutching to the hope that this would eventually lead to a semi-permanent support of an old military ally were all to prove false and ill-conceived. All these misjudgements could be traced to the intellectual hold of the Cold War mindsets and the discounting of the Afghan personality, as reflected in history. The United States, India and Pakistan, from their respective rationales, seemed to share the fear that the Soviet Union and the US would clash in a hot war around South Asia. When in office I must have told Ambassador Goheen and other envoys accredited to Delhi many times that the Soviet Union had no intention of throttling the oil artery because they knew it would be a *cassius bellum* to a new World War with consequences as serious as overwhelming West Berlin, Nuclear disarmament and détente had an inexorable logic, which could be delayed, but could not be denied. Although in January 1980 I was no longer Foreign Secretary but I was so gravely alarmed at the potential adverse consequences, particularly after our abstaining vote in the General Assembly that I considered it my professional duty to put my worry to the decision makers and those close to policy making. What follows I have hinted but never before made fully public.

I took the initiative to seek an interview with the Prime Minister Mrs. Gandhi but I received no indication of her willingness to receive me. On the basis of some malevolent advice, she is supposed to have held it against me, that having been appointed Foreign Secretary by her, I had continued with zest to serve the successor Janata government. (Her advisers did not tell her that, as it happened, I had negotiated more agreements in one year's overlap during her tenure than in two and half years for the Janata government and anyway more than any other officer. In any case as a pexmanent civil servant my policy recommendations had remained unaltered.) Having failed to see the PM, I called on the new Foreign Minister Narsimha Rao and he in turn asked me to see my successor Ram Sathe who of course was an old friend. To both of them I recalled the initiative which government had taken in 1978 after the Saur Revolution and so by pre-emptive diplomacy, we had assuaged the possible false alarm in Pakistan and cautioned US not to 'revive tensions' by resuming military aid to Pakistan. Sathe said further developments and specifically the impending visit of Lord Carrington on behalf of the European Union and Clark Clifford from the United States were awaited but he did not share the urgency and magnitude of my concern. In the middle of January, on the occasion of the visit of Mr Narsimhan who was then Under-Secretary-General in the UN, at a luncheon in his honour hosted by R. Venkataraman, the future President of India, I met, for the first time, A.R. Antulay then General Secretary of the Congress Committee (later Chief Minister of Maharashtra) who was known to be influential in the party hierarchy. Antulay seemed to have had some regard for me and invited me to his house in Pandara Road to discuss the policy approach on Afghanistan, which had aroused great public concern in India. I visited Antulay on three evenings and on each occasion, I had long conversations, once lasting up to midnight when I repeated to him the urgency of prophylactic diplomacy so that the subcontinent did not once again get riddled by rivalry of super powers based on false premises. He promised to speak to the PM, and if possible, to arrange a meeting with her.

When I heard nothing from him, in the third week of January I went to see B.K. Nehru who was then staying with his brother in Maharani Bagh. I took with me a two-page note arguing the importance for India to correct the prevailing misperceptions, which was likely to cast an ugly shadow on our economy and foreign policy. I told him that in view of the prospective meeting of the Foreign Ministers of the Islamic countries, announced to be held in Islamabad before the end of January, urgent steps were called for to keep the subcontinent Non-aligned. Unless Indian diplomacy showed that we were not rejoicing at the action of the Soviet intervention, the Muslim world will get confirmed in the old prejudice against India. B.K. Nehru (who alas passed away only recently) was one of the most distinguished and wisest of civil servants of post-independence India. He belonged to the Nehru family and was the uncle of the Prime Minster. For almost the whole of my career, he had shown affectionate indulgence towards me. I speculated in my note that if prompt diplomatic action was not taken, the subcontinent could soon have to bear a new burden of US $ 20 billion due to a competitive arms race. He read my note carefully and was inclined to agree with its thrust that if we did not take preventive action, grave economic and political damage would follow. I pleaded with 'Bijju Bhai', as one called him informally, that he alone could go and speak to the Prime Minister but he kept silent. The sum and substance of my advice in these conversations and pleas was that considering the possible consequences and penalties, India should express disapproval of the Soviet intervention. We knew that the Soviet action was not aggressive in intent but it was nevertheless misguided and contrary to the cherished Non-aligned principles. The alarm was unjustified and would adversely affect the subcontinent when the climate of relations, specially between India and Pakistan, had greatly improved. I repeatedly emphasized that it was in our national interest by timely diplomatic overtures to prevent the remilitarization of Pakistan. Some time later when my fears seemed to be coming true, I happened to ask 'Bijju Bhai' why, of all people, he hesitated to volunteer advice to the Prime Minister, he told me that he did not want to risk arguments with other inmates close to Mrs Gandhi in her official residence at Safdarjang Road. It is, of course, now a futile speculation but if only we had stuck to our Non-aligned guns, India's international standing and economy at home might well have been spectacularly stronger. The extent and details can be disputed but it can scarcely be gainsaid that we lost immeasurably by departing from our own principles.

Scholarly Misjudgements with a Few Exceptions

In the 1980s, in addition to the heaped diplomatic misjudgements, most scholarly analyses were equally far fetched and compounded the misperceptions. Most Western analyses—some of these are listed in the bibliography at the end of the book—reinforced the contention that the Soviet invasion of Afghanistan was a move on the strategic chessboard to establish a long-lasting Soviet tourniquet on the vital oil supply to the West and Japan and in any case the red flag over the country would never retreat. I have seen only some of the books but, in retrospect, the merit of most is only as historical fiction. The mindsets of the Cold War had remained embedded even when it was plainly waning in intensity. There was also a *Schadenfreude* satisfaction in Soviet defeats in the encounters and corresponding praise for the Afghan Mujahidins. Among the exceptions of books brought out more or less contemporaneously is one by Louis Dupree, the scholar emeritus on Afghanistan. He was in Kabul at the time of the Saur Revolution and thought that Daud and his cabinet were killed and his government removed by a series of accidents. (I met Dupree in Delhi in 1978-9 but, at that time he did not expect that the Soviet Union wanted to occupy the country). He wrote epilogues to the reprints of his book first published in 1977 and finally in January 1980.[1] The book and the supplements provide the most detailed description of Afghanistan's history, culture and politics and gave the first description of the rise of Mujahidin groups after the Saur Revolution. He was the first to hint at the Soviet disenchantment with Hafizullah Amin and Amin's desparate effort to regain the support of the disaffected tribal leaders prior to the Soviet invasion. Perhaps more interesting in retrospect are the Field Staff Reports, written after he left the country where he perceptively describes the hold of Islam and the Soviet fear of fundamentalist contagion spreading to the Soviet Central Asian Republics. Dupree, however, came to believe that Soviets having intervened, their presence was permanent. He has passed away and this is a tragedy for contemporary insights on Afghanistan.

The book jointly authored by Diego Cordovez and Selig Harrison *Out of Afghanistan*[2] has special value but it only came out in 1995. It has a detailed review of the developments after King Zahir Shah was deposed in 1973, the political oscillations of Daud between the neighbouring capitals and developments in Kabul prior to the Soviet intervention. The authors also conclude that the Soviets accidentally stumbled into Afghanistan. The authors describe the policy conflicts between the hawkish American 'bleeders' and the diplomatically inclined 'dealers' and the difference in the perspectives of the State Department, CIA, and the Pentagon. It is also revealing how many American Cold War warriors wanted to fight Soviet Union to the last Afghan! The authors, using KGB records now available, show that there were parallel differences between Soviet agencies in Moscow as there were in Washington. In Pakistan also, there were Islamic 'hawks' and realistic doves. The authors confirm how Zia-ul-Haq managed to manipulate the USA through direct contact with Casey, the Director of CIA and did so, at times, behind the back of Yaqub Khan, the then Foreign Minister. It was Zia, who developed the strategic vision of a Pak–Afghan confederation to give the country depth in defence. Cordovez was the UN Secretary-General's representative for Afghanistan and the book describes the six long years of tortuous efforts, with its ups and downs, which eventually

---

[1] Louis Dupree, *Afghanistan*, Princeton, 1980.
[2] Diego Cordovez and Selig Harrison, *Out of Afghanistan*, Oxford, 1995.

led to the signing of the Geneva Accords in 1988. The fundamental basis was an agreed 'symmetry' of withdrawal of USSR forces and the simultaneous stoppage in the flow of American arms aid to Pakistan intended for the Mujahidins. But in all the negotiations there was no discussion or concern to leave behind a stable political structure in Kabul, which would represent all the tribes and ethnic groups in Afghanistan.

Sir Martin Ewans, with experience of service with British diplomatic missions in Karachi, Kabul and New Delhi, in a book,[3] which came out only in June 2001, incisively summarizes the whole history of Afghanistan and does it in sophisticated style and objectivity with only a mild British bias. He perceptively sees that the Afghan wheel had come full circle, from Anglo–Russian rivalry in the nineteenth century to the Soviet–American proxy war 100 years later. In the end, he concludes the result will be the same—the Afghans will successfully purge the country of foreign occupation and the traditionalists will get back in the ascendant. Sir Martin Ewans, at the time of publication, expected political longevity for the uncompromising Talibans. (It could well be premature to write off the possibility of the reincarnation of Pathan conservatism and xenophobia.)

A Uniquely Missed Opportunity by India

My own writings in this compilation, in comparison, are limited in scholarship and scope, but they have some resilient merit, though only of an occasional nature. The articles concentrate on the pernicious consequences, born of outdated ideological mindsets, resulting in penalties specially for the region. More than once in these articles I expressed the view that there never was a better moment to rationalize the India–Pakistan relations and resolve the Kashmir problem than what existed in January 1980. For the first and only time, Pakistan seriously apprehended, even though falsely, that its own national integrity was under threat from the North-West (USSR assisted by Afghanistan) and *not* from the East (India). (This apprehension finds confirmation in the reference to the Afghan crisis in the essay by Pervez Iqbal Cheema, a notable Pakistani scholar, in a book on the Simla Agreement).[4] There was then no

[3] Sir Martin Ewans, *Afghanistan: A Short History*, Curzon, 2001.
[4] P.R. Chari and Pervez Iqbal Cheema, *The Simla Agreement: Its Wasted Promise*, Colombo, New Delhi: RCSS and Manohar, 2001.

infiltration across the Line of Control (LOC). With sensitive prophylactic diplomacy, India could have assuaged Pakistan's anxiety
as it did in 1978, and turned the LOC into an international frontier
and achieved what India missed doing, at least on paper, in
Simla in 1972. These papers will also show that India betrayed or
discounted the national will of Afghanistan to independence. (In
1996 when the Talibans took Kabul, even the functioning Indian
diplomatic mission was withdrawn/expelled.) Earlier when India had
a working diplomatic mission in Kabul, it blundered in the wishful
hope that the Soviet Union would never withdraw. Even when the
Soviet Union began to see the invasion of Afghanistan as a pointless
conflict in a barren cruel landscape and the average Russian soldier
became drug addicted and saw no reason to the operation, India
failed to draw the right conclusions. The irony is that had India
remained in step with the Non-aligned consensus, it could have
diplomatically facilitated the Soviet exit from the morass of
Afghanistan when the Soviets had no will to remain in Afghanistan.

I have learnt recently that in 1986 Gorbachev had called our
chargé d'affaires in Moscow and informed him of his intention to
withdraw the Soviet forces. He wanted India's help to ensure stability after the Soviet Union pulled out. Delhi's reply was to advise
Gorbachev 'to hasten slowly', in other words to discourage from
him from the proposed withdrawal. [5] In our own heart of hearts we
seemed to have wished that the Soviet army would persist and
strengthen its forces in order to prevail over the Mujahidin resistance. In effect it would have meant that nationalism and Non-
alignment should take a beating in the hope that secularism would
be on the ascendant and Afghanistan would permanently distance
itself from Islamic Pakistan. Every study on Afghanistan had testified
to the religious conservatism of the Afghan tribes. Our diplomatic
observers also failed to see that the Afghan people saw both Presidents, Babrak Karmal and later Mohammed Najibullah as foreign
(Soviet) foisted stooges; Najibullah proved a more efficient administrator and with the help of continuing Soviet supplied arms, he
managed to survive till 1992—three years after the Soviet army
withdrew but eventually, he was killed mercilessly in 1996 and his
body was strung up publicly and no Afghan shed tears at the
spectacle. It was a mistake to have given him an official welcome
in Delhi in 1988. My own discreet advice in the paper at the con-

---

[5] Interview with C.V. Ranganathan on 24 December 2001.

ference in Austin, Texas as early as 1989 was that Najibullah should voluntarily step down as he was transparently out of step with Afghan nationalism but alas our diplomatic antenna was deadened by anti-Pakistan habits of the mind and we deliberately befogged our crystal balls in looking for the definition of our own long term interests.

Superpower Withdrawal: Abandoning the Region

Andropov and more so Gorbachev after coming to power saw the financial cost and the political futility of Soviet misadventure in Afghanistan. Gorbachev gave a year's notice to his military for a successful conclusion but eventually withdrew outmanoeuvering the hawks in Moscow, Washington and after warning, bypassing the pro-Soviet Najibullah regime in Kabul. In his speech at Vladivostok in 1986, just one year after he came to power, he acknowledged that Afghanistan was a bleeding wound. Henry Kissinger told me in October 2001 that when he had called on Gorbachev soon after the latter had come to power, he was himself taken aback when Gorbachev dismissed the validity of the Brezhnev doctrine. Gorbachev did not see any benefit from an Afghan variant of a Mongolia (a Soviet backed Socialist State). The rigidified mindsets were exposed and discarded.

The paradox is that it was the Communists who were the first to perceive the non-validity of ideology and the folly of intervention in Afghanistan. Once the Soviet forces decided to withdraw in the spring of 1989, the Soviet General Gromov invited the full international media to witness his marching back across the bridge over the Oxus. Thereafter USA immediately jettisoned its many-sided commitments and not only changed its policy towards Afghanistan but rediscovered that Pakistan was indeed a military dictatorship, and a threat to US non-proliferation goals! Today out of the quadrilateral, which started the horrific Odyssey of misperceptions in 1979-80, only Russia can look on with comparative comfortable detachment, without any special national anxiety about the future. They were the first to apply what Barbara Tuchman describes, quoting the Greek stoic 'the thinking fire of Reason'.

The irony, and for Afghanistan the tragedy is that at the time when the USA withdrew, it showed no real concern for Afghanistan's well being and concern at the fate of the nation. With the Mujahidin splintering, Afghanistan was abandoned to civil war, chaos and factional rivalry. When the seven Mujahidin factions could not hammer a working unity at the Shura held in Peshawar (which meant the exclusion of the Shia Hazara tribe oriented to Iran) Pakistan saw it as an opportunity for direct involvement. The ISI which had been enriched with arms and finance provided by CIA and themselves fanned the fundamentalist zest. It was Pakistan's turn to overlook history and forget that the Pashtun can always muster the courage and the cunning to defeat the foreigner.

Vision Ahead via Joint Landmines Clearance and Respect for the Afghan Character

The last piece in this compilation, written in 1997, urged an Indian initiative, jointly with Pakistan but with the consent and cooperation of local Afghan authorities, to sweep the 10 million odd mines embedded in the hills, fields and pathways of Afghanistan. The whole country is a killing field for unwary civilians, women on their daily chores and children at play. 25,000 new victims, it was estimated, would be maimed accidentally by triggering explosions every year. The landmine menace was the focus of great international concern in 1997. Jody Williams had launched the International Campaign to Ban Landmines (ICBL) in 1992 but by an effective campaign, she had gathered strong international support. The International Red Cross had long supported the campaign and Princess Diana had got so identified with the effort that she was called the 'Princess with the tryst with Landmines'. The organization was chosen for the Nobel Prize for Peace. (The only other areas with a comparable density of landmines were Kampuchea and Angola.) Canada, Norway and Austria took the lead to canvas governmental endorsements of a draft treaty outlawing anti-personnel mines. When it opened for signature in Ottawa, it quickly got over 100 countries as co-signatories. Alas USA, Russia, China, Pakistan and India were amongst the few who stood aloof. Whether weighing our security considerations, we should have gone along is a separate question, but my suggested initiative for Afghanistan was born out of the recognition that there were few other countries which had greater stakes in the welfare of the Afghan people or more sparable expertise than India and Pakistan. Our sappers have similarity of training and near familiarity of language and landscape. Notwithstanding our continuing rivalry and mutual suspicions, jointly managing operations would have been of critical beneficial importance for Afghanistan. In the process of working together, it is conceivable we might have developed the habit of cooperation, rediscovered some commonalities in a wholly humanitarian mission in a third country. It evoked no interest but the challenge has now greater urgency and bigger dimensions.

My analysis owes a great deal to lessons of history distilled by perceptive observers of the past. Sir Martin Ewans unearthed and quoted from a 38-page dispatch by Mountstuart Elphinstone who was the first official of the East India Company sent in 1809 to make contact with the Emir of Afghanistan. Elphinstone sympathetically and astutely described the Afghan vices but also his love of liberty and his martial qualities. At the end of my own paper, written for the Kennan Institute I had quoted Churchill's analysis in powerful prose after his service with the Malakand Field Force in 1897 which identified the same characteristics.[6] The world is reaping the whirlwind for ignoring the consistent lessons of history. But it was not enough to understand the past and the people: a bold vision had to go with it.

I have always believed that professional objectivity should not be afraid of going against the prevailing 'truths' even though articulated by powers with longer independent history and better resources. For me it is no mean satisfaction that though these papers were written over nearly two decades, yet even with the benefit of hindsight, I would not wish to modify one jot from any of them. But this is not a question of personal satisfaction but of avoidable national damage and policy perspectives. These pages illustrate my old faith that India's foreign policy has to be a principled blend of ideological agnosticism, responsible developmental nationalism with 'sufficient militarization'—a phrase first used by Shevardnadze as Foreign Minister in a General Assembly address—which would permit the release of optimum resources for social justice. These are essential ingredients and collaterals to national security and in a sense merely the redefinition of Non-aligned principles beyond the predictable atrophy of military alliances. As I argue in the concluding chapter, notwithstanding past mistakes, India must seek to inch forward politically and economically, but to fully retrieve our international standing, we must exercise greater principled objectivity and show better anticipation than we did on Afghanistan.

[6]Sir Winston Churchill, 'The Mamund Valley', in *A Roving Commission*, New York: Charles Scribener's Sons, 1951.

Afghanistan, I am convinced, should never have been perceived—as it was all too frequently in the last five decades—as actually or potentially an enemy's enemy. It was and remains an extension of South Asia but we must not overlook that it is at the crossroads of the continent. Over time it proved a great mistake to treat Afghanistan as a playground for competitive political and economic gamesmanship. Running through these articles which follow is the focus on the penalties of misperceptions for all countries which were repeated over the last two decades showing nothing had been imbibed from history. But the other underlying thesis which will be illustrated in the subsequent chapters that with sensitive diplomacy, the terrible tragedy could have been averted. Afghanistan 1978-2001 is a sad story of *The March of Folly*. The challenge for the future, which will be addressed in the concluding chapter, is how to bring about a new chapter of cooperation in South Asia and trigger a fuller awareness of the dimensions of terror which confronts the whole world.

2

Déjà vu in South Asia

No doubt every country, including the Soviet Union, wishes that the situation in Afghanistan could be turned back to the state of affairs before the coup that overthrew the regime of Mohammed Daud in April 1978.

The Soviet Union, in occupying Afghanistan in December 1979, underestimated Afghan nationalism and the international consequences of overwhelming a century-old non-aligned 'buffer'. Washington misjudged the occupation as a step towards strangulating the Persian Gulf oil artery but also found it an additional ground to correct the perceived military imbalance with the Russians. For the countries of the region, the developments of 1979 were not merely strategic moves on the chessboard of Afghanistan but also posed dangerous problems at that their doorstep which still remain.

In this context, the lessons of the last 30 years are relevant. In the early 1950s, China established a military presence in Tibet, which was then considered a kind of military buffer, and Soviet forces were deployed across the frontiers of Iran and Afghanistan. In 1954, pursuing a policy of containing the threat of Sino–Soviet power and compulsive ideological expansionism, America concluded an arms agreement with Pakistan; this was followed by the creation of the South-East Asia Treaty Organization (SEATO) and the Middle East Defence Organisation (Baghdad Pact). Even at that time, there was a barely concealed divergence between America's perspectives and the attitudes of its regional allies. Pakistan had no heart to provoke or fight the Communist bloc, but by going along with American strategy it was able to obtain military supplies for defence or use against the perceived threat from India.

*New York Times, 24 April 1981. The Reagen administration, after assuming the office was proposing new measures to contain the Evil (Soviet) Empire and contemplated resuming military aid to Pakistan which inevitably led to a setback to the regional easing of tensions.

The consequences of this ambivalence were disastrous, it polarized the subcontinent. It led to two India–Pakistan wars and further fragmented the political map and resulted in the diversion in India and Pakistan of scarce resources from national development. Eventually, SEATO and the Central Treaty Organization, the Baghdad Pact's successor, had to be buried, and Pakistan, like its neighbours, reverted to Non-alignment. Moreover, it enfeebled American diplomacy in the region, including with Pakistan.

The Reagen administration after assuming office revived the alarm that the Soviet policy was to pose a strategic threat to the West in the important but vulnerable Middle East.

A strategic consensus is again being considered, this time involving Egypt, Israel, Saudi Arabia, the Gulf, and Pakistan, with the promise of American arms. This would presumably be integrated with a rapid-reaction strategy against Soviet expansionism. The region is, no doubt, strategically important to the superpowers, but every country, it must be remembered, has its own geography, internal politics, and complex relations with neighbours. The proposed policy could intensify internal ferment and regional instability, precipitate a new India–Pakistan arms race, and lead increased great power involvement in the region.

In the last five years, there has been a creeping recognition in both India and Pakistan that they have a stake in each other's stability and must cooperate economically. While maintaining cautious vigilance against rival powers, the United States, Soviet Union, and China have separately welcomed this trend. The Soviet Union, except during the Bangladesh crisis and since 1980, has maintained friendly relations with Pakistan. So far, it has refrained from supporting the Baluchi and Pashtun separatist movements which could further dismember Pakistan.

However sizeable the quantity of arms it receives from Washington, Pakistan cannot confront or deter the Soviet Union. Meanwhile, such military aid would be interpreted by Pakistan as a moral sanction to delay the quest for democratic legitimacy that is the military regime's declared goal.

The problem of regional strategic balance and stability must be thought through incisively. For the frontline States, punitively raising the cost of occupation would scarcely amount to an enthralling policy objective. The remote hope of reverting to the pre-April 1978 situation may lie in regional cohesion insulated from competitive superpower militarism. Pakistan, facing the burden of 1.7 million refugees and numerous internal problems, has to choose between its domestic agenda, together with regional non-hostile, Non-alignment, and adjustment to the global strategies of one of the superpowers. The Islamic conference may provide economic and moral support but ignores the security dilemma that flows from Pakistan's geography.

Realistically, a solution in Afghanistan can only follow international détente, not remain a condition for it. Even if there is no immediate withdrawal, it is unlikely that the superpower dialogue will not be resumed sometime. Afghanistan, like Cambodia, may then become another sideshow, overtaken by other crises or the cyclical play between confrontation and co-existence. On the other hand, new great power competition may lead to internal and external tensions and further destabilization, which would be a calamity for the region and a worse quandary for all interested powers.

3

Solution in Afghanistan: From Swedenization to Finlandization

I

'Internally the political situation in Afghanistan is stable. President Daud remains very much in control and faces no significant opposition. The process of political institution building is going apace.' This was stated on 16 March 1978, in a testimony before the US House Subcommittee on Asian and Pacific Affairs, by Ambassador Adolphe Dubs, speaking as Deputy Assistant Secretary of State for South Asian Affairs. The following month, on 28 April 1978, President Daud along with members of his family and four senior members of his government had been killed and the Democratic Republic of Afghanistan, led by the Communist-inclined coalition of Khalq and Parcham parties with Taraki as President, established. Later in the same year Adolphe Dubs went on to become the US Ambassador to Afghanistan and in February 1979 was himself killed as a hostage in a Kabul hotel by the new Republic's security guards, in an inept endeavour to overwhelm his captors, who were suspected of being Islamic militants.

In January 1980, after the Soviet intervention in Afghanistan, President Carter declared that the Soviet action posed the gravest threat to world peace since World War II and propounded the Carter doctrine, which committed the United States to defend the Persian Gulf. The US administration also made it known that every step possible would be taken to compel the withdrawal of the Soviet forces.

---

* Paper prepared at the Woodrow Wilson Centre at Washington DC, adopted and circulated by the Kennan Institute of Advanced Russian Studies in 1981-2. In the meanwhile military aid for Pakistan had become official policy even though it was clear that the Soviet Union had no intention to disrupt the oil flows to the West.

Only nine months later, in October 1980, during the US presidential campaign, when major issues of external as well as internal policy were being debated in a national television hook-up lasting 90 minutes, neither President Carter nor President-to-be Reagan even mentioned the problem of Afghanistan!

These three episodes, separated in time by no more than two and a half years, reflected extraordinary changes in American perceptions of the Afghanistan situation and its international significance.

Before the Saur Revolution of April 1978, Afghanistan had caused no serious anxieties for East–West relations. However, when the Soviet intervention occurred, in December 1979, Afghanistan was at once linked in the American view to Yemen, Angola, Ethiopia, and Vietnam's action in Cambodia. The Soviet action was judged to be based on the confidence derived from the improved military balance of the Warsaw Pact vis-a-vis the North Atlantic Treaty Organisation (NATO). The Soviet Union, it was argued, was attempting to realize the old Russian ambition to reach warm waters and aiming to dominate South and South-West Asia, and there by seeking to control or even throttle the oil artery on which the industrialized West was critically dependent. It was believed the timing of the Soviet intervention was related to the hostage crisis in Iran which was then baffling the United States. It was also seen as a signal to Ayatollah Khomeini and the Tudeh Party that the Soviet Union would react in the event of a US intervention in Iran. At the time, the United States and indeed most Western governments and analysts saw the Afghan developments as moves in the Kremlin's global strategy against the West.

The Soviet official position on Afghanistan has been equally changeable and contradictory. After President Daud's last visit to Moscow in February 1977, the joint communique reaffirmed friendship, trust, understanding and satisfaction, and the determination to consolidate economic cooperation on 'an equal and mutually advantageous' long-term basis. A 12-year Treaty for Economic Cooperation was signed, detailing specific fields for joint development, which in its preamble recalled the old treaties of 1921 and 1931 of 'Neutrality and Non-Aggression'. When Hafizullah Amin visited Moscow in May 1978 after the overthrow of Daud, the communique with Andrei Gromyko referred to the same treaty—'signed during the time of V.I. Lenin'—and reiterated confidence in the 'unbreakable friendship, all round cooperation and good neighbourliness between the two countries'. After the Soviet invasion in December 1979, the

April 1978 Revolution was still applauded, but its mastermind, Hafizullah Amin, was now found to be an agent of the CIA and was roundly criticized as a dictator, oppressor, and traitor and accused of terror, violation of legality, etc. The turn-about became more anomalous when the Soviet military intrusion was claimed to be a response to the request from the Afghan government of which Amin himself was at that time the head. More ironically, the legal basis cited were Article 51 of the UN charter (which gives the right of individual and collective self-defence) and Article 4 of the 1978 Soviet–Afghan Treaty that had been negotiated by Amin himself. The many shifts in the Soviet positions, even after April 1978, when they had a privileged position with the Afghan government, reveal a striking failure to understand the Afghan people and their political attitudes.

The substantive thrust of the Soviet defence for the violation of Afghan neutrality was that imperialism had planned an aggression to mend the holes in the strategic arc created by loss of the Shah's Iran. A commentator in *Pravda* even suggested that the imperialists were planning a return to Kabul in triumph. The Czech government, in supporting the Soviet intervention, wrote more honestly that the USSR acted in 'the spirit of internationalist solidarity of revolutionary and anti-imperialist forces'—an oblique reference to the so-called Brezhnev doctrine, which had been advanced for intervention in Czechoslovakia.

The successive votes in the UN condemning the Soviet action, and demanding Soviet withdrawal from Afghanistan, showed that even two years after the intervention, the Soviet explanations have carried little international credibility. Indeed the Soviet invasion of Afghanistan has probably caused the biggest setback in the history of Soviet relations with the Third World. It was the first direct use of Soviet combat troops outside the Yalta demarcations and the only time such troops had been employed in a non-aligned country. As long as the Soviet presence continues, Soviet diplomacy will be left to depend on the mistakes of the West, or seize opportunities which may arise out of national or regional conflicts and circumstances. It has seriously undermined decades of efforts of the Soviet Union to portray itself in the decolonized world as a principled supporter of independence, nationalism, and Non-alignment.

In any case neither the US nor the Soviet variants of the dreaded Armageddon has come to pass. Notwithstanding continuing mention in public statements, Afghanistan has slowly slid away from the focus of international attention and anxiety. But within Afghanistan, defiant insurgency has not died down or been smothered.

Meanwhile, the Soviet intervention had triggered a chain of reactions. On the subcontinent, it has been leading to the massive rearmament of Pakistan, and in turn of India, a process sure to strain their economies and intensify regional tensions. The US response, based on the Carter perception, was a central factor in the creation of the Rapid Deployment Force, a greatly increased American- and Soviet-naval presence in the Indian Ocean, and the effort to reach an anti-Soviet strategic consensus. The premises proved unfounded, but the reactions generated developed a momentum of their own.

II

A final understanding of what led to the Soviet decision to intervene in Afghanistan will remain buried in the secret archives of the Kremlin. Predictably, the *ex post facto* Soviet explanation referred to the threat of subversion of the established Democratic Republic of Afghanistan, chiefly from the United States and China through Pakistan. In denying the charge of aggression Soviet leaders, including President Brezhnev, sought to deflect criticism by referring to East–West problems. Cited were the Camp David process, the upgrading of the US nuclear and conventional arsenal, the changed US attitude to the ratification of SALT-II, the US build-up in the Indian Ocean, the development of the US–China military relationship, etc. These explanations, however, lacked plausible causal or chronological connections with the developments inside Afghanistan.

One could safely surmise, in fact, that the Soviet Union had grossly underestimated the adverse consequences which flowed from its intervention. The operation itself did not prove to be a quick surgical exercise. The mix of military coercion, economic aid, and pro-pagandistic fraternization (with the help of ethnic and religious comrades of neighbouring Central Asian republics) failed to produce quiet acquiescence by the Afghan people and reasonable, if not enthusiastic, support for the installed Karmal regime. Nor did Soviet diplomacy expect to be so put on the defensive, not just in the Non-aligned world and the community of Islamic nations, but in the Communist fraternity itself. Incidentally, it was also a set back to Cuba's hopes articulated at the Summit meeting held in Havana in September 1979 of leading the Non-aligned Movement to look upon the Socialist bloc as its natural ally.

Very little has been heard in the last two years of the Asian security system which, in effect, was the Soviet design for the containment of China's influence and expansion in that part of the world. On the contrary—and this too may not have been foreseen—the Soviet action in Afghanistan, along with the fall-out from Vietnam's action in Cambodia, gave an unexpected boost to Chinese diplomacy in much of South Asia and the ASEAN region. In fact, the geopolitical Soviet gain from the occupation of Afghanistan was no more than slightly improved logistics and somewhat better tactical capability in the event of a major regional conflict involving the superpowers. But this was a marginal advantage in a hypothetical contingency. In any case, as compared to the United States, the Soviet Union always had an operational advantage in the Gulf region, barely 700 miles from its own southern frontier.

On the American side, as stated earlier, the immediate reaction, like a conditioned reflex, was to posit a worst case strategic scenario. One can, however, safely speculate that domestic political factors were, at least in part, responsible for the exaggerated significance attached to the Soviet action. Had the Soviet intervention taken place in 1978 instead of the year before the US presidential elections and, had it not coincided with the baffling humiliation of the American hostages being held in Iran, the reaction of the Carter administration might have been less agitated and better balanced.

It can be argued that the embargo on exports of grain and on the flow of Western credits and technology, the boycott of the Olympics, and the general international alarm may have averted further military moves planned in the Kremlin. Without internal evidence such a contention cannot be proved or disproved, but it does not appear very convincing. Except for the Olympic boycott, the American response caused embarrassment and damage to the American policy and in no way advanced the goal of a Soviet retreat from Afghanistan, and the grain embargo was eventually withdrawn unilaterally.

One cannot escape the conclusion that both the easy-win confidence of the Soviet Union, with its anticipation of minimal fall-out, and the excessive alarm on the American side were gross misperceptions. What was common to the fallacious judgements of both the US and the USSR was that every action or development was appraised from their respective global strategic perspectives instead of by an objective assessment of the complex dynamics of local events and regional circumstances.

The ups and downs in Soviet–American relations might have been no different even if there had been no Soviet invasion of Afghanistan. Possibly the crisis in Afghanistan encouraged Solidarity and Polish nationalism, and the unexpected political and military difficulties in Afghanistan may have restrained the Soviet Union from another direct intervention. What is relevant in this context is that the Soviet move into Afghanistan and the immediate militaristic reactions in the West have made the restoration of stability in the whole region vastly more complex and difficult.

To find explanations for the unexpected developments, the chronology of events needs to be objectively reviewed as it developed and was perceived both internally and externally. But before doing so, it would be useful to recall some historical background. While it has been ignored or discounted by the principal powers, it can yet illuminate the present and perhaps suggest a way out in the future.

III

No country outside the parameters of the European concert had an historical experience of the ebb and flow of empires comparable to that of Afghanistan. Straddling the crossroads between Europe and Asia, Afghanistan was important millennia before anyone had reflected on the strategic importance of distant lands. Since Alexander's march to the Indus, the Hindu Kush and its subsidiary ranges, which are the Afghan homeland, have been witness to some 25 invasions. However diverse in origin and ethnic hue, every emperor who fancied himself as a world conqueror attempted to cross Afghanistan on the way to the Orient. The Bactrians, the Persians, the Turks, and the Mongols came and crossed, or stayed for a while, and then were obliged to withdraw. Napoleon and Hitler sought the agreement of their counterparts in Russia to smooth their passage to India. The only advance from the south was that of the Mauryan Empire, three centuries before the Christian era, when the message of Buddha was propagated in these lands. Eventually, in the seventh century after Christ, Islam came from the West, took root, and the Sunni faith became the dominant religion of the Afghan tribes.

When the European powers finally reached India by sea, Afghanistan became the diplomatic and military battleground between two competing empires, both European. The Great Game was played for half of the nineteenth century, between the Czarist Empire expanding southward and the British advancing from the east and wanting to establish a safe strategic frontier for their dominion over the sub-continent. The Game was played with military adventures, diplomacy, intrigue, and deceit. But, even then, the Afghans were to contest the foreign giants for their homeland. The Afghan rulers and tribal chiefs played the British off against the Russians and vice versa—and inflicted military and political humiliation on both powers. Afghan tactics were even then full of courage and cunning. They included assassinations, ambushes, denial of supplies, use of captured arms, double dealings, and deception. In the end it was the defiant hostility of the Afghan tribesmen which compelled the 'forward' imperialists of both Russia and Britain to yield to pragmatic counsels to leave the Afghans to their own tribal polity. Afghanistan was the only Asian country which, having faced full-scale repeated invasions from different powers, did not end up as part of an European Empire. The experience of coping with the Great Game of two empires had, however, catalyzed Afghanistan, starting with Emir Abdur Rahman, into taking the first step towards the creation of a modern State.

In its foreign relations, the Afghan Emirate maintained a sagacious policy of not getting involved in the European political game or serving as strategic instrument of any power. Afghanistan defied both Russia and Britain and remained neutral during the First World War. When after the War Britain was militarily exhausted, the Afghans launched an invasion into British India in an attempt to get back the tribal areas east of the Durand Line. It failed in this purpose, but by the treaty of 1919, Afghanistan obtained recognition of its full independence.

After the end of British control over Afghan external relations, the first major decision of the Afghan government was to recognize and conclude a treaty with the revolutionary government established after the October Revolution in Russia. Afghanistan was the first country to buy aircraft and arms from the Soviet Union, and in 1925 Amanullah was the first monarch to visit the capital of the revolutionary Communist State. Afghanistan, however, did not bind itself exclusively to its northern neighbour. Apart from maintaining the old links with Britain and Russia, it enlarged its diplomatic contacts and established economic and cultural links with Germany, France, and the Islamic world.

The external environment around Afghanistan altered more radically after the Second World War. The British withdrew from the subcontinent, and Pakistan came into existence. Iran under Reza

Pahlavi gathered strength and later oil wealth. The United States emerged as the other great power in the new Great Game. In 1954 when a bilateral security treaty was concluded between Pakistan and the US, Afghanistan was not even informed by the US. Afghan suspicions were aroused that the US supported Pakistan on the Pakhtunistan question. Although Afghanistan had earlier considered getting arms from the US, after the US–Pakistan alliance, it refused to join the Baghdad Pact or even the Regional Cooperation and Development (RCD) agreement, though it was claimed the latter had only an economic focus. The post-War international landscape confirmed Afghanistan's perception that its security was best assured through its traditional policy of Non-alignment with any great power, but economic cooperation wherever beneficial, and friction-free relations with the powerful neighbour to the north. Not even the United States seriously questioned the rationale of this policy.

But while remaining sensitive to Soviet interests and keeping the USSR as pre-eminent amongst its partners, Afghanistan systematically enlarged its pattern of bilateral economic relations with Communist and non-Communist countries—notably with the USA, Federal Germany, China, Czechoslovakia, Yugoslavia, France, the United Kingdom, Japan, and India. The USSR concentrated on the development of power, gas, minerals, and communications; US aid was primarily for Helmand valley development and support for education and the national communication infrastructure. The USSR built the road from Herat to Kandahar and the USA continued it to Kabul. Western studies made in the 1960s and early 1970s—long before détente—had commented that, at least in Afghanistan, there was a kind of complimentarity in the developmental field between the otherwise competing powers.

The most serious external problem which Afghanistan had to face in the last three decades was with Pakistan on the Pakhtunistan question. The issue came to ahead on several occasions and led to a slowdown and sometimes to an actual blockade in transit of Afghanistan's seaborne commerce, which traditionally only went through Karachi. In the worst crisis of 1960-1, the Soviet Union purchased and airlifted Afghan products and by doing so permanently strengthened Soviet–Afghan trade relations. But it should be noted that, except for a statement made when Bulganin and Khrushchev were in Kabul in 1955, the Soviet Union did not categorically endorse the concept of Pakhtunistan.

Those who make an argument for the hidden hand of the USSR in the Saur Revolution (as part of a grand design) have suggested that the Soviets had become apprehensive about President Daud becoming hostile and therefore masterminded his overthrow in 1978. But there is little proof of serious Soviet dissatisfaction with Daud before April 1978. If anything, for two decades Daud was looked upon as the architect of a closer Soviet–Afghan relationship. It was during Daud's tenure as Prime Minister in the 1950s that Afghanistan invited Bulganin and Khrushchev to Kabul. The visit launched the substantial Soviet-assisted economic programme in the country, and led to the agreement by which the Soviet Union re-equipped the Afghan armed forces. The Soviet Union was the first to recognize the Afghan Republic when Daud dethroned his brother-in-law, King Zahir Shah, in 1973 and exuded satisfaction and confidence at Afghan–Soviet relations. *Posthoc* analyses have grasped at isolated and minor indications of suspected Soviet dissatisfaction with Daud, such as his allowing Western technicians and UN experts to work on development projects north of the Hindu Kush near the Soviet border. But it cannot be shown that these ever added up to real concern or led to a tangible deterioration in Soviet–Afghan relations. As compared to the relations with her Islamic neighours, Iran and Pakistan, Afghan relations with Communist Russia had been free from serious tensions up to 1978.

It is a fact that both before and during Daud's presidency many Afghan civilians, and officers of the armed forces had been educated and trained in the Soviet Union. In the process, outside their professional courses, they must have been exposed to propaganda and ideological persuasion. One can safely assume both the Khalq and Parcham parties had long-standing contacts with the Soviet Union and must have received support from Soviet agencies. The Soviet Union is acknowledged to have been instrumental in uniting these factions in 1977. However, such non-governmental investment and efforts are the features of the diplomacy of all great powers but they have generally yielded abysmally dismal dividends. In Afghanistan the strength of pro-Soviet sympathizers prior to 1978 was never considered by any observer to be of revolutionary timber or capability. Training abroad, be it in the USSR or China, has often produced more ideological sceptics than brainwashed anti-national converts. Or to put it another way, just as many students have been attracted to distant socio-economic models without any direct or indirect foreign contacts. In the case of Afghanistan none of the principal radical faction leaders were trained in the USSR. Taraki was self-

educated and had served in the Afghan embassy in Washington and
even worked for the US embassy in Kabul. Babrak Karmal, now the
President, was educated only in Kabul. Amin became a Marxist in
his years with the Teachers College in Columbia University, New
York. The fact is that all too frequently sincere Communists with
firm and loyal commitment to Moscow or Peking have found
themselves out of line with the twist and turns of the policies of the
respective Communist mentor states. The intellectual antecedents of
the leaders or even the party link with Moscow do not really provide
a plausible clue to the course of Afghan developments starting with
the overthrew of Daud.

IV

How then did this country, which preserved its independence and its
native identity against great odds and with dexterous diplomacy and
was accepted as a neutral non-aligned buffer by all powers, become
a victim of a coup and an invasion jeopardizing its successful
traditional policies? If the events are followed objectively, it would
appear that a series of sudden and unplanned turns provide the most
plausible explanation for the Afghan developments.

From every reliable account, including those of Western observers
in Kabul at the time, the coup of 1978 happened and succeeded
unexpectedly. Some analysts now argue that this coup was planned
for August, but no one denies that when it occurred, it was as great
a surprise to Moscow as to the rest of the world. According to Louis
Dupree of the American University Field Staff, with a lifetime of
scholarly expertise on Afghanistan, who was in Kabul at the time, a
series of accidents, combined with inefficiency and ineptitude, led to
the violent overthrow of the Daud government. The success of the
coup, he suggested, surprised even its makers.

All commentators agree that the killing of Mir Akbar Khan, a
popular Parchamite figure, triggered the initial protests at a time
when social and economic discontent was on the increase. The Khalq
group succeeded in exploiting the killing to arouse public indignation. With the support of some units of the army and the air force,
the protest demonstration was turned into a kind of march on the
Bastille—the Presidential palace—where the assembled senior
members of the government and their families were summarily
killed. The numbers of Khalq–Parcham members and active sympathizers in the defence forces—some no doubt well placed—were

probably no more than a few hundred. Hafizullah Amin sub-sequently claimed that he executed a master plan, but this must be discounted as emanating from the triumph of victory and power.

Ten days passed between the murder of Mir Akbar Khan and the overthrow of the Daud government. With a modicum of adminis-trative foresight and a security alert, by bringing in units from the provinces as a precaution, it might have been a different story. In any case, the important fact was that the developments were local and unforeseen. The Soviet Union had no doubt helped bring about the reunification of the Khalq–Parcham factions in 1977, but the killing of Mir Akbar and its improvised exploitation do not reveal any Kremlin design or manipulation aimed at overthrowing the Daud regime.

The Soviet Union was understandably quick to recognize the unexpected and welcome the change in Afghanistan. Almost all countries, including those of the West, followed suit within weeks because the seizure, however brutal, was local and internal. The USSR had an obvious interest in seeing the socialist regime conso-lidate itself. Economic help and technical advisers were readily provided to the new government, and had an important role in the civil administration and the security forces. But the pattern and policies of the new Afghan leadership were based on their under-standing of the Soviet model, rather than on prior guidance or direction from the Soviet embassy or from Moscow. The Parcham faction initially accepted the Khalq leader, Taraki, as President and 'father of the nation', and Soviet comments echoed this local variant of the cult of personality. When within weeks the coalition dis-integrated, it did so not on policy issues, but because of the personal rivalry and competitive ambitions of Amin and Babrak. The USSR went along with the results of the power struggle. It did not demur at the expulsions of the Parchamites, when Babrak and others were dismissed.

Amin, who emerged as the driving force of the new republic, was a convinced votary of the economic and social theories of Marx and the socialist system as installed by Lenin. Based on such textbook knowledge and Amin's understanding of the Soviet example, the new government launched forth on a programme for a quick trans-formation of Afghanistan into a socialist country. A barrage of decrees were issued: 'tyranny' and usury were abolished; the equality of ethno-linguistic groups was proclaimed; large and middle-sized landholdings were redistributed; education and health services were made free; women were liberated and ordered to attend adult literacy classes; natural resources were nationalized and the judiciary was revamped. A new secular national flag in Communist red instead of Islamic green was adopted. This amateur radicalism—socialism by decree and fiat—ignored the culture and sociology of the old tribal society. The new rulers also overlooked the incapacity of the governmental machinery—further enfeebled by purges and disoriented by newly appointed, young, inexperienced political cadres—to implement such reforms. The economic and administrative dislocations which naturally followed soon forfeited the support of the urban populace. The onslaught on religion and the entrenched social ethos provoked the anger of the Mullahs and the tribal chiefs in the countryside. The initial expectancy soon turned into disillusionment and hostility toward the regime.

All such opposition was predictably dismissed as the reaction of vested bourgeois interests, and the regime's response was only to intensify the repression. First the suspected Daud supporters, then, in turn, the Parchamites, the Islamic leaders, and later even nationalist sympathizers and army officers who had helped the coup were imprisoned. The arrest of each group increased the estrangement of the regime from the people. Within months the new rulers came to be looked upon as godless and foreign. The culmination was the revolt in Herat in March 1979 when units of the Afghan army mutinied, joined the insurgents, and even killed a number of their Soviet advisers. Again, the response to this growing insurgency was not retreat from the proclaimed socialist programme or accommodation with the Islamic elements, but more ruthless suppression. The assumption of all effective powers by Hafizullah Amin as Prime Minister in March 1979, leaving Taraki only as a figurehead, symbolized the persistence of this ruthless, doctrinaire course.

Throughout this period (from April 1978 to about June 1979) there was no evidence that the Soviet Union had any hesitation in backing Amin as the emergent power in Kabul. He claimed to be and was accepted as the most loyal friend of the Soviet Union. The Treaty of Friendship between the USSR and Afghanistan (December 1978) was actively promoted by Amin as Foreign Minister. When Brezhnev referred to Afghanistan as a new member of the Socialist Commonwealth, he was expressing not just satisfaction at the year's developments in Afghanistan but also confidence in the leadership of the country, where Amin was really at the controls. Some *post hoc* analyses hint that the Soviet Union had long harboured doubts about Amin and was all the time nursing Babrak Karmal. But until the spring of 1979 the Soviet Union was publicly unreserved in its support for Amin, who was seen as a zealous guardian of Soviet interests.

V

It was only in the summer of 1979 that the Soviet Union became alarmed that the radicalism and ideological militancy of Amin were proving dangerously counter-productive. The incidents in Herat, Jalalabad, Kandahar, Mazar-i-Sharif, Pakthia, etc., and the general spread of insurgency in the country were patent evidence of the alienation of the people from the regime and their hostility towards the Soviet Union. The Soviet Union is known to have said to its friends that Afghanistan was proceeding too fast on the road to socialism. At this stage some gentle attempts to moderate policies must have been made. But it could not be easy for the first Socialist State to curb an ideological militant so unabashedly pro-Soviet. Having rejoiced in the Saur Revolution and backed the Khalq government, the Soviet Union now became apprehensive that the advent of socialism was likely to jeopardize, instead of strengthening, Russian security and turn a traditionally friendly country into a hostile neighbour.

It was in this defensive anxiety that the Soviet Union contemplated the political if not physical elimination of Amin. Earlier the USSR had acquiesced in the attenuation of Taraki's power (because he was not effective enough). In the dilemma of anti-Soviet disaffection being created by a pro-Soviet regime, the Soviets concluded that power should be restored to Taraki precisely because he had a greater nationalistic appeal and was less ideologically militant!

According to all analysts the dethroning of Amin was planned when Taraki stopped in Moscow on his way to and from the Havana Non-aligned Summit. It seems to have been agreed that Amin was to be defrocked, in whatever way possible, immediately after Taraki's return to Kabul.

But modern Russians may again have overlooked their own nineteenth-century experience that an Afghan reacts against becoming the instrument of a foreign power. It appears that Tarun, the head of Afghan security who had accompanied Taraki, tipped off Amin of the plans to dethrone him. When, on 14 September, Amin finally went to the palace in response to Taraki's invitation (after, it is reported, personal assurances of safety had been given by the Soviet Ambassador), he brought his own armed escort with him. In the shoot-out, Taraki was injured by Amin's guards and Tarun was killed, but Amin managed to escape.

The Soviet Ambassador, it was reported, was present in the palace at the time of the shoot-out. Amin must have become dramatically alive to the reality that, far from being the Soviet Union's preferred leader, he had lost their confidence and they sought his removal. What was perhaps even more important, the Soviet embassy knew that Amin had discovered the Soviet intention to unseat him; indeed, Amin was reported to have said as much to some East European diplomats a few weeks later. His fears were confirmed when three senior pro-Taraki ministers took refuge in the Soviet embassy after the palace shoot-out.

At all events, Amin immediately assumed all Taraki's titles and sought to consolidate his position. He declared Tarun a national hero, and he purged the remnants of the security forces of anyone he suspected of being pro-Parcham, pro-Taraki or pro-Soviet. But unlike the consolidation attempts when he became Prime Minister, this time he did not turn to the Soviet Union for advice or support. Indeed, he demanded the recall of Soviet Ambassador Puzanov—a most unusual occurrence within the Socialist commonwealth. Belatedly Amin sought to retreat from his earlier unpopular positions, to appeal to nationalist sentiments, and to broaden his political base. He even tried to mollify the Mullahs and the alienated Islamic opinion. The death sentence on the nationalist Qadir, whom he himself had arrested the previous year, was commuted. It was during this period when referring to the persisting insurgency, he made a point of declaring that 'We would not ask our foreign friends to shed blood for us.'

The failed September palace coup was the critical episode which made the subsequent direct Soviet intervention inevitable. There could be no compromise with an alienated Amin still in power. The Soviet Union faced the possibility of a total reversal in what had promised to be gratuitous gain. During the summer months independent contingency plans on how to prevent the country from turning hostile may have been prepared by Soviet security agencies. After September 1979 mere Soviet responsiveness to decision-making in Kabul was over. The Kremlin must have feared that, given time to marshall internal nationalist consolidation and secure external support, Amin, the loyal ideologue, would turn into a defiant Tito or even a nationalist Dubcek. There may even have been the worse fears that Amin might become a Sadat, abrogating the agreements through which he himself had cemented Afghan–Soviet relations, ask for the withdrawal of Soviet military and civil advisers, and reach out to establish an American link.

The intervention had to be on a scale sufficient to simultaneously remove Amin and his supporters, disarm the Afghan army, take control of the towns and communications, and tackle the widespread insurgency. This required an operational capability and logistic support which could not be assembled in a hurry. At the same time, while plans and preparation were under way the intentions had to be carefully concealed.

These three critical months between September and December 1979 must have been a battle of wits and deception between the Soviet embassy and Amin. Superficially the mutual *bonhomie* continued. Friendly, but not effusive, protocol messages were exchanged on the anniversary of the October Revolution and the Afghan–Soviet Treaty. Even diplomatic observers failed to notice the crisis of confidence and the aroused suspicion between the two governments, but the dye was cast. The visits of General Ivan Yepishev, with experience of Czechoslovakia in 1968, General Pavlovsky, and General Papukin of the Soviet Ministry of Interior must have been intended not to curb the insurgency—as might have been alleged—but to plan for the military intervention in the country. During this period, Amin seems to have been fed information to keep him nervous and dependent on Soviet support. An offer to take Amin's nephew to Moscow, after he was wounded in December, might have been intended to make him believe in the Soviet Union's benign interest in his personal and political welfare. On the eve of the intervention, deliberately warned of impending big insurgent attacks in Kabul, Amin may have even reluctantly agreed to let a small armed Soviet contingent be brought in by air. These mobile units took quick control of the Kabul airfield and later facilitated the induction of airborne troops before the main force rolled in across the frontier. This permission may be what was referred to by the USSR as the invitation for a Soviet intervention.

However, after his narrow escape on 15 September 1979, Amin must have had premonitions of the danger of direct intervention by the Soviet Union. His own counter strategy, planned as discreetly as was possible under the circumstances, seems to have been to regain popularity at home, diversify his external contacts, and eventually to wriggle free of the Soviet embrace. At this stage Amin, who had been so hostile in the past, made friendly overtures to Pakistan. Having earlier been so aggressive on the Pakhtunistan question, Amin may have even decided that it would be expedient to go back to the lines of agreement which were being explored in 1978, between Bhutto and Daud, and hence Agha Shahi, the Foreign Minister of Pakistan, was invited to Kabul. Amin's quick change of attitude may also have had a more far-reaching purpose. He may have thought to use Pakistan as a conduit to send a signal to the United States that he was anxious to revert to the traditional pattern of Afghan non-alignment.

In these months, for the first time after Ambassador Dubs was killed, there were, in fact, indications of some slight improvement in Afghan–US relations. The US embassy was strengthened and the anti-West rhetoric was muted. The announcement of a date for the Pakistan Foreign Minister's visit (it was postponed at the last minute) may have clinched for the nervous Kremlin, the timing of the landing of the Soviet airborne contingent. (It could also be assumed that the Western world would be caught preoccupied with Christmas festivities.)

Even at the time the Kremlin's motive may be most plausibly described as a defensive anxiety at the prospects of a hostile alienation of Afghanistan, rather than the desire to advance the Soviet Union's strategic or ideological frontiers. However, the world was shocked and came to fear that the USSR was now prepared to intervene militarily even in the Third World on the basis of the 'Brezhnev doctrine'.

VI

The contention of this essay is that the Afghan crisis culminating in the occupation of the country by Soviet forces was the product of misadventures and mishaps, compounded by internal mishandling and international misperceptions. Prior to April 1978 the pace of modernization of Afghanistan was admittedly slow. Political expectations had been awakened, and dissatisfaction with the Daud regime had grown as attempts to economic progress, social justice, and political democracy proved sluggish or outright failures. Pockets of radicalism existed amongst students and intellectuals in Kabul, but despite all the investment in propaganda and indoctrination of officials, the 'Communist' factions and Soviet sympathizers in Afghanistan were still insignificant in numbers or influence. The tribal hold on the country was so strong and the influence of Islam so entrenched that no observer prior to 1978 predicted that Afghanistan was ripe for revolution.

That Daud was trying to increase and diversify technical and economic cooperation with non-Communist countries was true. This included Egypt, Pakistan, the Islamic nations, and also India. He was seeking additional economic assistance from the Western countries. But there was no intention to or likelihood of diluting Soviet pre-eminence, particularly in the defence sector.

More significant could have been the prospects of massive aid, totalling US $ 2 billion, which the Shah at one time held out to Daud. The Shah had talked of a resolution to the old Helmand river dispute and of providing help to build a rail link that would reduce Afghanistan's exclusive dependence on Karachi for its seaborne commerce. The Shah, no doubt, envisaged that Afghanistan, like the Gulf, would come under Iran's protective umbrella. He may have tried to sell his concerns about the dangers and designs of 'Islamic Marxists'. But, almost a year before the direct Soviet intervention, the Shah and his grandiose dreams had collapsed. It is only in the light of hindsight that Soviet fears of a change in Afghan foreign policy have been advanced as an explanation for the Soviet invasion in December 1979.

Afghanistan has been a tragedy because it need not have become such an intractable international problem. Daud could have moved faster to fulfil his promises of social and economic progress and more broad-based politics; he need not have excluded the Parchamites from the coalition or, in his republican incarnation, been so repressive of a handful of radicals; following the funeral of Mir Akbar Khan in April 1978, Daud could have acted with more administrative acumen. Amin could have been less impetuous with his radical reforms. Similarly the Soviet Union could have restrained Amin much earlier, instead of initially giving him unquestioned support for his headlong transition to socialism and his brutal repression. But all these errors and misjudgements and improvised reactions were local in nature. Not until September 1979, it would seem, was direct Soviet intervention decided—or, by the Kremlin's logic, considered unavoidable.

President Brezhnev was not deceiving President Carter when he had assured him in Vienna in the spring of 1979 that the Soviet Union had no intention of direct intervention in Afghanistan. Earlier in 1979 Dupree himself had thought an intervention by the USSR was unlikely. The circumstances which compelled the Soviet invasion occurred subsequently. In fact, ironically, had the September coup succeeded and Amin been eliminated, and the more pliable and moderate Taraki reinstated, there might not have been a Soviet invasion of Afghanistan!

Setting aside these hypothetical conjectures, two features of overriding importance can be distilled from the chronology of the crisis. First, in a situation where a conflict emerged between advancing or consolidating the professed ideology and security anxieties, and both could no longer be ridden in tandem, it was the security consideration which prevailed in Soviet decision-making. If this were not so, the USSR would have backed Amin more massively and not displaced him; nor would Babrak Karmal, after being installed, have been allowed to backtrack on the socialist programme initiated by Amin.

Secondly, whether it was the opposition to the socialist decrees put out after April 1978, or the persistent challenge to the Soviet army after it moved in, the Afghan will to independence—call it nationalism—was stronger than was anticipated. The religious, cultural, and social ethos of the land rejected alien ideas even when they were put forward by sons of the soil. They defied the Taraki–Amin regime and have continued to rebel against the Babrak Karmal government because the traditional independence and personality of the country was being outraged.

The critical importance of these two factors—Soviet perceptions of its security and the sturdy individuality and nationalism of the Afghan people—could have been gleaned from the history of Russia's relations with Afghanistan. In the past, Afghans had come to respect Russian security sensitivity, and the Soviet Union had learned not to offend the social and political personality of Afghanistan. As a result of misperceptions and misadventures these resilient imperatives were brought into cross-purposes. The heart of the problem now was how to assuage both Afghanistan's nationalism and Soviet apprehensions of its security.

VII

The spur to the resolution of the Afghanistan problem now rests squarely on the recognition that the present situation could lead to an unpredictable deterioration for both global and regional powers. The blood-letting inside the country has inflicted terrible suffering on one of the poorest countries in the world. The mounting burden of refugees—exceeding two million and still growing—could be a disaster for the political unity and economic health of Pakistan. Afghanistan is not an island and the Durand Line cannot become a Maginot Line. The present situation inherently bears the risks of border incidents, hot pursuit, and counter infiltration across a notoriously permeable frontier. The ripples of tension and, with it the lava of instability, could spread eastward to the subcontinent, southward to Baluchistan and the Gulf, westward to Iran, and even northward to the Central Asian republics. The terms of disaffection are a mix of national, sub-national, tribal, religious, and socio-economic factors. They are all but immune to the vigilance of conventional frontier customs and security forces, especially in this part of the world. There could be other Afghanistans—in the sense of sudden dissidence-ignited internal turmoil, followed by violent suppression and alienation, global linkages and alarm. No power, be it global or local, should be confident or complacent enough to think that persisting instability can be so controlled as to harm only the adversary, without damage to its own immediate or long-term interests. Hence, not just in the interests of Afghanistan but also of any or all nations with stakes in the area, the need to prevent such spillover lends urgency to the political solution to the Afghan problem.

However, as of now, neither the beginning of a solution nor the sense of urgent quest is anywhere evident. The paradox is that there has been a surprising measure of common ground on the broad ingredients of an ultimate solution. There has been implicit recognition that stability could not be restored unless Afghanistan is neutralized against great power presence or competition. Even the recent study by Anthony Arnold of the Hoover Institution (who sees the crisis as proof of aggressive Soviet strategy against the West) agrees that Afghanistan must revert to 'its traditional role as a nationally free, truly non-aligned and independent country'. The proposal put forward on behalf of the European Economic Community by Lord Carrington also aimed at the evacuation of Soviet forces in return for the guaranteed neutrality of the country. The resolutions of the Islamic Conference, the Non-Aligned Foreign Ministers Conference, and the UN resolutions had differing nuances, but all demanded the restoration of Afghanistan's non-alignment. In his speech of 22 February 1980, even President Brezhnev offered to withdraw Soviet forces but only after 'all forms of outside interference' had ended. Predictably the Soviet position continues to confuse causes and consequences, but what comes through various Soviet comments is that (unlike the situation in Poland), the primary Soviet concern is to prevent Afghanistan becoming a hostile base rather than to retain Afghanistan as a strategic ally or hold it up as a model Socialist State. The proposals advanced in the West also acknowledge that any solution would have to ensure that Afghanistan would not become a base to stir up trouble in Soviet Central Asia. Anthony Arnold, for example, acknowledges that the Afghans cannot afford to have permanently bad relations with the USSR any more than they could afford permanent hostility towards Britain prior to 1947.

All these proposals in effect, amount to wanting Afghanistan to be reverted to the position which prevailed before 1978—namely, non-aligned, sensitive to Soviet interests, but free to develop economic relations with non-Socialist as well as Socialist countries, and able to evolve and modernize according to its own national religious and social ethos. The problem is thus not really to discover the outline of the end-solution, but to determine how to move forward toward it when it seems to demand going back and undoing the complex legacy of bitterness and suspicions interjected by the misadventures and mistakes of the last three years.

The parallels of Finland and Austria have been recalled both for the similarity of the end objective and the modalities of reaching it. The Soviet–Finnish Treaty led to the evacuation of the Soviet base at Porkkala in return for a pledge that Finland would not join a military arrangement hostile to the USSR and that the latter would retain the right to intervene if Soviet security were threatened. The Austrian Treaty of 1955 which ended the post-war four-power occupation and restored Austrian sovereignty was on the condition that the country would remain neutral.

The situation and circumstances of Finland and Austria were, however, very different from those of present-day Afghanistan. Both Austria and Finland had well-established democratic national traditions. The elected governments of the countries were in a position to speak for the national consensus, that to secure the withdrawal of the foreign presence, imposed neutrality would be an acceptable sacrifice. No one can at present speak authoritatively for the Afghan nation. No one, certainly not the Soviet Union, can be confident that if the Soviet troops were to be withdrawn, the bitter feelings of the Afghan people would evaporate and the country would not become revanchist and hostile to Soviet interests and security.

To identify, or to assuage, Afghan nationalism is beyond the capabilities of the concert of great powers. Moreover, when the Austrian State Treaty was negotiated—soon after Stalin's death—there was a brief easing of Cold War tensions, at least in Europe. In the present glacial international environment, every proposal emanating from one of the major powers is suspect as a move to advance or consolidate the strategic advantage over the other superpower. It was not surprising that the Soviet Union summarily rejected the EEC proposal of a two-stage international conference under UN auspices. Similarly, the proposal of 14 May 1981 from Kabul, endorsed by the USSR, for direct talks with the neighbours could not but be seen in the West as merely an attempt to secure legitimacy for the present regime, ignoring the evident alienation of the Afghan people.

There was, however, an aspect of the resolution of the problems of Finland and Austria which is pertinent to the search for a solution in Afghanistan. The withdrawal of Soviet presence from Austria was possible because Poland, Czechoslovakia, Hungary and Rumania provided a security buffer for the USSR. The restoration of full Finnish independence hinged on the presumption that Sweden would remain neutral and not join NATO. Selig Harrison[1] in urging 'Exit through Finland', has underlined that the Soviet withdrawal would have to be coupled with the guarantee of the non-alignment of Iran, Pakistan, and India.

Could a similar cushion—a penumbra of neutrality around Afghanistan restored to non-alignment—come into being? This is the critical question—a precondition to possible further steps for the eventual resolution of the Afghanistan crisis. The Kremlin's reaction to the idea of withdrawing as from Austria or Finland is likely to depend on whether Pakistan (and for purposes of the argument, Iran) is to be a Federal Germany, armed as a frontline State, or a Switzerland—neutral and non-hostile between the great powers. The question is not so hypothetical as it may seem. The anti-Soviet strategic consensus was conceived on the presumption that Afghanistan was a springboard for a further southward thrust into Pakistan and the Gulf. If the US was still pressing for the military containment of USSR and envisaged a strongly armed anti-Soviet Pakistan (Iran,

[1]Selig Harrison, 'Dateline Afghanistan: Exit through Finland?', *Foreign Policy*, No. 41, Winter 1980.

for the moment is out of the question), then there can be no hope of Soviet evacuation of Afghanistan. Indeed, it would amount to volunteering a *post hoc* justification for the Soviet intervention and providing the sanction to perpetuate the Soviet presence in the country.

The USSR, on the other hand, was engaged in damage-limiting diplomacy to assuage the apprehension that had been aroused in the region, especially amongst the neighbours of Afghanistan. Even in the face of strong denunciations, the USSR had maintained a posture of cool non-hostile detachment toward the Islamic regime in Iran, be it only as a political investment in an uncertain future. With Pakistan, Soviet relations since the Saur Revolution have gone through phases of sharp accusations and even threats but have remained short of actual manifestations of hostility. Judging from public statements made during the visits of Vice Foreign Minister Firyubin in the autumn of 1981, both countries have reaffirmed friendliness and commitments to enlarged economic cooperation. It is pertinent to recall that even though Pakistan remained tied to the West, in the last two decades, especially after the Soviet mediation in Indo–Pakistan problems at Tashkent, the Soviet Union has sought to maintain good relations with Pakistan. It has tried to balance the developing Sino–Pak relations. It had noted that Pakistan was critical of US policies on Vietnam and the Middle East. As mentioned earlier, the Soviet Union has refrained from supporting Afghan demands for Pakhtoonistan. Contrary to some expectations it has not yet given encouragement or material support to the Baluchistan dissidents. Whatever the future may hold, USSR has not yet played its anti-Pakistan cards or acted to enfeeble Pakistan's internal unity.

From its side, Pakistan has however tried to simultaneously follow two divergent lines of policy. On the one hand, it has pursued the diplomacy of non-alignment and of non-provocation of the USSR; on the other, it has sought to improve its defence capability on grounds of the threat from the USSR through Afghanistan. A digression on Indo–Pakistan relations would reach beyond the scope of this article, but assuming that Pakistan's main security anxieties are *vis-a-vis* India, this ambivalence could still be dangerous for Pakistan. Pakistan risks actual deterioration of its relations with the USSR, increased pressure on its Afghan border, and heightened tensions with India, all of which could aggravate her internal problems. Therefore, while unresolved ferment in Afghanistan and the Soviet presence on its border may gain Pakistan enhanced security capabilities, its leaders must recognize that the same ferment and presence in Afghanistan was fraught with heightened military dangers and of economic and political strain for the country.

If it is accepted, as this interpretation has sought to suggest, that the Soviet intervention in Afghanistan grew out of local and unexpected defensive anxieties, then the West should be able to refrain safely from counter-measures initiated on the erroneous suspicion of a grand aggressive design. The oil flows have not been threatened, and the Gulf is as secure (or as fragile) as it was before 1980. The urgent need to militarize the region to block the Soviet threat has lost its proclaimed rationale. To persist with the military containment of Afghanistan prevents the creation of the belt of neutrality, and could further strain the stability of the whole region.

VIII

If a serious attempt at a political solution is to be made, the foregoing analysis would suggest the following sorts of step-by-step modalities.

1. A regional conference of countries closely affected by the present situation in Afghanistan should be convened in the capital of one of them. The obvious participants would be Pakistan, Iran, India, Kuwait, Saudi Arabia, the UAE, Bahrain, Qatar, and Oman, or as many of them as would be willing to attend it. All these countries subscribe to the principles of Non-alignment. In some cases even in the face of strong 'persuasion' to the contrary, they have refused to provide military bases and operational concessions for the great powers. They can thus credibly affirm their opposition to the permanent presence of Soviet troops in Afghanistan and endorse the objective of reverting Afghanistan to non-aligned status. As an assembly of the region for the region—outside of the UN—the conference could assert immunity for itself from the competitive manoeuvres of the great powers. At the first stage, the problems inside Afghanistan itself would not be the focus of their attention—so Afghanistan need not be invited. The initial purpose would be to create a climate of mutual interest in regional stability, insulated from the strategic militarization of the South-West and South Asia by outside powers. Its aim, in effect, would be the Swedenization of the region (in the sense of voluntarily reaffirming neutrality and detachment from military blocs) as a step towards the eventual Finlandization of Afghanistan (statutorily imposed neutrality).

To realize this purpose and safeguard against the threats of fresh interventions from outside the region, the ministers could agree to meet periodically, say every quarter, and in the process promote regional economic cooperation and harmonization on the pattern of ASEAN.

2. Once this non-aligned or neutral regional buffer has been established and gained credibility—which might even take a year or two—the conference might seek the addition of selected non-aligned nations from other regions to enhance its international standing. Such an enlarged grouping might include, for example: Algeria, Jordan, Nigeria, Malaysia, Indonesia, Senegal, Tanzania, Male, and Guinea, all of them having sizeable Muslim populations. A function of this larger non-aligned assembly would be to choose an observer group of five nations for a peacekeeping role in Afghanistan. The observer group could be of countries both from within and outside the region. The countries so selected would be expected to provide the personnel and support facilities for a protracted peacekeeping commitment in Afghanistan.

3. Given the likelihood of widespread international endorsement for its mission, especially after the surrounding region has demonstrated its detachment from the global strategic competition, there would be an even chance of the non-aligned observer group being accepted for installation in Kabul by the Afghan government and the Soviet Union. Once established in Kabul, the first tasks would be to seek to defuse the insurgency, help restore internal confidence, facilitate the return of the refugees, and create conditions for a Loya Jirgah of representative Afghans to assemble in Kabul. The settling on a new basis would be difficult under the circumstances, the membership of the Loya Jirgah so could be broadly along the lines of the last such assembly (held in January 1977). The Jirgah would be expected to draw up a new constitution for the country as was done in 1963-4. The observer group's task would be only to facilitate and, if required, advise the constitution-making process of the Afghans.

4. On the basis of the new constitution, the non-aligned observer group would assist in organizing and supervising general elections in the country. The group would have to determine its own procedures, but in some respects the role of the Commonwealth observers in Rhodesia/Zimbabwe in 1980 might provide

some useful guidelines. During the election process the primary responsibility for law and order would have to continue to rest with the Afghan government's civil security forces; but electoral officers from the observer group countries would help to supervise the elections. Through negotiations, a thinning and grouping of the Soviet forces could be arranged prior to the elections.

The assistance of the world community, including the great powers, would be necessary to facilitate the rehabilitation of the refugees on their return to the country. Further, in cooperation with the Afghan government, the observer group could act as funnel and supervisor for urgent measures to restore the shattered economy of Afghanistan.

Needless to say the task of the non-aligned observer group would be delicate and difficult. It would be helped or hindered to the extent credibility was established for its non-ulterior and non-aligned purposes.

5. On the basis of the supervised elections, power could be transferred to the chosen representatives of the Afghan people, and a government could be formed according to the new constitution of the country.

6. The new government, once established, could negotiate to formalize the neutrality of Afghanistan and the withdrawal of the residuary Soviet forces and conclude an Afghan–Soviet Treaty on the lines of the Soviet–Finnish Treaty. The treaty could be formally endorsed by the UN so that in the final instance all great powers would be committed to respect Afghan neutrality and non-alignment.

These are tentative ideas with some deliberate and some doubtless inadvertent omissions set forth primarily with a view to provide a basis for discussion. They can be modified with better counsel and through a process of confidential diplomatic consultations. It is easy to anticipate flaws and pitfalls in this framework. Indeed, the proposal may be as much a non-starter as the other suggestions but the step-by-step sequence seeks to incorporate the following conclusions which emerged from this analysis.

(a) The present drift is dangerous for all countries interested in this strategically located country and region.

(b) A solution that will reduce tensions, restore peace, and obtain the eventual withdrawal of Soviet forces must emanate and be controlled from within the *region* and not sought to be imposed by mutually suspicious, adversary great powers.

(c) The creation of an outer belt of neutrality around Afghanistan has to be a pre-condition for the withdrawal of Soviet forces from Afghanistan.

(d) Only a non-aligned group of nations can command sufficient confidence and respect both to assuage the suspicions of the Afghan people and the anxieties of the Soviet Union about its future security.

(e) The Afghan people are entitled to determine their own form of government.

(f) During this protracted process, the security interests of regional or great powers would not be adversely compromised.

The approach offered here deliberately limits the involvement of the great powers. It is, however, obvious that no such effort could get off the ground without the assurance of their benign acquiescence in an endeavour to see Afghanistan restored to its traditional non-aligned role and the region freed from the dangers of further tensions and instability.

IX

The foregoing pages have repeatedly reaffirmed that Afghanistan remains a serious problem and the present drift is dangerous. A radically different paradigm—which maintains that there is now no longer the same urgency to a political solution of the Afghanistan situation—cannot be overlooked. The unresolved problem of Afghanistan has ceased to stand in the way of the superpower dialogue. The US–USSR arms control talks had started before the declaration of martial law in Poland. There is a belated recognition that Soviet intervention was local and not a step in an aggressive grand design directed against vital Western interests. Since the USSR is now there—and that too by force—in a kind of reverse linkage, the Afghan problem can be used further to contain Soviet expansionism and generally to buttress Western diplomacy and strategy against the Soviet Union.

The significant unspoken thought in this point of view, is that the Soviet Union is militarily bogged down, economically under strain, politically stumped, and internationally on the defensive because of

Afghanistan. Babrak Karmal's government, despite attempts to reverse its own harsher decrees and win back Islamic opinion, remains cribbed, confined, and alienated from the Afghan people. The Afghan rebel leaders—religious, tribal, and secular—though unable to unite on a common command or platform, remain irrevocably hostile to the USSR. In these circumstances, the Soviet Union should not be given an easy way out, much less the political kudos that would result from a voluntary withdrawal. Instead, with little risk and limited costs, Afghanistan should be turned into a Russian Vietnam. To this end, the insurgents should be provided with automatic rifles, anti-tank guns, and portable rockets against helicopter gun-ships, all preferably of Russian design. Even though intensified insurgency may never dislodge the Russians, the drain of men and resources, together with the loss of empathy in the Muslim world and in the Central Asian republics, would be a deterrence against similar adventures elsewhere.

Intellectually, this extrapolated *realpolitik* argument is carried even further. The Soviet Union, by its intervention, has given a new legitimacy to the *droit de limitrophe*—that disregarding international law and morality, other great powers can exercise the right to take military action in a neighbouring country for reasons of perceived threats to their national security. One has even heard, admittedly in a seemingly jocular vein, that the South African policy in Namibia and its pre-emptive armed forays into countries supporting the liberation movements can be defended as not essentially different from the Soviet action in Afghanistan.

In the United States, the Soviet presence in Afghanistan has been cited in marshalling public support for increased defence expenditures. It was used to justify the programme of massive rearmament and put on the defensive those who urged arms control talks and détente. Some plausible dovish arguments have also been adduced to reinforce the *realpolitik* approach. For example, one hears argued that even the reunification of Germany was shelved in order to preserve international peace, and Afghanistan is far less important than Germany. An incidental benefit, it is claimed, has been that Soviet frustrations in Afghanistan had saved Poland from Afghanistan's fate.

This compendium of reasons—some Machiavellian, some realistic, and some merely wishful—crystallizes into a policy judgement that the Soviet occupation of Afghanistan offers the West political advantages without serious corresponding dangers and risks. Carried to its analytical conclusion, this would amount to an unspoken and no doubt unintended parallelism of interest between the USSR and USA in the non-solution of the Afghanistan problem. Whether such considerations have been seriously entertained in responsible official circles is difficult to confirm based on published information only. But if in fact a tacit reconciliation to a permanent Soviet presence in Afghanistan is accepted in the US, the change would amount to a *volte-face*. Not that parallel interests between the superpowers should in principle cause surprise or regrets. The prevention of a major nuclear conflagration, the quest for arms control, détente, and international stability hinge on their sense of global responsibility. Indeed, it is worth recalling that there developed an unspoken parallelism of interest between the USA and USSR in a political solution in Vietnam so that the US could withdraw with some honour. (China at that time was urging a continuing military struggle.) But the present situation would be of the reverse kind, as it would amount to reconciliation in an ongoing conflict and ignoring of the strength and validity of Third World nationalism.

There should be no illusion that this kind of superpower in-difference to local or regional instability would not further damage their diplomatic credibility and standing. Like Kampuchea, Afghani-stan should not become a sideshow. But the serious misjudgement in this approach is the presumption that the USSR or the US had the capacity separately or, even together, to quarantine the problem inside Afghanistan and prevent or manage any spillover outside. It would, in fact, not be possible to insulate a low-level conflict—whether it should prove seriously damaging or merely irritating to the USSR—so that it had no fall out in space or time. The sources of instability will not fade away. On the other hand, a benign support for a South and South-West Asian peace process could translate the negative acquiescence in no solution, with all its hazards, into a positive quest for regional stability which would better safeguard the legitimate security and economic interest of both superpowers. A peace process might even catalytically revive the climate of détente—the hope and expectation of most countries including members of the NATO and Warsaw Pacts.

It needs underlining that the search for a political solution in Afghanistan has relevance and wider importance for the stability of the whole connected area, from the South Asian subcontinent to the Middle East. Following the assassination of President Sadat and given Israel's persisting intransigence on the Palestine question, the entire Middle East is likely in the future to be more divisive and tense. The appeal of Pan-Islamic fundamentalism, cutting across political and ideological frontiers, and defying, both the conservative and secular governments is likely to grow. The social evolution and modernization of these traditional societies is likely to be erratic and could, for a while, even be regressive. A strong feature of the prevailing sentiments in the entire Arab-Islamic world is a growing wariness towards both superpowers. The governments in the region may try, through arms purchases or economic cooperation, to sue one or the other to their advantage. But no government is likely to openly embrace either of the superpowers in total trust or dependence. None of these countries, not even post-Sadat Egypt, wants to be seen as in alliance with the East or West. The Gulf Cooperation Council may plan on regional military cooperation but they remain opposed to Western bases in their countries. Only Israel has taken a positive attitude towards the proposed strategic consensus. As happened in Iran and Iraq, the superpowers may find themselves to be exasperated spectators to sudden new turbulence and dramatic rejections. (Significantly neither Iran nor Iraq switched to embrace the other superpower.) Afghanistan for the Soviet Union, and Iran for the United States, were demonstrations of the hazards of excessive involvement or intrusion without heed to the sociology and nationalism of countries which did not share the military perspective of the big powers. To face similar contingencies (which, like the abortive coup in Bahrain, may ignite locally), the wisest policy for both superpowers may be to shift deliberately from over anxious and overzealous involvement to a posture of benign detachment and responsive friendliness. While the Arab–Israeli problem is becoming more complex, if not impossible of peaceful resolution, the Afghanistan problem provides, for the moment, an opportunity to demonstrate a change of stance and image before new shocks of xenophobic hostility and local turmoil burst upon the Middle East landscape.

A demand for detachment and restraint from superpowers can, of course, be dismissed as unrealistic non-aligned utopianism. In the West it is likely to be castigated as lacking in understanding of the dynamic and expansive nature of Soviet strategic ambitions and of the stakes for the industrialized West. Soviet suspicions of the proposed solution would be equally deep but more restrained in expression, at least until it becomes evident whether it will gather regional and international support. But from the point of view of both superpowers, cohesive non-alignment, starting at the regional

level, offers a better chance to ensure stability and dampen the future
dangers of similar protracted Afghanistans or sudden Irans. Further,
one may speculate that the Soviet Union wishes to regain some
positive credibility in its diplomacy in the Islamic world. It is
therefore more likely to respect and respond—and less likely to
ignore and defy—a collective regional initiative if it follows successful efforts to create a buffer belt of neutrality and so assuage its
security anxieties on its southern flank.

The anatomy of the Afghan crisis reinforces lessons from other
cases of armed intervention, where nationalism and local circumstances were ignored or misunderstood. Apart from the US
intervention in Vietnam and the Russian involvement in Afghanistan, military action as a form of coercive diplomacy when tried by
China against Vietnam met with the same nationalistic resistance
and ended in political, if not military, failure. In Kampuchea, the
Heng Samrin government has sought to capitalize on being more
humane than the brutal Pol Pot regime, but it remains to be seen
whether it can gain 'acceptance' as long as its sanction is only a
massive alien military force. In this context, India's withdrawal from
Bangladesh within 100 days was uniquely wise and thereby avoided
an immediate nationalistic backlash. One might even speculate that,
if in the Bay of Pigs, there had been initially a military success instead
of failure, that accomplishment might have led to a worse quagmire,
involving military occupation and guerrilla warfare.

Where international tensions have been defused, withdrawals
effected, and comparative stability restored—as in Cuba after the
missile crisis, or between India and Pakistan after Tashkent, or in
Finland and Austria—it was through the kind of superpower restraint advocated here. Such restraint did no harm to the strategic
interests of either superpower. Strategic vigilance between the two
superpowers to the extent warranted by their respective threat
perceptions could continue, but deterrence should rely on the
multiple options contained in their strategic armouries, without
intruding into and complicating the politics of nations and regions.
Their strategic launchers can be safely kept 'off the horizons' of the
turbulent developing world. Is it too broad a generalization to
observe, that in a democratized, differentiated, but universalized
system of nation-states, political globalism has mainly courted
frustrations and disasters. On the other hand, under the arch of the
superpowers' balance of terror, persisting and resurgent nationalism
and regionalism—economic and political—has been relentlessly

creeping ahead in Asia, Africa, the Caribbean, and even in Europe and looks like the wave of the future. Statesmanship demands adjusting to this all-too-obvious trend rather than ignoring, resisting, or seeking to discipline it to globalist strategic paradigms.

In conclusion it bears repetition that in Afghanistan the problem started locally and developed with its own dynamics. It was mishandled at home and misperceived abroad. The sturdy nationalism of its people and the country's long experience of guarding its identity and independence without drastically offending its northern neighbour was overlooked in an impetuous involvement. A nation in this situation, from any point of view, must be a buffer; a people with this courage and faith must be left alone to evolve in their own way.

Sir Winston Churchill, as a young subaltern campaigning against these same Pathans on the Indian frontier, came to this perspicacious judgement way back in 1897. His observation merits quotation, even at perhaps excessive length, for its prose as well as its prophecy.

Neither the landscape nor the people find their counterparts in any other portion of the globe. Valley walls rise steeply five or six thousand feet on every side. The columns crawl through a maze of giant corridors down which snow-fed torrents foam under skies of brass. Amid this scene of savage brilliancy, there dwells a race whose qualities seem to harmonise with their environment. . . . Every man is a warrior, a politician and a theologian. Every large house is a real feudal fortress made, it is true, only of sun-baked clay, but with battlements, turrets, loop-holes, flanking towers, drawbridges, etc. complete. Every village has its defence. . . . Every family cultivates its vendetta, every clan its feud. The numerous tribes and combinations of tribes have their accounts to settle. Nothing is ever forgotten and very few debts are left unpaid.

Into this happy world, the nineteenth century brought two new facts: the breech-loading rifle and the British government. The first was welcomed as an enormous luxury and blessing; the second treated an unmitigated nuisance. . . . The convenience of breech-loading, and still more of the magazine, rifle was nowhere more appreciated . . . (than in the Indian highlands. A weapon which would kill with accuracy at fifteen hundred yards opened a whole new vista of delights to every family or clan which could acquire it.[2]

Of course history marches on; old style empires disappear and new nations emerge with new ambitions or new concerns. Techno-

---

[2]Sir Winston Churchill, 'The Mamund Valley', in *A Roving Commission*, New York: Charles Scribner's Sons, 1951.

logy advances and weapons become more destructive but the will to independence keeps matching the will to conquer. The Duke of Wellington, as good a military strategist in his time as any, may have had far-seeing wisdom when at the time of the disastrous First Afghan War he cautioned from London, 'Our military success will only be the beginning of our political problems.'

The Duke of Wellington's caution translates into non-alignment and non-intervention in today's times. The militarily weak are strong in defiance, but if left alone, they will not be the instruments of contending powers in what they perceive as extraneous confrontations. The Afghan still insists on being master in his own homeland. It was in nobody's interest that he should be used merely as a convenient argument. A Swedenized South and South-West Asia followed by Finlandized Afghanistan may provide a way out from the impasse created by the failures and frustrations of superpower globalism and give greater hope for stability to a region which is of importance to the whole world.

4

A Neutral Solution

The ongoing crisis in Afghanistan is the result of misadventures and misjudgements, compounded by internal mishandling and international misperceptions. Nobody anticipated the Saur Revolution of April 1978, in which a coalition of the Khalq and Parcham Communist-inclined parties overthrew the then President Mohammed Daud and proclaimed the Democratic Republic of Afghanistan. Few envisaged that a Soviet invasion would later take place to remove a regime headed by a leader earlier considered to be a pro-Soviet ideologue. Far from following some grand design, the course of the revolution was determined by unforeseen developments. The bloodletting goes on interminably, inconclusively, and possibly dangerously. Paradoxically, a broad consensus exists among contending and interested powers that a return to the pre-1978 status quo would be a satisfactory solution to the crisis over Afghanistan. The problem is how to turn back the clock, how to assuage outraged Afghan nationalism and obtain the disengagement of the Soviet Union, which through mishaps and mistaken impetuosity has alienated a never unfriendly neighbour.

When the Soviets intervened in Afghanistan 20 months after a revolution they viewed as a welcome surprise, the West interpreted the move as a threat to its strategic interests. The Carter administration viewed the Soviet action as a first step toward fulfilling Russian ambitions to secure warm water ports as well as to dominate the Persian Gulf and thereby control or even cut the West's oil lifeline. According to this view, the Soviets timed their intervention to take advantage of the hostage crisis in Iran that was preoccupying the United States. President Carter denounced the invasion as possibly the gravest threat to international peace since World War II and

Foreign Policy, Summer 1982. This is expressly a summary of the paper circulated by the Kennan Institute (Chapter 3).

proclaimed the Carter Doctrine, which committed the United States to defend the Persian Gulf against any outside threat. Washington also made it known that it would take every possible step to compel the withdrawal of Soviet forces from Afghanistan. Yet, within less than a year Afghanistan faded from active international diplomacy.

The Soviet position on Afghanistan also has been riddled with changes and contradictions. Before Daud was overthrown, every indication suggested that Moscow was satisfied with its relations with Afghanistan and committed to Daud, who was after all the architect of closer Soviet–Afghan relations. After the Democratic Republic was proclaimed, the USSR held a position of privileged insight into the country. It is thus striking to note the numerous shifts in the Soviet attitude toward Afghanistan.

Initially the Soviets welcomed the Khalq–Parcham coalition led by President Noor Mohammed Taraki, then acquiesced in the exclusion and banishing of Babrak Karmal and the Parchamites, and ultimately supported Khalq leader Hafizullah Amin when he seized power. Yet after the Soviet invasion, while Moscow continued to applaud the revolution, it denounced the revolution's mastermind Amin and installed Karmal as head of the government. These changes in the Kremlin's official stance can scarcely be explained by a well-organized Soviet plan to control and manipulate the revolution.

Meanwhile the Soviet intervention triggered a chain of reactions. It led to the massive rearmament of Pakistan and, as a result, of India, thereby straining both their economies and exacerbating regional tensions. If also led to the formulation of the Carter Doctrine, the constitution of the Rapid Deployment Force, and the US campaign to establish an anti-Soviet strategic consensus, and greatly increased US and Soviet naval presence in the Indian Ocean.

The United States erroneously based its appraisals of every development on its own global strategic perspective instead of the complex dynamics of local events and regional circumstances. The Soviet Union acted impetuously to tidy over a situation that had deteriorated unexpectedly, justifying its action in globalist terms of pre-empting imperialist ambitions. The Soviet move into Afghanistan and the militaristic reactions in the West have thus made the restoration of stability in the region vastly complicated and difficult to achieve.

What has transpired is both surprising and tragic since it is almost a replay of the great power game played in Afghanistan during the last century. The lessons of history were clearly overlooked. The struggle over the strategic highlands astride the historical invasion route between Europe and Asia arose from the competition and confrontation between Czarist Russia, which was expanding to the south, and the British Empire, which wanted to protect the outer perimeter of its dominion over India. The Afghan tribes even then did not prove to be docile spectators as the foreign giants vied for their native homeland. In the end, the defiant hostility of the Afghan tribesmen forced both Russia and Great Britain to abandon their ambitions and leave Afghanistan alone. Modern Afghanistan was born in a struggle against conquest, and it has never lost that will to remain independent.

Since 1880 the rulers of Afghanistan have maintained a sagacious policy of not becoming involved in the European political game or serving as the strategic instrument of any power. In its strategic location, Afghanistan recognized that to preserve its independence the country must remain neutral in great power conflicts but with special care not to provoke the security-related sensitivities of its powerful neighbour to the north.

Even though it was governed by a conservative monarchy, Afghanistan quickly recognized the Communist government in Russia. As early as 1921 Afghanistan concluded a treaty of neutrality and non-aggression with the Soviet Union and shortly thereafter started buying arms and aircraft from it. While remaining sensitive to Soviet interests, Afghanistan developed a pattern of economic relations with countries of different social systems. Considering Afghanistan's location, the United States never questioned the rationale for Afghan foreign policy. For its part, the Soviet Union respected and made no determined effort in those 60 years to undermine the social system and Islamic culture of the country. After World War II and until 1978 the only serious problem that Afghanistan faced was with Pakistan on the Pushtunistan issue—that is, Afghanistan's desire to unite the Pushtun tribes.

But a series of unexpected developments quickly precipitated a crisis. Following the murder of a popular Parchamite leader, Mir Akbar Khaiber, the Khalq–Parcham group seized power in April 1978 in a quickly improvised coup at a time of increasing economic and political discontent. The ineptitude and growing conservatism of the Daud regime contributed to the surprising success of the revolution. The initial cohesion of the Khalq–Parcham coalition disintegrated not over principles but because of internal rivalries.

Amin, who emerged as the driving force of the new republic, was a convinced votary of the economic and social theories of Karl Marx and the socialist system as pursued by V.I. Lenin and adopted a staunchly pro-Soviet attitude in his approach to international politics. Based on such textbook knowledge and Amin's understanding of the Soviet example, the new government sought to transform a deeply religious society into a modern secular state through a series of fiats and decrees. The result was widespread disenchantment and resistance; within months the new rulers were looked upon as godless and foreign. The repressive measures that followed only further alienated the people and made them militantly hostile both to the regime and to the USSR.

All through 1978 and the first half of 1979 the Soviet Union supported Amin and his policies, including the ruthless suppression of the insurgency. But by the summer of 1979 the Soviet Union realized that the impetuous imposition of socialism by a pro-Soviet ideologue was turning a traditionally friendly country into a hostile neighbour. The Soviets came to recognize that despite all his ideological fidelity Amin was becoming a liability to Soviet security. The Kremlin therefore decided that power should be restored to Taraki precisely because he had a greater nationalistic appeal and was less ideologically militant. The Soviet Union schemed with Taraki to remove Amin from power at least politically, if not physically. This intention seems to have been betrayed by the chief of security and, as a result of the palace shoot-out on 14 September, Taraki was injured while Amin escaped.

The aborted palace coup was the critical episode that led to the internationalization of the developments in Afghanistan and made the subsequent Soviet intervention inevitable. It turned Amin, the loyal ideologue, into an anti-Soviet nationalist. In the Kremlin's embarrassment and nervous anxiety at the failure of the conspiracy with Taraki, Moscow saw no scope but of intervention which was sufficient to simultaneously remove Amin, neutralize the Afghan army, and to tackle the intensifying insurgency. The Kremlin probably feared that Amin, in his disillusionment with the Soviets, would renounce the treaty of friendship and ultimately demand their total withdrawal from Afghanistan—following the example of Egyptian President Anwar Sadat. The Soviets thus faced the possibility of reversal in what had promised to be a gratuitous enlargement of the Socialist commonwealth.

Amin, angry at his repudiation and suspecting Soviet malevolence, attempted to consolidate his position. Belatedly, he sought to retreat from his earlier unpopular positions, appeal to nationalist sentiments, and broaden his political base by pacifying the Mullahs and his alienated countrymen. Similarly, he sought to diversify his external contacts—most noticeably with Pakistan and possibly through it with the West—in the hope of eventually wriggling free from the Soviet embrace. The Soviet invasion put an end to these plans.

Militarily and politically, the Soviet move was an impetuous reaction to local circumstances and dynamics. The Soviets never expected their forces to meet such resistance from the Afghan people. Much less did they anticipate that their move would provoke such a storm of criticism and condemnation from the Third World and even from international Communist parties. It has seriously undermined Soviet appeal and diplomacy in the decolonized world, where Moscow has long sought to promote the ideals of independence, nationalism, and non-alignment.

It retrospect the USSR probably recognizes that a genuinely non-aligned Afghanistan pursuing non-radical policies was a better guardian of Soviet interests. In the past, Afghans had come to respect Russian sensitivity concerning security, and the Soviet Union had refrained from undermining the social and political structure of Afghanistan. As a result of misperceptions and misadventures, there was a clash of the imperatives of Afghan nationalism and Soviet apprehensions about security. The heart of the problem now is how to assuage both.

Preventing Spillover

The spur to the resolution of the Afghanistan problem can come only from a recognition that the present situation could lead to an unpredictable deterioration, affecting both global and regional powers. The bloodletting inside the country has inflicted terrible suffering on one of the poorest countries in the world. The mounting burden of refugees—exceeding 2 million and still growing—could lead to disaster for the political unity and economic health of Pakistan. In the present situation there is an inherent risk that counter-infiltration across the notoriously permeable frontier between Afghanistan and Pakistan will escalate and lead to border incidents and even hot pursuit. Tension and instability could spread eastward to the subcontinent, southward to Baluchistan and the Persian Gulf, westward to Iran, and even northward into Central Asia.

The germs of disaffection—a mix of national, sub-national, tribal, religious, and socio-economic factors are all but immune to conventional frontier customs or security forces. Other crises in the area could easily occur. No power, global or local, can be confident or complacent enough to think that persisting instability can be controlled to harm only its adversary, without damaging its own immediate or long-term interests. The need to prevent such spillover therefore lends urgency to finding a political solution to the Afghan problem, not only for Afghanistan but for any or all countries with stakes in the area.

At present, neither the beginning of a solution nor a sense of urgency is evident. Nevertheless a surprising measure of common ground on the broad ingredients of an ultimate solution has emerged among the various interested parties. Many have implicitly recognized that stability cannot be restored unless Afghanistan is neutralized against great-power competition. A recent study by the Hoover Institution's Anthony Arnold, who sees the crisis as proof of aggressive Soviet strategy against the West, agrees that Afghanistan must revert to 'its traditional role as a nationally free, truly non-aligned and independent country'. The European Community proposal, articulated by former British Foreign Minister Lord Carrington, also aimed at the evacuation of Soviet forces in return for the guaranteed neutrality of the country. Resolutions passed by the Islamic Conference, the Non-aligned Foreign Ministers Conference, and the United Nations all demand the restoration of Afghanistan's non-alignment. Even Soviet President Leonid Brezhnev has offered to withdraw Soviet forces but specified that he would do so only after 'all forms of outside interference' had ended. Most significant, the various Soviet comments seem to imply that the primary Soviet objective is to prevent Afghanistan from becoming a hostile base rather than to retain the country as a strategic ally or as a model Socialist State.

All these proposals in effect call for the restoration of Afghanistan to its pre-revolutionary status—non-aligned although sensitive to Soviet interests, free to develop economic relations with all countries, and able to develop according to its own religious and social ethos. Thus the general outline of a solution that could satisfy all parties already exists. But what in essence represents a return to the pre-

1978 status quo cannot be achieved without eliminating the bitterness and suspicion created by the events of the last three years.

Some have suggested that a settlement similar to those reached by Finland and Austria after World War II might work for Afghanistan. The Soviet–Finnish Treaty led to the evacuation of the Soviet base at Porkkala in return for a pledge that Finland would not join a military arrangement hostile to the Soviet Union and that Moscow would retain the right to intervene if Soviet security were threatened. The Austrian Treaty of 1955, which ended the post-World War II four-power occupation and restored Austrian sovereignty, requires the country to remain neutral.

The situation and circumstances of post-war Finland and Austria, however, differed greatly from those of present-day Afghanistan. Both Austria and Finland had well-established democratic governments that could speak for the national consensus and decide that imposed neutrality was an acceptable sacrifice to secure the withdrawal of the foreign forces. No one can at present speak authoritatively for the Afghan nation. No one can confidently assert that if the Soviet troops withdraw the bitter feelings of the Afghan people will evaporate and they will not become hostile to Soviet interests and security.

One aspect of the Finnish and Austrian settlements, however, is pertinent to the search for a solution in Afghanistan. The Soviets could afford to withdraw from Austria because Poland, Czechoslovakia, Hungary, and Romania provided a security buffer for the Soviet Union. The restoration of full Finnish independence hinged on the presumption that Sweden would remain neutral and not join the North Atlantic Treaty Organization. Selig Harrison has pointed out that Soviet withdrawal from Afghanistan would similarly require a guarantee from Iran, Pakistan, and India to remain non-aligned.

The Kremlin's attitude toward withdrawal from Afghanistan will depend on whether Pakistan becomes a heavily armed, pro-Western ally or a neutral state between the superpowers. America's anti-Soviet strategic consensus rests on the assumption that the Soviet Union intends to use Afghanistan as a springboard for a thrust into Pakistan and the Persian Gulf. As a result, the United States has sought to enlist countries such as Pakistan in a strategy of military containment of the Soviet Union. Yet any kind of military arrangement or alliance with the West will eliminate all chances of Soviet evacuation from Afghanistan. Indeed, it will provide justification for the Soviet intervention and continued Soviet presence in the country.

The USSR for its part is engaged in damage-limiting diplomacy to alleviate the fears its invasion of Afghanistan have aroused in the region. Even in the face of strong denunciations, Moscow, has maintained a posture of cool restraint toward the Islamic regime in Iran.

Since the occupation of Afghanistan, Soviet relations with Pakistan have gone through phases of sharp accusations and even threats, but they have not been actively hostile. In fact, during the fall 1981 visit to Islamabad of Nikolai Firyubin, a Soviet Vice Foreign Minister, the Soviet Union and Pakistan reaffirmed their desire for friendly relations and their commitment to enlarged economic cooperation. Even though Pakistan had remained tied to the West for over two decades, the Soviet Union has sought to maintain good relations with Islamabad, especially after the development of Sino–Pakistani friendship. Moscow has refrained from actively supporting Afghan demands for Pushtunistan, and it has not given encouragement or material support to the Baluch dissidents. Contrary to many expectations in the West, the Soviets have not acted to enfeeble Pakistan's internal unity.

Meanwhile, Pakistan has tried to simultaneously follow two divergent lines of policy. On the one hand, it has pursued a diplomacy of non-alignment and has tried not to provoke the USSR; on the other hand, it has sought to improve its defence capability on the grounds of the concern it shares with the United States about the Soviet threat through Afghanistan. But under the current circumstances, this dual policy may no longer be tenable for Pakistan. It risks deterioration of its relations with the Soviet Union, increased pressures on its Afghan border, and heightened tensions with India. These pressures could also aggravate the country's already grave internal problems.

Steps Toward Peace

The Western policy of military containment of the Soviet Union in the area, based on the erroneous view that the Soviet invasion of Afghanistan was the first step in some grand design, now threatens to make a solution to the Afghan problem impossible to achieve and may even further strain the stability of the whole region. The oil flows have not been threatened, and the Gulf is neither more nor less secure than before 1980. The reason given for militarizing the region, namely, to block the Soviet threat, has lost its proclaimed rationale.

If there can be a belated recognition that errors of judgement have led to the present unsatisfactory and possibly explosive situation, then all the parties involved can be in a position to attempt the following sequential diplomatic steps. These steps can facilitate a movement toward a real, lasting political solution.

A regional conference of countries closely affected by the present situation in Afghanistan can be convened. Pakistan, Iran, India, Saudi Arabia, the United Arab Emirates, Bahrain, Qatar, and Oman could meet in the capital of one of these countries, all of which belong to the Non-aligned Movement. In most cases they have refused to provide military bases or the use of facilities to the superpowers, even in the face of strong pressure. They can thus credibly affirm their opposition to the permanent presence of Soviet troops in Afghanistan and endorse the objective of returning Afghanistan to non-aligned status.

Unlike a conference under UN auspices, an assembly of countries from the region could operate outside the competitive manoeuvres of the superpowers. At least initially the conference would not focus on the problems inside Afghanistan, and so Kabul need not be invited. The meeting would first aim to create a climate of mutual interest in regional stability. Specifically, it would seek an agreement by which all countries reaffirm their neutrality and detachment from military blocs, in effect the 'Swedenization' of the region. This declaration and policy must be the first step toward the eventual 'Finlandization' of Afghanistan. The participants could also agree to meet periodically to sustain the region's new status in order to safeguard against the threats of further political upheaval and fresh interventions from outside, and to promote regional economic cooperation and harmony on the pattern of the Association of South-East Asian Nations.

Once this non-aligned buffer is established and has gained credibility, the conference may seek the addition of selected non-aligned countries from other regions to enhance its international standing. Such an enlarged grouping could include, for example, Algeria, Jordan, Nigeria, Malaysia, Indonesia, Senegal, Tanzania, Male, and Guinea, all of which have sizeable Muslim populations. The function of this larger non-aligned assembly would be to choose an observer group of five countries to perform a peace-keeping role in Afghanistan. This group could include countries from both within and outside the region. They would be expected to provide the personnel and support facilities for a protracted peacekeeping commitment in Afghanistan.

Given the likelihood of widespread international endorsement for the observer group's mission, especially after the surrounding region has demonstrated its detachment from global strategic competition, the Afghan government and the Soviet Union would have strong incentive to accept the group in Kabul. Once installed, the group's first tasks would be to defuse the insurgency, help restore internal confidence, facilitate the return of the refugees, and create conditions for a Loya Jirgah—the traditional gathering of Afghan tribal representatives—to assemble in Kabul. The Loya Jirgah could be held on the basis of the last such assembly in January 1977. It would be expected to draw up a new constitution for the country. The observer group would facilitate this process but advise only if required.

On the basis of the new constitution, the non-aligned observer group would assist in organizing and supervising general elections in the country. The group would have to determine its own procedures, but in some respects the role of the Commonwealth observers in Zimbabwe in 1980 might provide some useful guidelines. During the election process the primary responsibility for law and order would have to continue to rest with the Afghan government's civil security forces. The observer group would be expected to help supervise the elections and could negotiate the thinning and grouping of the Soviet forces prior to the elections.

The newly elected government would conclude an Afghan–Soviet Treaty along the lines of the Soviet–Finnish Treaty and negotiate the withdrawal of the remaining Soviet forces. The treaty could be formally endorsed by the UN so that in the final instance all major powers would be committed to respect Afghan neutrality and non-alignment.

Benign Detachment

In the present military and political quagmire, achieving such a solution is bound to be extremely difficult. Only diplomatic consultations could work out the details and essential refinements of these step-by-step proposals.

The entire process deliberately limits the involvement of the superpowers, but it could not begin without their benign acquiescence in an endeavour to see Afghanistan restored to its traditional non-aligned role. The assistance of the world community would, however, be necessary to facilitate the resettlement of the refugees and provide humanitarian aid. In cooperation with the Afghan government the observer group could act as a funnel and supervisor for urgent measures to restore the shattered Afghan economy. The essence of the proposal—to create an outer belt of neutrality as a precondition for the Finlandization of Afghanistan—would ensure no damage or danger to the security of the superpowers or the region. But the proposal assumes that only non-aligned regional powers can assuage both Afghan nationalism and Soviet anxieties about the future security of the USSR, and in no way increases the threat to the oil artery, so vital to the West and much of the world.

The effort to arrest the present drift will be challenged or rejected by those who see the situation as, on balance, affording some gratuitous advantages to the West. Thus, according to this view, a little covert military and financial support to the Afghan Mujahidin can transform Afghanistan into a Soviet Vietnam.

The Soviet Union is militarily bogged down, economically strained, politically hindered, and internationally on the defensive because of Afghanistan. Babrak Karmal's government, despite attempts to reverse the harsher socialistic decrees and win back Islamic opinion, remains alienated from the Afghan people. The Afghan rebel leaders—religious, tribal, and secular—although unable to unite on a common leader or platform, continue to be irrevocably hostile to the USSR. In these circumstances, according to some, the Soviet Union should not be given an easy way out, much less the political benefits of a voluntary withdrawal. Although an intensified insurgency may never dislodge the Soviets, the drain of men and resources, together with the loss of empathy in the Muslim world and in the Central Asian republics, can be a deterrent against similar adventures elsewhere.

Proponents of such a course carry the intellectual argument even further. The Soviet Union, by its intervention and disregard for international law, has provided legitimacy for other great powers that perceive a threat to their national security to take military action in a neighbouring country. Even South Africa's policy on Namibia and pre-emptive South African armed forays into countries supporting the liberation movements can thus be defended as no different, in essence, from the Soviet action in Afghanistan.

In the United States, hardliners have used the Soviet presence in Afghanistan to marshal support for increased defence spending and to deflect pressures favouring détente. Some hint at a similar US need to police Central America.

This compendium of reasons—some Machiavellian, some realistic, and some merely wishful—crystallizes into a policy judgement that the Soviet occupation of Afghanistan offers the West political advantages without serious corresponding dangers. Carried to its ultimate conclusion, such an approach suggests an unspoken parallelism of interests between the superpowers. Each would benefit from a continuation of the Afghanistan stalemate.

This kind of indifference to local or regional instability by the superpowers would, however, only damage further their diplomatic credibility and standing. Like Kampuchea, Afghanistan is on the way to becoming a sideshow, another victim of globalism. The presumption of such a policy—of fuelling a simmering low-level conflict with no attempt at political solution—is that the USSR, or the United States, has the capacity, separately or even in concert, to quarantine the problem inside Afghanistan and prevent or manage any political or military spillover. This would be yet another serious misjudgement. In contrast, support for a South and South-West Asian peace process could help achieve progress toward regional stability. It would thereby safeguard the legitimate security and economic interests of both superpowers. A peace process might even help revive détente.

The search for a political solution in Afghanistan has relevance and wider importance for the stability of the whole area from the subcontinent to the Middle East. The assassination of Sadat, the lack of progress on the Palestinian question, and the recent violence on the West Bank and in Jerusalem have further increased tension and division in the Middle East. Under these circumstances the appeal of pan-Islamic fundamentalism, cutting across political and ideological frontiers and defying both conservative and secular governments, will continue to grow. The governments in the region may try, through arms purchases or economic cooperation, to use one or the other superpower to their advantage. But no government, not even post-Sadat Egypt, is likely to embrace openly either superpower in total trust or military dependence. As happened in the war between Iran and Iraq, the superpowers may find themselves to be exasperated spectators to sudden new turbulence and dramatic rejections.

Washington's debacle in Iran and Moscow's in Afghanistan demonstrate the hazards of excessive involvement or intrusion in countries that do not share the perspective of the superpowers. The wisest policy for both superpowers, therefore, would be to shift to a posture of benign detachment and responsive friendship. Many will dismiss such superpower detachment and restraint as unrealistic non-aligned utopianism. But from the point of view of both superpowers, cohesive non-alignment offers a better chance to ensure stability and avoid future dangers similar to those in Afghanistan and Iran.

The lessons of the Afghan crisis reinforce those from other cases of armed intervention where nationalism and local circumstances were ignored or misunderstood. Apart from the US intervention in Vietnam and the Soviet involvement in Afghanistan, Chinese military action against Vietnam met with the same nationalistic resistance and ended in political, if not military, failure. In Kampuchea, the Heng Samrin government has sought to capitalize on being more humane than the brutal Pol Pot regime, but whether the present government can gain acceptance as long as its only sanction is a massive Vietnamese military force remains to be seen. Where international tensions have been defused, withdrawals effected, and comparative stability restored—as in Cuba after the 1962 missile crisis or between India and Pakistan after Tashkent, or in Finland and Austria—the kind of superpower restraint advocated here was a crucial factor.

It has become clear—as it was at the end of the last century's great game—that a country in Afghanistan's situation must be a buffer and that a people with such courage and faith must be left alone to evolve in their own way. A Swedenized South and South-West Asia and a Findlandized Afghanistan may provide a way to break the impasse created by the failures and frustrations of superpower globalism. Together, both could bring greater stability to a region that is important to the superpowers and to the whole world.

5

The Author Replies – I

I wish to thank those who have written to comment on my article [carried in the Summer issue of 1982 of *Foreign Policy*].

I have not suggested that a satisfactory solution to the Afghanistan imbroglio would be easy to achieve. A scrutiny, free from any globalist predispositions of the chronology and development of the crisis, seeks to suggest that the proposed step-by-step approach might provide the basis for resolving the central problems of Afghan independence and regional peace and stability. Other suggested solutions have ignored Afghan nationalism or Soviet security concerns and so, predictably, have failed.

The present Western policy is to provide limited no-risk military support to harass the Soviets. The measures initiated since 1980 were predicated on the false assumption that the Soviet invasion was a step to threaten Persian Gulf oil flows, and were meant to contain Soviet southward expansion. These plans have by now failed or been abandoned. The Rapid Deployment Force has been constituted, but it has been rejected by the countries directly affected by the invasion, who have chosen to remain neutral. Incidentally, Soviet presence in Afghanistan could improve only marginally Soviet military capability in the region. The distance from the Soviet border on the Caspian Sea to the head of the Persian Gulf is shorter, and to the Straits of Hormuz no longer, than from any potential base in Afghanistan. Reactive preparations based on false premises persist, but it is difficult to perceive the outlines of a Western policy which could restore Afghanistan's sovereignty.

I neither condone the Soviet presence nor believe that the continuing ferment is due primarily to outside support for the Mujahidin. I do not suggest that the Soviets independently are pursuing actively an opportunity to withdraw. I do believe that a carefully, integrated

---

*After the *Foreign Policy* published the article entitled, 'A neutral solution'. The Soviet forces were increasingly harassed by the Afghan Mujahidin.

diplomatic process could create conditions and pressures that might induce the Soviets to restore Afghan independence.

Pakistan's policy seems somewhat different from some articulated [Francis Fukuyama's] expectations. No doubt Pakistan, like all of South-West Asia, is concerned by the Soviet military presence on its borders. But while Pakistan obtained a pledge of substantial US military aid, it does not, evidently, share US perceptions of Soviet intentions. Despite earlier Soviet verbal threats, both the USSR and Pakistan have affirmed that their relations remain cordial. Pakistan has even agreed to indirect talks with Afghan President Babrak Karmal's government. Similarly, contrary to some expectations, the USSR has not played the Baluch card or reactivated the old Afghan case of a separate Pakhtunistan.

Pakistan does face the burden of two to three million Afghan refugees who have fled their homeland. But they were not, as Fukuyama implies, pushed out by Soviet and Afghan forces deliberately to intimidate Pakistan. Easing this burden, which compounds other internal problems, depends on a political solution in Afghanistan.

I have not suggested international negotiations regarding the form of Afghanistan's government. The Afghan people must choose their own constitutional arrangements but only non-aligned observers can enable them to choose freely by minimizing international pressures. The adversary powers must first detach themselves, allow Swedenization, and give non–alignment a chance. Such actions would be consonant with the emerging reality of Third World nationalism and non-alignment rather than seeking unsuccessfully to make Afghanistan and other Third World countries adjuncts of global strategies.

It is asked whether Finlandization would also be commended in the Caribbean, southern Africa, or Indo–China. The circumstances— geographical and historical—for every country and region differ, but the tragic failures or frustrations of interventions against nationalism from Vietnam onward point to a negative lesson. The proposition that living with non-alignment is a lesser hazard than intrusive military interventions holds good everywhere.

In Afghanistan nationalism has not been smothered; it continues to undermine Soviet foreign policy. 'Swedenization' in the region might allow for the restoration of Afghan independence and even ease the burdens for the USSR. Finland has been fully independent internally and in its economic relations. Afghanistan is in a similar location to Finland. For almost 100 years Afghanistan preserved its independence by adopting a non-hostile attitude toward its northern neighbour. The mistaken intervention by the USSR has not disproved the validity of the policy. To embody this position in a treaty registered with the United Nations would not really derogate Afghan sovereignty. The desire to harass the Soviet Union should not be the pretext for, in effect, inflicting continuing punishment on the Afghans.

Let me repeat that this carefully integrated approach may not secure Soviet withdrawal from Afghanistan. If Swedenization is sincerely tried first, however, the USSR may find plausible rejection of this approach difficult. In any case, a regional approach could be a catalyst for better understanding within South Asia and economic cooperation with South-West Asia. Even if the Afghanistan problem is not solved, the consequences of Soviet action can be arrested, bilateral tensions submerged in a broader discipline, and the fragile hopes for stability in the region strengthened. Regionalism centred around non-alignment and economic complementarities might lead to dampen a future crisis and temptations of interventions, based on pre-conceived but non-objective analyses, by outsiders.

6

The Author Replies – II

I have seen the letter from Said Mohd. Malwand, Chairman of the Malwand's Trust of Afghan Human Freedoms, commenting on my articles on a framework for a solution to the Afghan imbroglio.

I have myself acknowledged the formidable difficulties in unscrambling a tragic situation precipitated by mistakes and misperceptions. But the danger now, especially for the Afghan nation and the region, is from the present drift and continuing bloodletting. The expectations that Soviet forces will go on to the oil and warm waters of the Gulf have been belied. But the involvement of the United Nations (UN) provides the *ex-post* justification for Soviet military operations and long-term consolidation, including the deployment of sophisticated weaponry.

If the aim is to restore Afghanistan to non-alignment and genuine independence, then conditions must first be created so that Soviet security will not be perceived to be endangered by a revanchist anti-Russian dispensation in and around the country. A regional initiative, with the full moral backing of the Non-aligned Movement, can possibly make the Soviet Union review its policy. The integrated step-by-step approach might rescue the USSR from a no-win military situation and a politically calamitous involvement. The initial creation of a regional buffer might find the Soviet Union agreeable to scaling down and grouping its forces while the Afghan people determine their own constitutional framework and the entire Non-aligned world acts as an objective umpire.

The resolutions of the Islamic conferences and the proposals and initiatives of the UN, not unexpectedly, have not got off the ground because they ignore the Soviet Union's security sensitivities. The Soviet-sponsored proposals sought to bypass Afghan nationalism. What I have urged, if followed sequentially, runs no serious risks but safeguards both factors. It may be flawed but somewhat like Churchill's definition of democracy, it may be the worst possible solution, except for all the others!

The eventual Finlandization of Afghanistan through regional Swedenization might, just conceivably, obtain restoration of Afghanistan's national personality and offer some promise for one-sixth of the Afghan people to regain their homelands. It is worth trying. In any case, it is unrealistic to expect that a great power, however mistaken it may have been, can be harassed or punished into surrender and withdrawal.

7(a)
Afghan Imbroglio – I

For the West, Afghanistan has become a sideshow or at best a convenient argument. It is now widely recognized that the Soviet invasion did not pose a danger to world peace. Nor was it a first step in a Soviet grand design or even a threat to the oil from the Gulf. The West still seems to hope that Afghanistan would remain a smouldering Soviet Vietnam. But in any case the measures for compelling a Soviet withdrawal have been all but abandoned.

Back-burner

The Soviet Union also probably now recognizes that its military intervention in a non-aligned neighbour has exacted a far heavier price militarily, economically, and diplomatically than it anticipated. The argument that Soviet involvement and the subsequent failure to pacify Afghanistan was due to external support for the Mujahidin has carried little international credibility. As long as the Soviet Union persists in its military action, Soviet foreign policy at least in the Third World will not regain a positive buoyancy. The USSR is probably relieved that the focus of international attention has shifted to other theatres such as Lebanon where the United States abetted the aggression and now faces its own frustrations. But propaganda rhetoric aside, Afghanistan has moved to the back-burner as far as the global powers are concerned.

For South and South-West Asia, the continuing bloodletting in Afghanistan and its actual and potential consequences remain a serious, if not a dangerous, problem. Pakistan is now burdened with two to three million refugees, which has compounded its political and economic travails. It has accelerated the arms race between Pakistan and India and correspondingly the enormous opportunity

---

* *Indian Express*, 24 August 1982 (summary of Chapter 3 for the Indian readers).

costs to their national development. Instability could spread in all directions from this old Asian crossroad. The real agony is for Afghanistan and its people. A brave old nation is being destroyed, just as Kampuchea was fatally damaged by American intervention in 1970.

Afghanistan was the only country in Asia and Africa which resisted and defeated imperialist intervention and that too both from Czarist Russia and British imperialism. For close to a century, it succeeded in safeguarding its independence by skilful detachment from great power politics. Ironically now in the post-colonial era the country faces the threat to its personality and its nationalism. If the Non-aligned world also gets reconciled to such external intervention, it would increase the temptation for similar adventures against weaker neighbours and further undermine the validity and strength of the movement as a whole.

Special Tragedy

Afghanistan is a special tragedy. No one anticipated the internal turmoil, much less that it would lead to internationalized tension before 1978. A careful scrutiny of the chronology after the unexpected success of the Saur Revolution suggests that a combination of internal dynamics, ineptitude, misperceptions, and mistaken impetuosity determined the course of developments in Afghanistan. Hafizullah Amin emerged as the principal decision-maker in 1978 and the Soviet Union welcomed and responded with support for the policies pursued by the newly established Democratic Republic. However in the summer of 1979, the Soviet Union found that the ideological militancy of Amin was actually turning a country—never in the past unfriendly to the USSR—into a security liability. The Soviet Union tried first to moderate, and when it failed, planned to have him displaced. The abortive attempt to install Taraki failed, but as a consequence, turned the pro-Soviet Amin, still in power, into a nationalist and a potential Sadat. The Soviet intervention was, no doubt, prompted by defensive anxieties and not aggressive expansionism. But they overlooked their historical experience in Afghanistan and the frequent lessons that nationalism and liberation movements are further fuelled, and not dampened, by a foreign presence, even in poor and backward nations.

Political Solution

There is now common ground that there can be neither a military defeat of the Soviet Union nor pacification through arms to Afghanistan. Only patient and skilful diplomacy towards a political solution can restore peace to the region. There is also common ground that such a solution must seek to revert Afghanistan to the pre-1978 dispensation of an independent but Non-aligned country. Even the West recognizes that Afghanistan cannot be allowed to be hostile to Soviet security interests.

The heart of the problem is how to safeguard Soviet security concerns and simultaneously to assuage outraged Afghan nationalism. How are the apprehensions and anger generated in the last four years to be eradicated? In effect, the problem is how to go forward when it involves going back to the beginning. The Carrington initiative, on behalf of the EEC, and the Soviet proposals came to nought because they did not satisfy one or the other of these basic ingredients.

Parallel Interests

The United Nations (UN), which must perforce deal with member governments, can also make little progress as it can have no access to the nationalist insurgents. Moreover, the UN cannot go very far in defiance of one or both superpowers. In the present international climate, both superpowers are either stymied by each other or are becoming indifferent to regional conflicts. When the superpowers appear to be developing a parallel interest in letting the Afghanistan problem recede from the urgent international agenda, the Non-aligned countries, especially those belonging to the region, detached from global militarism, must wrest the initiative to resolve what is essentially a regional problem.

7(b)

Afghan Imbroglio – II

In the light of the foregoing analysis of the Afghanistan question, the following step-by-step approach may provide a framework for a solution which aims at reaching broadly-shared goals.

A conference of the Non-aligned nations bordering on Afghanistan or directly interested in the stability of South-West Asia should be called. Pakistan, Iran, Saudi Arabia, Kuwait, United Arab Emirates Bahrain, Qatar, Oman, and India suggest themselves as possible participants. Kuwait, which has the closest relations with all or most of them and with both the superpowers, may be most suited to play host. With the commitment of these countries to regional stability, the purpose of this conference should be to individually and collectively reaffirm, as they have already done in different contexts, their determination to remain detached from globalist military strategies. The declaration and policy would be in line with the Swedish policy of military neutrality between NATO and the Warsaw Pact. (It may be recalled that it was only because Sweden chose neutrality that the USSR withdrew from the Porkkala base in Finland. The Soviet withdrawal from Austria in 1955 may also not have come about if Eastern Europe did not provide a cushioned buffer against the NATO powers.)

Credibility

Once the Swedenization of the region surrounding Afghanistan has won international credibility—and this process must take some months, if not longer—a larger conference of Non-aligned nations from other regions and continents, along with the original group, should be assembled. (The participation can be determined at the first conference.) The purpose of this second meeting should be to

---

* *Indian Express*, 25 August 1982 (summary of Chapter 3 for the Indian readers).

choose a five-nation group which could play a peace-keeping and observer role in Afghanistan. In the light of regional Swedenization and reinforced by the backing of a bigger cross-section of Non-aligned nations, there should be reasonable prospects of the five-nation group being accepted by Kabul and not being opposed by Moscow.

A Non-aligned peace-keeping group (which is bound to include some Islamic countries), once established in Kabul, should seek to obtain a ceasefire and an end to insurgency and facilitate the return of the refugees who have fled the country. Thereafter, a Loya Jirgah on the basis of the Afghan tradition (the last was held in 1977) could be called to draft a new constitution for the country. The five-nation group could assist, if asked, in drafting the constitution but in any case (as in the case of the Commonwealth observer group in Rhodesia), it should superintend and observe the election under the new constitution.

On the basis of the results of the elections, a new Afghan government could assume the reins of power in Kabul. The first task of the new government would be to negotiate a treaty with the USSR on the lines of the Soviet–Finnish Treaty (embodying a commitment to respect Soviet security interests). Thereafter, the residuary Soviet forces should be totally withdrawn from the country.

Way Out

These proposals, it must be acknowledged, are riddled with deliberate gaps and would, no doubt, face unforeseen difficulties. The framework will have to be refined through diplomatic consultations. The spur to the effort must come from the fact that the alternative of continuing drift is potentially dangerous. But at all events the initiation of this process could be a catalyst to economic regionalism in South and South-West Asia.

The Afghan problem may well be more amenable to a Non-aligned initiative than, for example, the undoing of Israeli aggression in Lebanon and the arrest of the suicidal conflict between Iran and Iraq. The success of the process would, no doubt, require the acquiescence, if not benign support, of the great powers but the envisaged process does not adversely affect their defensive security interests. In any case, the writing is on the wall. The superpowers will have to shift from a policy of overzealous military involvement to one of restraint and responsive economic friendliness in the developing world. Their globalist military strategies will have to be kept off the horizon if only because they have courted resistance and frustrations in so many parts of the world. A Swedenized South and South-West Asia, followed by the Finlandized Afghanistan, could restore peace and meaningful independence to Afghanistan and help the quest for stability in a region important to the whole world. Indian diplomacy will also gain immeasurable vigour and credibility, within the region and internationally, if our commitment to a political solution could be given concrete shape and translated into reality.

8

Central America and Afghanistan

No analogies are exact, but the Soviet problems in Afghanistan may provide a more instructive parallel than Vietnam to US problems in Central America.

The Afghan revolution of April 1978 succeeded because the Marxist-inclined factions were able to exploit the increasing disaffection with social and economic conditions. The Kremlin did not trigger the revolution but of course welcomed the gratuitous extension of 'socialism'. Before long, the ideological militancy of President Hafizullah Amin led to the disintegration of the revolutionary coalition, as the nationalists and the conservative tribes and Mullahs who at first supported it became alienated from it.

When insurgency showed that the country was turning hostile to the Soviet Union, the Russians tried to eliminate Amin, but the attempt misfired. In nervous impetuosity, the Kremlin then launched the ill-fated military intervention.

Today, although the government installed by the Russians has retracted many socialist measures, it has not gained domestic legitimacy. The presence of 'foreign infidels' has turned the insurgency into a holy crusade. What was a local irritant has become a running sore and an international embarrassment.

The Soviet Union will not be defeated by the Afghan rebels, but the intervention has been a strategic and political disaster. It led to the shelving of the second strategic arms limitations accord, the creation of the US Rapid Deployment Force and an increased American presence in the Indian Ocean, and constituted a near-fatal blow to détente.

Moreover, it shattered the claims of communism as a principled supporter of peace, anti-imperialism, and non-alignment. It revived the arms race in the subcontinent and invited overwhelming condemnation from the Islamic community and the United Nations.

*New York Times and International Herald Tribune, 13-14 August 1983.

Clearly, too, Afghanistan has become a quagmire for the Russians, who now use Western alarm at the intervention and covert CIA assistance to the rebels as justification for their continued presence.

All this has lessons for the United States. In El Salvador, too, the insurgency won't go away. Honduras is being militarily bolstered as Pakistan was after the Soviet intervention in Afghanistan.

The Contras—the Nicaraguan counter-revolutionaries—are being trained and armed as the Afghan rebels and refugees were. Cuban support of the Sandinista government and Salvadorean guerrillas is as marginal as the outside backing for the Afghan rebels. A naval quarantine will not frighten the Sandinista into abdication but would probably strengthen their resolve and internationalize the conflict.

In a better world, each superpower could profit from studying the other's experience. They might find themselves in agreement that defiant nationalism is stronger than military power used to coerce small nations. They might even acknowledge to each other that all problems are not wholly or largely due to the other's conspiratorial malevolence.

They could both disengage with dignity by letting regional powers who have vital interests in peace and stability in their areas 'circle the wagons' against all political and military interference. This is the role that the Contadora countries—Mexico, Venezuela, Colombia, and Panama—seek to play in Central America and that the countries surrounding Afghanistan could work out for South and South-West Asia.

In both Afghanistan and Central America, the superpowers have fuelled, not smothered, next-door nationalism. They would risk much less if they learned to live with it.

9
Letter to the Editor of NY *Times* Reply to Dr Brzezinski

Sir,

I was interested to see Dr Brzezinski's article on 6th October linking the two crises of Afghanistan and Nicaragua. Through the courtesy of your columns on 12th August 1983 I had also argued that Soviet Union's dilemma in Afghanistan provided a more instructive parallel for the United States policy in Central America than Vietnam. Elsewhere (*Foreign Policy*, summer 1982) I had urged that the solution in Afghanistan could be from 'Swedenization to Finlandization'. This encapsulated definition is not as elegant as Dr Brzezinski's formulation of 'external neutralization and internal self-determination' but the goal is not dissimilar. I had urged that under the supervision of five Islamic and regional countries, chosen and carrying the moral backing of the entire non-aligned fraternity, through sequential steps, the Soviet Union's security anxieties could be assuaged and Afghanistan could be restored to its pre-1978 non-alignment. In a conference held at this school on Third World Militarization in 1984, it was suggested that the Contadora group could supervise a similar process for Nicaragua.

For years now, Afghanistan and Nicaragua have suffered terrible human and economic distress because problems which were essentially socio-economic and nationalistic in origin were instinctively interpreted as moves in the East/West politics and strategies. The real interests of the US and USSR have not been jeopardized but, as a result, South Asia and Central America as a whole are being destabilized. Meanwhile, neither USA nor USSR is able to advance or retreat from their respective political and military quagmires.

New York Times, 10 October 1983.

Both situations may indeed be amenable to patient regional or subregional diplomacy if the USA and USSR could tacitly agree not to frustrate the regional initiatives. USSR, however, is as unlikely to accept USA and China as guarantors in Afghanistan as the USA would not acquiesce to a similar permanent position for the USSR in Central America. But genuine nationalism, which is allowed to thrive domestically and is not smothered from the outside could not really pose a threat to the next door superpower. In fact, by a provision similar to that in the Soviet–Finnish Treaty any provocative departure from enforced neutrality of the small country would give the right of intervention to the neighbouring giant.

Even after 3 years, the UN proximity mediation have not made much progress on Afghanistan. The fact is that in the present climate, the world body cannot be wholly inoculated against the play of East/West suspicions, especially when a permanent member of the Security Council is involved. Moreover, the Secretary-General's representative can only deal with the established governments. He cannot ascertain the wishes of the people, especially if they are in refugee camps, in deep jungles, or in barren mountains. A process, outside the UN which is supervised by medium, non-aligned regional countries would have a much better chance to obtain internal self-determination and external neutralization. What is more, these regional powers would have a continuing stake in 'circling the wagon' against unwarranted intervention, subversion and great power politics in their neighbourhood.

LBJ School of Public Auther   J.S. MEHTA
The University of Texas, Austin

10

The Prospects in Afghanistan: Can India be Indifferent?

The Soviet Union intervention in Afghanistan in December 1979 proved to be the final impetus in changing the direction of the Carter administration's foreign policy—from measured steps to improve East–West relations, to revived suspicions and coercive containment of the Soviet Union. President Carter was already unnerved by the US diplomats being taken hostage in Iran and its likely effect on his re-election. He pronounced the Soviet invasion of Afghanistan as the greatest threat to world peace since World War II. The United States shelved SALT-II, decided to boycott the forthcoming Moscow Olympics, put an embargo on grain exports to the Soviet Union, constituted a Rapid Deployment Force, and seemed geared for an impending Soviet attack on the Gulf or at least the throttling of oil flows to the West. Almost every commentator in the West viewed this first direct Soviet intrusion beyond the Yalta demarcations with alarm. For weeks Afghanistan dominated the world media.

International Indifference

However, only a few months later Afghanistan became for the West one of the plethora of unresolved Third World problems. It was not even mentioned by either Carter or Reagan during a ninety minute televised debate when, in October 1980, the two presidential candidates debated world and domestic problems. The grain embargo was unilaterally lifted, the legacy of the boycott of the Olympics was a retaliatory boycott of the Los Angeles games—much regretted by the American organizers and a precedent for the further politicization of international sports. The Rapid Deployment Force of course stands in vigilant readiness; it has held one or two major exercises and must have prepared many contingency plans. But it

Annual Foreign Policy Review, 1985, Ed. Prof. Satish Kumar, JNU, 1986.

may be weary of sustaining an alarmist alert and baffled at the modus operandi in possible operational situations. The search for a strategic consensus died because no country except Israel found participation a military necessity, or a political expedient.

But the violence and bloodletting in Afghanistan has continued. It has lasted longer than the Vietnam war and the Iran–Iraq conflict. According to the *Third United Nations Human Rights Report*, prepared by Professor Armacora, an Austrian lawyer, and released recently, violence and the use of sophisticated weapons and methods in Afghanistan has increased. Some 5,00,000 refugees fled Afghanistan in 1985 and the total now approximates 5 million. Since the intervention began, about one million people have been killed and one and half million have been injured or maimed. Schools, mosques, and dispensaries continue to be destroyed by bombing and ground action. Some 35,000 civilians have been killed in the past twelve months, of which 99 per cent were by government or Soviet forces. The situation, the report warned, has become more serious than ever.

Yet, in reality, Afghanistan has long ceased to be central to world politics. No doubt, international declarations (like that of the Non-aligned and the Islamic nations), innumerable joint communiques, and speeches in the UN have alluded to Afghanistan. Since January 1980, the UN General Assembly has passed resolutions seven times, which, with rare consistency, have rejected Soviet explanations and demanded the unconditional withdrawal of Soviet troops, and the restoration of the independence and non-aligned status of Afghanistan. It has been repeatedly urged that the country should have the right to determine its own economic, political, and social system and that conditions must be created for the Afghan refugees to return to their homes. Even after six years, the vote against the Kabul government and the Soviet Union has not been diluted. On the last count it went up slightly with 122 in favour (as against 120 the previous year) with twenty opposed and fourteen abstentions. (India has been in the abstaining minority.)

From these international declarations and resolution, however, one cannot pretend that the crisis in Afghanistan has been moderated. The ongoing conflict provides a convenient argument for the West, but the international pleas of the retaliatory measures have made no difference to the course of developments within Afghanistan. One cannot also claim that the evolution of international politics is stalled or even affected by Afghanistan. A Summit meeting has taken place between Reagan and Gorbachev; arms control talks have been resumed; in general, the East–West trade relations have not been impeded. The Reagan administration has, no doubt, openly increased aid for the Afghan 'insurgents', now reportedly US $ 250 million, and is also providing very sophisticated weapons. But there is no indication of any policy goal behind or ahead of Washington's approach except that the USSR should continue to suffer military, economic, and political haemorrhage. It is not claimed that this aid and arms would dislodge Soviet presence or even obstruct the Soviet operations.

False Alarms

The exaggerated fears expressed in 1980 after the invasion of Afghanistan stand falsified. The USSR has not moved into Pakistan and through it to the warm water coasts; the oil flows were never throttled; the Central Asian Republics have not been subverted through the contagion of Islamic fundamentalism. Even Baluchistan has not been destabilized by the USSR or the Babrak Karmal regime; there have been no serious incidents of purposeful hot pursuits into the North–West Frontier Province of Pakistan, much less clashes between Pakistan and the Soviet forces in Afghanistan. China has not indulged in a counter intervention through the thin Wakhan strip; and India and the Soviets have not colluded in a pincer squeeze on Pakistan. The success or failure in the progress towards either détente or deterioration is not contingent on a solution in Afghanistan. None of the wider strategic dangers and consequences have come to pass. With no framework of policy in evidence, the fact of the matter is that the plight of the country and its people has become a sideshow of international concern.

One cannot help suspecting that by now countries do not see their own vital interests being seriously affected by the six-year old, and still continuing, conflict in Afghanistan. After expressing regrets and sympathies, cynical though it may sound, the majority of nations are likely to be quickly reconciled if Afghanistan became a footnote in history.

The Afghan People

Undaunted by the brutal commentary on the realities of international ethics and power politics in the twentieth century and even when the dice seems so heavily loaded against them, the defiant and heroic Afghan people are not prepared to resign themselves to the destruction of their nation. No other Asian or African peoples had harassed and defeated the simultaneous imperial encroachments—the Czarist and the British interest of the nineteenth century. No country could claim to have practised a form of neutrality (which we now call non-alignment) for so long—since 1890—and done so through two World Wars.

The magnitude of the present odds against the Afghan nation has, however, no parallel in the past. The punishing tragedy that Afghanistan is suffering is more grim than the brutality of the racist regime in South Africa. In terms of numbers killed, it is only slightly less gruesome than what was inflicted by the Pol Pot regime in Kampuchea. In contemporary defiance against the foreigner, the Afghans can only compare with the struggle of the Vietnamese against the US intervention in their country.

The Afghan people, however, are pitched against a neighbour and not a distant superpower. The USSR had deployed over 1,00,000 troops using the most modern weapon systems, including obliterating firepower, ruthless and unchallenged aerial power, and the deadly helicopter gunships.

Even so, initially without outside support and later gratefully welcoming help and arms from the USA and Muslim nations, the traditional will and determination of the Afghan people has not been broken. The Babrak Karmal regime has not succeeded in establishing even a semblance of internal legitimacy. According to most estimates, some 80 to 85 per cent of the country remains beyond the secure control of the Kabul government. The economy of the country must be in chaos and most people must have been reduced to a low level of subsistence. If the reports which come out of Afghanistan are even fractionally true, Afghanistan must be the most hapless land on earth.

Victims of Afghanistan

PAKISTAN

Next to the agony of Afghanistan itself, the most pernicious consequences of the Soviet invasion and the internal conflict in Afghanistan have fallen on Pakistan. Three or perhaps four million Afghan refugees in Pakistan can become the nucleus of a State within the State. The Afghans in Pakistan are also proportionately much larger than the Palestinians in Lebanon, which has been the subject of international and Indian concern. Pakistan could not possibly take the kind of action against these fellow Islamic brethren as, at one time, was conducted against the Palestinians by Jordan and later by the Syrians. Notwithstanding aid from international agencies and from the Muslim nations, Pakistan's future economic viability stands in jeopardy, made worse by the rumbling political volcano.

No doubt, through agile diplomacy, the Afghan development enabled Pakistan to capitalize on the international alarm caused by Soviet actions and intentions. It was able to repair its relations with the US which had sunk to a low ebb in 1979. After the Reagan administration came to power in 1981, Pakistan obtained a major allocation of US $ 3.2 billion in arms and economic aid. It is worth recalling that since 1965, the US had stopped military aid to Pakistan. In the 1970s, Pakistan had even failed to get the licence to purchase A-7s, a subsonic fighter from the USA. It has now acquired some squadrons of F-16s which are one of the most sophisticated medium range strike aircraft in the world. Pakistan also now has a radar screen and marginally improved capability on the Pak–Afghan front. In the process, it has significantly augmented not only its defensive but also its offensive capabilities against India. But Pakistan could scarcely feel secure against the military might and logistic ease commanded by the Soviet Union. It would be naive for Pakistan to bank confidently on the hope that the United States would come to its defence when the tensions or even conflicts were transparently local or regional.

The United States is not likely to risk a major conflict with the USSR simply for the sake of Pakistan. There are also lessons for Pakistan to learn from the way the US jettisoned Marcos. In any case, with all its improved military capability against India, Pakistan has been more than out-trumped by the superior modernization, military muscle, and the indigenous ordnance and industrial capacity of India. Whatever the short-term gains, Pakistan remains not only under increasing economic pressure but, in any hypothetical sce-nario, its security remains as problematic as at any time since the Soviet intervention in Afghanistan.

INDIA

Next to Afghanistan and Pakistan, India has been the indirect victim of the Soviet intervention. After the Bangladesh crisis and the far-reaching fiscal restraints following the first oil shock in 1974, India's defence outlay increased only gradually. However, since 1980 and with the build-up of Pakistan's military, our defence budget has more than doubled. We have acquired, or are in the process of acquiring, sophisticated aircrafts of diverse origins and capabilities, heavy battle tanks, aircraft carriers (which will carry Sea-Harriers), nuclear powered submarines, and a blue-water surface fleet. The economic burden of the subcontinental arms race has fallen on the Indian people while a great share of the benefits has gone to the arms suppliers. The situation has coincidentally acquired more dangerous dimensions with India and Pakistan's mutual suspicions regarding the other's nuclear weapons capability. No doubt, our economic growth has shown an upsurge. But we too face a small variant of the long-term American dilemma confronting the Reagan administration—mounting deficits and increasing national debt; falling exports and a looming balance of payment crisis; the dread of inflation and a gigantic resource constraint for development and modernization, especially against poverty and the social agenda of the nation. All this casts a shadow not just on the Seventh Five Years Plan but also on our long-term economic and political health and in the final instance, on meaningful independence in our domestic and foreign policies.

Indo–Pakistan problems have, of course, deeper roots and manifestations than the outflow from the Afghanistan problem. The Punjab crisis, for example, is essentially internal, but the succour and support for extremists by Pakistan now comes in the way of marrying Pakistan's proposed simple No-War Declaration and the Indian counter-proposals for a Treaty of Friendship which would rule out foreign bases and external military links. The suspicion that Pakistan and Sri Lanka are developing a military nexus will become another inhibiting factor in improving Indo–Pakistan relations. But these old and new impediments aside, the shadow of Afghanistan has fallen on India.

For more than thirty years, the policy objective of non-alignment has been to insulate our country from the play of great power politics so that we can pursue our developmental goals with our own strategies. This prophetically enlightened policy never realized its optimal potential because the Indo–Pak Cold War got enmeshed in the superpowers Cold War. A slow process of decoupling the two Cold Wars was under way in the 1970s. The Soviet intervention, in a kind of *déjà vu* repetition, has relinked the US and Pakistan in the same way as they were linked in a military security and alliance relationship in 1953-4.

After three decades, especially after Rajiv Gandhi became the Prime Minister, slowly but significantly a broad national consensus has emerged that improved relations with our neighbours must have a greater priority in our national objectives. However, the good neighbourly policy and the future of the South Asian Association for Regional Cooperation (SAARC) cannot go much beyond semantics and minimal agreements when a mutually reinforcing arms race continues.

The US now professes friendship towards Rajiv Gandhi's India and has removed some old restraints on technological transfers. The Festival of India has buried the old complaint that the American people are indifferent to India and its heritage. But the United States has not changed its primary foreign policy goal—of competing with, containing, and militarily outmatching the Soviet Union and pursuing anti-Soviet economic and diplomatic policies. Because of the Soviet presence in Afghanistan, even in the face of India's apprehensions (and three decades of experience), the US is now considering a new pledge of US $ 4.02 billion of military and economic aid to Pakistan—Pakistan's request was for 6.5 billion dollars. Even this advertised reduction is bound to give a new and vicious spurt to the subcontinental arms race. The quintessential fact is that if the Afghanistan problem persists, the whole gamut of the national goals of Pakistan and India will stand jeopardized and slip further out of their respective controls.

The full opportunity costs of Afghanistan cannot be computed but no one can deny that they have been horrendous. Was this unavoidable or was it a failure of timely judgement and diplomacy? More to the point, is it possible to move towards a solution which would recapture a greater measure of latitude for our worthy national goals? To summon the courage to answer these questions with all their in-built obstacles, one must nail down the false hypotheses on Afghanistan which have complicated most analyses.

Afghanistan: An East–West Issue?

In broad terms and contrary to what continues to be frequently argued, the Afghanistan development was not originally an East–

West problem. It is the hypnotic hold and vested interests of diverse hues that transformed a local development into the familiar mould of Cold War analysis. Both superpowers as usual are guilty of transposing cause and consequences. In spite of being a neighbour, the Soviet Union had not exported communism to the monarchical and oligarchic regimes in Afghanistan in the six decades since the October Revolution. Even the United States, until 1978, never seriously accused the USSR of subversion of the regime of King Zahir Shah or President Daud. Indeed, six weeks before the overthrow of Daud, the Deputy Assistant Secretary of State, Ambassador Dubs, had testified to a congressional subcommittee that 'President Daud was very much in control and the processes of institution building was going on apace.' There were not more than a few hundred members of the Khalq and Parcham parties. No doubt, both were Leftist, but they had been refused admission in the world communist movement. The fact is that the revolution took place locally and was not manipulated by Moscow. It was successful because of growing socio-economic problems and the administrative ineptitude of the Daud administration in handling the anger of the people at the killing of the popular leader Mir Akbar Khan. The USSR promptly welcomed a government which proclaimed ideological affinities in a neighbouring country. The subsequent dynamics ending in Soviet intervention flowed from decisions made in Kabul, not Moscow. For nearly a year and a quarter, the Kremlin merely played a supporting role and in hindsight, it would privately acknowledge, not a far-sighted one. The United States had lost what little role it had after the Democratic Republic of Afghanistan had been established in April 1978. Until the summer of 1979 Hafizullah Amin received support because he acted as the most loyal votary of the USSR. At the special session of the UN on Disarmament in June 1978, Amin was more vociferous in his denunciation of the West than the Soviet delegates themselves. It was Amin who, believing in socialist solidarity, negotiated the Treaty of Friendship which Taraki signed as President with Brezhnev in December 1978.

If Amin was not the favoured leader of the Kremlin (as is now suggested in Moscow and also in the West), Babrak Karmal and the Parcham group could not have been banished in June 1978; nor could Taraki, while remaining President, have been reduced to a figurehead and Amin himself have become, in March 1979, the all powerful Prime Minister and been provided muscle and support for his repressive policies. It was only when Soviet advisers were killed that the USSR recognized that his ideological militancy in trying to turn Afghanistan into a Leninist state had turned the country into a security liability for the Soviet Union. The Soviet attempt to moderate and later, on 15 September 1979, to physically or politically eliminate him, misfired. Instead of Amin, the more pliable Taraki who was President was killed. It exposed the Soviet game and only then did Amin turn into a nationalist. This led to the Soviet invasion of December 1979.

There are many ironies and falsehoods which can be traced to the ambience of the Cold War. The West would like to make-believe that Amin was always an anti-Soviet nationalist, but there is no evidence prior to the summer of 1979 to prove this. The Soviet contention is equally implausible when, in *post hoc* explanations, it seeks to denounce Amin as a CIA agent. The Soviet Union's defence that it intervened to save the revolution from external takeover, carries little conviction. Under more direct Soviet tutelage, Babrak Karmal, who was installed by the Red Army, has dismantled some of Amin's socialist superstructure. Mosques have been reopened and new ones built, and Mullahs and tribals and now non-Communists have been placated.

With a calmer and more shrewd judgement, it should, even in December 1979, have been clear that the Soviet Union intervened not for expansionist or ideological reasons, but because of defensive anxieties. The impetuous reaction of the Soviet Union can be understood in the context of the traditional Russian security paranoia. But it overlooked Russia's own experience of the Afghan capacity of defiance and the more recent experience of the United States in Vietnam.

Nationalism Underestimated

If the Soviets had succeeded in politically eliminating Amin earlier—like the US decided to ditch Diem (President of Vietnam)—the need for direct involvement might not have arisen. Initially for a year and a half, there was minimal outside arms support for the Afghan freedom fighters and tribals. Significant CIA support only followed the Soviet invasion. Like the USA in Vietnam, the Soviet Union underestimated the capacity of modern day nationalism to defy an outside power on the homeground. The USA enfeebled itself at home and abroad but finally, when it suffered military reverses it could extricate itself. The Soviet Union may not be defeated. It has also suffered military humiliation and political embarrassment, but it is more reluctant to vacate a contiguous country. The USSR has also suffered a serious setback in its foreign policy projection in the Third World which recalls the US self-inflicted damage from Vietnam. Along with Kampuchea, it has given gratuitous advantage to China. Moscow will be inhibited and carry less conviction of sincerity when it protests against the American gunboat diplomacy in interventions such as in Grenada and around Nicaragua and now the brazen attack on Libya.

There is ample evidence that if Soviet security could be effectively guaranteed, it would welcome Afghanistan reverting to its almost 100 years old traditional neutrality which was always careful not to impinge on the vital interests of Russia. Gorbachev's statement at the recent Party Congress hints at a new flexibility and possible willingness to be rid of this running sore in the no-win military and diplomatic situation. Indeed, there is an implicit consensus across the ideological spectrum amongst the nations that a political solution should be a kind of formalized *status quo*—a return to an independent non-aligned Afghanistan and, by implication, the total withdrawal of Soviet troops and the exclusion of other outside interventions.

The question is how to go back to the beginning. With the Soviet forces and a nation of fanatic tribal kamikazes locked in a deadly struggle, the legacy of hatred and bitterness against the USSR will not easily evaporate. It is for this reason that it is difficult to find a risk free, long lasting, and dignified solution acceptable to all the contending parties.

Limitations of the UN Role

After the failure of the West and the pleas of the Non-aligned world and others, the world has been content to consign the problem to the lap of the UN. For three years Diego Cordovez, as Special Representative of the UN Secretary-General, has had intermittent talks with the governments in Kabul, Islamabad, and Moscow. These five rounds never quite reflected the agony of Afghanistan or the desperate human urgency of finding a solution. Last year (in 1985), the UN envoy drew up a four part agreement which provided for the withdrawal of Soviet forces, affirmation of the principles of non-interference supported by international guarantees, and the return of refugees in safety and honour. But the negotiations have been stumped on the issues of the interrelationship between the constituent parts such as the conditions, priority, and time of Soviet withdrawal. After Diego Cordovez's recent shuttles between Islamabad and Kabul and talks in Delhi, some hopeful statements have been made as preparation for further talks, scheduled for May 1986.

In my view, the UN role was always flawed and finding a solution was going to be difficult. It is not just because the UN has had a poor record in the resolution of international conflicts. The proposal to have a standing peace-keeping cadre, to give the UN the nucleus of an independent muscle to overcome sovereign defiance by nations, was not incorporated in the UN Charter. The UN is at a special handicap where one of the parties happens to be a permanent member of the Security Council. (The UN never tried to mediate the Vietnam war.) While the UN Charter begins by affirming its ultimate sanction on behalf of the people, it remains a body representing governments regardless of whether or not they are in tune with the will of the people they represent. The ultimate trump card in the Afghanistan situation is held by the Afghan people and their will to independence. The Secretary-General's Representative has no means to ascertain the wishes of the Afghan people. The special envoy cannot even reach the 5 million Afghan refugees who are now in Pakistan and Iran. Under what conditions would the Afghan rebels/freedom fighters call off the Jehad and stop fighting the foreigner in their land or accept a timetable agreed upon without their knowledge even if it were accepted by Moscow, Islamabad, and the government in Kabul? A procedure which cannot question the legitimacy of the Kabul government, and must treat the Afghan people as if they had no standing in the negotiations, has a fatal weakness. We can keep hoping that Diego Cordovez will find a solution, but the limitations of the UN inherently weakens the chances of success.

Is there, then, no alternative for a solution of the Afghanistan imbroglio? A wholly different approach and procedure is called for in order to get back to where we were before this crisis.

The Key Elements

Three key facts are sought to be identified in this paper which must be recognized and embodied in any framework for a peaceful solution.

1. The real stakes reflecting the agony and the urgency—are first and foremost for the Afghan people and second, for Pakistan and India. The interests of other powers are marginal. Their postures may be convenient arguments or propagandist ploys for reasons extraneous to the problem, or simply declaratory affirmations.
2. Postures aside, Afghanistan neither was nor is an East–West problem in the strategic sense. Whether there is détente, arms control agreements, or protracted tension and, God forbid, an East–West war, it is not critically dependent on the present dimensions of conflict in Afghanistan.
3. The ideological arguments—expansion or containment—are a misleading superimposition on a situation which developed due to its inner dynamics, not from outside manipulation. The Soviet Union will decide whether and when to withdraw, to uphold or jettison Babrak Karmal,[1] on the basis of its own security considerations and political balance sheet and not for ideological reasons.

Steps Towards a Possible Solution

If the foregoing analysis has any merit, then India alone can make the difference to whether the present tragic drift continues or is arrested and reversed. India alone can explain to the USSR that the Afghanistan issue has also led to a punishing fall-out for India. It brought back the US involvement in the subcontinent and has resulted in a debilitating diversion from development. In giving the benefit of doubt to Soviet explanations for the intervention, we have found ourselves alienated from our neighbours and the bulk of the Non-aligned fraternity. Paradoxically, the damage from our friendly indulgence also compromised our role as a friend of the USSR. After our speech and vote in favour of Soviet Union in the UN General Assembly in January 1980, we have, in fact, been ineffective in promoting the understanding that the Soviet Union was not launched on a grand design which threatened South and South–West Asia. More relevant for the fundamentals of our interests, it has been a setback to the enlightened goal of Non-alignment of insulating the

[1]Since this article was written, Babrak Karmal has been replaced as the General Secretary of the ruling party by Mr Najibullah, although he continues to be the President of Afghanistan. The country is ruled collectively by Babrak Karmal, Najibullah, and Prime Minister Kisthmand.

region from the Cold War. My own experience with the USSR has convinced me that in the final instance, Moscow inwardly recognizes—perhaps more realistically than many Indian friends of the Soviet Union—that an India which is seen to be non-aligned is a greater asset than if its is compromised to look like a docile camp follower of Moscow.

Given these assumptions and the skill of our diplomacy to put it across persuasively but firmly, we could initiate, in sequence, the following steps towards the solution of the Afghan problem.

1. We should decide to vote with the overwhelming majority of the Non-aligned (and the international community), urging the withdrawal of foreign troops and the restoration of independence and non-alignment to Afghanistan. It should be possible to explain this to the USSR.

2. Next, we should take the initiative to convene a regional conference of countries in South and South-West Asia. This might include Pakistan, Bangladesh, Nepal, Sri Lanka, Bhutan, Kuwait, Saudi Arabia, the United Arab Emirates, Bahrain, Qatar, and Oman. Iran and Iraq could both be invited if there is a ceasefire, but neither if the conflict between them continues. This conference should reaffirm their pledge as Non-aligned countries and as members of the Gulf Council that they will not give bases to, or forge military arrangements with either bloc and remain neutral on East–West issues which may impinge specifically on South and South-West Asia. (This is what I had once called the Swedenization of the region, implying voluntarily affirmed neutrality. Because Sweden refused to join the NATO, in 1955 the Soviet Union withdrew from the Porkkala base in Finland.) Having affirmed their non-alignment, these regional powers should collectively affirm their sensitivity to the defensive security concerns of the USSR and simultaneously demand the withdrawal of Soviet Forces from Afghanistan.

It follows that countries like Pakistan will have to re-examine some aspects of their present, open or covert, commitments. It may be recalled that Pakistan's discretion to obtain military supplies by purchase, loan, or as gift was not questioned by the Indian Foreign Minister in 1981. It would be unrealistic to terminate existing commitments but the future arms acquisition programme could be re-examined. Pakistan will have to review whether it should allow the country to be a conduit for military help to Afghan insurgents. Pakistan, in other words, will have to squarely face the problem of whether it wants to live with the present dangers or work for a non-aligned Afghanistan. When India joins in the initiative, the question will have a wholly new imperative and logic.

3. After a regional commitment to Swedenization, a meeting of the entire Non-aligned Movement should be called and asked to choose five or seven countries which are prepared to provide an observer corps for Afghanistan. A possible list from which the countries may be chosen might be India, Kuwait, Algeria, Malaysia, Indonesia, Tanzania, Senegal, Nigeria, and Peru. The majority might be countries with a sizeable Muslim population and none which have older subsisting military arrangements with the West. If Pakistan starts diluting its obvious tilt and perceived involvement in East–West military strategy, it could also qualify for consideration in the Non-aligned observer group. At all events, the selection of the countries must carry the collective backing of the Non-aligned Movement.

4. After Swedenization, the selection of the peacekeeping observer group, and the preliminaries are worked out, the chosen spokesman/chairperson of the group should request the governments of the USSR and Afghanistan to allow the observer corps to assemble in the Afghan capital. With the backing of the Non-aligned Movement, refusal would not be so easy. Once in Kabul, the observers should be deployed in consultation with the Kabul government at strategic points in the country.

5. The Non-aligned observer group should thereafter negotiate for disengagement, thinning, regrouping, and withdrawal of a substantial part of the Soviet/Afghan military forces to their barracks around important cities or locations in the country. This could be on the pattern of the grouping and withdrawal of White Regime forces during the Rhodesian elections in 1979.

6. The Non-aligned observer group must then work to obtain a ceasefire by the insurgents as a prelude to permitting the refugees to return to their homes. It would be an important part of the task of the observers to monitor the ceasefire and the repatriation of the Afghans in 'peace and honour'. The observer group could also become the conduit for urgent emergency economic assistance from the world community to rehabilitate the people and repair the destroyed infrastructure in the country. The Non-aligned group and the international community would have to muster all its persuasive powers with the United States

and other nations with sympathy and aid capabilities. As in the famine disaster in Ethiopia, it could become a massive international relief operation under non-political direction.

7. The next stage would be to call a traditional Loya Jirgah to determine independently whether Afghanistan should revert to the 1973 constitution or adopt a new one. The observers should observe but no non-Afghans, should have a part in these deliberations on constitution making.

8. On the basis of the chosen constitution, an election could be held in Afghanistan. The Non-aligned Observer Group would be required to observe and supervise the election process in the country. The ruling Parcham faction could, of course, field its own candidates. The subordinate government machinery would have to be utilized, but as in Rhodesia, the role of observers would be critical and must be transparently independent.

9. On the basis of the supervised-elections a new Afghan government could be formed. The first major task of the new government would be to negotiate and formalize a declaration of neutrality and non-alignment of Afghanistan. Thereafter this government, representing the freely expressed wishes of the Afghan people, should negotiate a Soviet–Afghan Treaty on the lines of the Soviet–Finnish Treaty.

10. Finally, the residuary Soviet troops could be withdrawn from Afghanistan. The Treaty could formally and, hopefully, without any opposition, be endorsed by the UN General Assembly.

This is a bare outline which could incorporate refinements through diplomatic negotiations. The sequential steps may seem protracted, but it could be completed in less time than that for which the UN envoy has been unsuccessfully geared to the task. It requires no great perspicacity to call it unrealistic if not Utopian. However, I would claim in favour of this framework that it is the worst possible solution except for all the others, including the political solution being worked out by the UN.

The ten stage sequential plan embodies some fundamental preconditions for a constructive resolution of the Afghan situation: first, the solution of a regional problem will emanate from the region and not be imposed from outside. Second, only a non-aligned group can affirm an outer belt of neutrality which would assuage Soviet anxiety, permit withdrawal, and give a chance of restoring Afghanistan to independence and non-alignment. Finally, only the Afghan people are both Hamlet and the Prince of Denmark. If they do not have a say in determining their government in keeping with their national personality, there may not be any ceasefire, return of refugees, and a commitment to Finlandization.

India's interest lies in a step-by-step quest for a solution which arrests and reverses the shrinkage of non-alignment in South and South-West Asia. No doubt, Indian diplomacy would have to face delicate and different challenges. It would have to carry credibility that the proposal of a non-aligned South and South-West Asia is not a cover for India's hegemony of the region. India's role would also have to lay at rest the suspicion that its purpose is not only to rescue the USSR militarily, but also to perpetuate Soviet political influence.

India will have to carefully, consistently, and conceptually project a vision that India's own interests are inextricably geared to peace, stability, and respect for nationalism in Afghanistan and other South Asian countries. The ecological and economic interdependence of the region is such that none—not even India—can prosper much, unless all our neighbours also do so.

India Misses an Opportunity

Afghanistan has been about the worst example of intellectual failures, false judgements, and misperceptions on the part of almost all countries. India's failure has been particularly unfortunate and unnecessary. In 1980 India might have, after the Soviet invasion, seized a real opportunity to permanently rationalize Indo–Pak relations.

Unfortunately, the Soviet invasion coincided almost exactly with the Indian general elections of 1980. The rhetoric of the election campaign of the Congress party contained pledges of reinforcing relations with the USSR, allegedly damaged by the Janata government. This pushed us into unthinkingly accepting that the legitimate government of Afghanistan invited the Soviet troops, a contention summarily and consistently rejected by 122 countries. My guess is that if Mrs. Indira Gandhi had been in power since 1977 or Morarji Desai had continued till 1982—he was voted out in July 1979—India's reactions would have been different. If Mrs. Gandhi were to have gone along with the Non-aligned consensus and asked for a Soviet withdrawal in 1980 (as she was to do in Saudi Arabia only three months later), the whole climate in South Asia could have been different. If India had adopted the friendly postures taken towards

Pakistan, which Foreign Minister Narsimha Rao did in June 1981, the more serious adverse consequences including the induction of supersonic aircraft by Pakistan might have been avoided. President Carter who was in power in 1980 was critical of Pakistan's human rights record and, in anger at Soviet action in Afghanistan, he offered to Pakistan only US $ 400 million in military-cum-economic aid, which the Pakistan President described as 'peanuts'. A timely sensitivity for Pakistan's genuine if unfounded anxieties (somewhat similar to our apprehensions of China's intentions in 1962), and a call to both blocs to withdraw from actual or intended intervention at an assembly of South and South-West Asian countries, could have created the climate for the agenda left unfinished at the Simla Conference. A historic opportunity for consolidating non-alignment in South Asia slipped by.

But it is not too late to recognize that Afghanistan cannot be left to drift towards destruction. India must not be resigned to the Durand Line permanently becoming a Cold War frontier. That could correspondingly mean the failure of non-alignment for us and our region. If this is agreed, then it must also be recognized that our effective role would require the beginning of a chemistry of trust with Pakistan. Complete success in any initiative for a solution in Afghanistan can neither wait for improved relations with Pakistan nor independently precede it. The two problems are linked and must be pursued patiently and purposefully in tandem in order to achieve a breakthrough in both or either.

Scope for Indian Initiative

From this view point, despite manifest difficulties, there is no reason to despair of a breakthrough. Some fallacies, no doubt widely and deeply entrenched, would have to be exorcised by statesmanship in India. It is, for example, a false fear, our own variation of the Cold War hypnosis—which suspects that the Soviet Union is averse to improved Indo–Pakistan relations. Second, whatever may be stated openly, the USSR does not truly believe that all Afghan insurgents are under the inspiration or control of Pakistan and/or USA. The third fallacy is that the Soviet Union is intrinsically hostile to Pakistan. Since the signing of the accord in Tashkent except in crunch situations as in the later stages of the Bangladesh crisis, the USSR has sought to improve bilateral relations with Pakistan (partly with the object of balancing Chinese influence). This came out in speeches when only two years ago, the Soviet supported steel mill was opened in Pakistan. Even in the context of Afghanistan, and notwithstanding periodic warnings, Soviet–Pakistan relations have not plummeted as some Indian analysts had expected and some Pakistani spokesman has claimed. The Soviet Union does not see an either/or choice between India and Pakistan. But while the USSR does not necessarily want India as a dependency or a military ally, it recognizes that India is, by far, its most important non-socialist friend. Finally, Rajiv Gandhi's India, even in 'American eyes and despite all manner of differences on world politics, is not equated with Pakistan. Democratic India even with its internal crisis and giant size problems is an anchor of stability in the Indian Ocean arc. If we understood these realities, it could reinforce our confidence in a vigorous initiative.

There is another important reason which should spur an Indian initiative for stability in South Asia. Looking beyond the tenure of the present administration in Washington, the chances are of a slow but significant improvement in superpower relations. General Secretary Gorbachev, now securely established with a mandate confirmed by the 27th Party Congress, will still be around. For the Soviet Union under Gorbachev (like China under Deng-Hsiao-Ping), while not running security risks, the overriding concern is to reverse the lagging pace of its technological, managerial, agricultural, and industrial modernization. This would point to easing the economic burden through arms control agreements and improved relations with the USA and the West. Though not as seriously as the USSR, for reasons of macro-economics and alliance policies, a post-Reagan administration may also want to get back to the détente track. If one were to go by the succession of unilateral gestures to the USSR, like the cessation of underground tests, and freeze on intermediate range weapons, it is more than possible that in three years time the two superpowers may get into a quiet tango above the heads of respective friends and allies. (Gorbachev has also proposed a minuet of the five permanent members of the Security Council on nuclear disarmament, significantly omitting India.) The strategic significance of Afghanistan including the incremental advantage of Soviet presence has been exaggerated by those who play war games on super computers.

The whole area of South and South-West Asia is like a Soviet backyard, just as Central America and the Caribbean is for the USA. But the ultimate reality is the strength of nationalism defying the military strength of the alien intervention. For these reasons, rather than wait for superpower deals or bank on a political rabbit being produced by the UN, we must get off the mark to quarantine our region internally from the play of superpower politics.

In sum, the totality of circumstances, and above all, the more long-term twenty-first century goals which Rajiv Gandhi cherishes for India, suggest that it is not too late for an Indian initiative on Afghanistan. India must always be seen to be everywhere on the side of independence and nationalism; otherwise we will not be able to redeem our own tryst with destiny. No doubt, this will require skilful forward looking intra-regional diplomacy. But this is within our capability once vouchsafed with political benediction and geared to a conceptual vision of a genuinely non-aligned South and South-West Asia. Moscow and Washington will most likely acquiesce with these goals. Even if they did not, we could still inch forward if we stopped overestimating their power to coerce and undervalue our concern for our own future which is inextricably enmeshed with stability in South Asia as a whole.

11

The Afghan Scenario: Why India Stands Marginalized

Everyone agrees that Afghanistan must revert to become non-aligned and stable but no single country nor any feasible combination of countries appears to be able to lead it back to the beginning. Consistent with Indo–Soviet friendship, Ambassador Vorontsov came to Delhi to share the Soviet assessment and possibly its anxieties. From the Indian capital, he reiterated confidence in the Kabul government and voiced warnings to Pakistan and the United States. But the Soviet media had already publicized the relief felt by the Soviet contingent when Afghanistan was behind their backs. Not military power, but the skill of Diplomacy and only material support are being marshalled to help the Kabul government to prevail. Meanwhile, the USSR itself has moved quickly to establish its political position in West Asia and the Islamic world and even effected a rapprochement with fundamentalist Iran. One cannot but conclude that for the Soviet Union, Afghanistan is of secondary importance to its new global politics and domestic economic priorities. Pakistan, having given refuge to three million Afghans, has been well-placed to influence at least the Sunni insurgent groups. But despite geography, a shared faith, and Pakistan providing a conduit for arms, the Afghans are no more likely to accept becoming a province of Pakistan than acquiesce being a Soviet republic. But Pakistan has won credit for being on the side of nationalism, as India was in the struggle for the liberation of Bangladesh.

Kabul's Writ

Our own future standing in Afghanistan has got very narrowly identified with a government which the overwhelming majority of Afghan people distrust, and much of the international community

* *Indian Express*, 30 March 1989.

considers as militarily besieged and politically at bay. The possible immediate prospects are diverse: the government may hold the towns but is unable to extend its authority; continuing rampant tribal warlordism has all major groups swearing allegiance to Zahir Shah; the new Islamabad-based coalition gaining militarily with further international recognition; there is hopes of a broader grouping when joined by Iran-based Mujahidin.

Two things are clear. Peace is not round the corner in Afghanistan and India stands marginalized to protracted chaos in the neighbourhood. Future historians, with no vested interest in the present politics, are likely to be critical at the avoidable jeopardy of our interests and the damage to the traditional regard of the Afghan people for India.

The insurgency and defence of the People's Democratic Party of Afghanistan (PDPA) government in Kabul began soon after the Saur Revolution in 1978, even before Soviet intervention and outside aid to the Mujahidin (1981). The Brezhnev Politburo overlooked that both the British and the Czarist empires had suffered frustration and defeat at the hands of the Afghan tribals. It was not the lack of additional Soviet military capacity or the American-aided fire power of the Mujahidin but Gorbachev's statesmanship which openly acknowledged the folly of Soviet intervention. This dramatic decision was crucial in winning credibility for the historic transformation brought about in Soviet foreign policy and world politics.

In January 1980, there was a more promising opportunity to normalize on all Indo–Pakistan problems than at any time. In the past including at Simla in 1972, Pakistan was truly worried about its security and, for the first time, recognized that the primary threat did not emanate from India. India was in the position to assure the world that the Soviet intervention, no doubt disastrously misconceived, was defensive in intent and the Western alarm that Soviet forces would cross into Baluchistan, and go on to throttle the oil flow to Japan and the West was wholly fallacious. This is not hindsight wisdom; within a fortnight, representations were made to decision-makers to launch a diplomatic initiative. That there were no threats of a wider conflagration was shared with and reported by the visiting correspondent of *The Economist*. Instead of echoing the *post facto* rationalization that Soviet intervention was at the invitation of Hafizullah Amin's government, in prompt show of understanding and sympathy, in word and concrete gesture, to Pakistan, could have been followed by leading South and South-West Asia collectively to ask both for Soviet withdrawal and warn the West against counter-intervention. Admittedly, after the American hostages were taken in Iran, the Carter White House had turned hawkish, but we might have wrested the initiative to insulate the region for non-alignment. A step-by-step sequential plan for a neutral solution in Afghanistan was urged which might have enabled India, along with other non-aligned countries, to play a constructive role.

We sided with the Soviet Union not because of Non-aligned principles (which have been fundamentally on the side of nationalism, liberation struggles, and against great power interventions) but because in the superimposition of the Cold War on the subcontinent, the Soviet had been a well-tested friend of India. The irony is that had we taken the same position as the non-aligned majority, far from damage to Indo–Soviet relations (just as Soviet relations with the other 120 countries were not damaged), we would have advanced our national interests and also rescued the Soviet Union from a no-win situation and, in the present dilemma, helped in the search for a broad-based government.

In the UN vote on Afghanistan, where all of India's neighbours voted differently from it, India allowed itself to be misconstrued as justifying intervention by a big country in disregard of the sovereignty of a small neighbour. It reversed the developing promise of improved bilateral relations with China. In subsequent months we showed qualified disapproval of the Soviet intervention. If we had taken the same position promptly and publicly and had we shown the same understanding for Pakistan as reflected in the speech of our Foreign Minister in Karachi in June 1981 (which conceded Pakistan's right to somewhat improve its defence capability), we might have reduced if not averted the massive military aid programme launched by the Reagan administration. Even the Carter administration, alarmed as it was, offered when General Zia-ul-Haq dimissed as 'peanuts'. We did not read the writing on the wall when Reagan, in his election campaign, pledged to re-establish military superiority and aid countries in the 'frontline' against USSR.

Diplomatic Moves

Too many in India had quietly assumed that the Soviet Union was bound to marshal the resources necessary to succeed in Afghanistan even if it took some years to do so as this would dilute for ever the threat to India from Pakistan. We failed to anticipate that the Soviet Union's policies, transcending ideology, would overcome the old nervous apprehension of Western threats to its security. Beyond occasional statements of sympathy, we did not agonize with impatience at the tragic violence in our region, and so remained indifferent to the prospect in Afghanistan. We activated our diplomacy only in 1988 after the Soviet Union changed course, implying that Afghanistan was not considered worth Soviet blood and treasure.

We would no doubt prefer a secular dispensation in the country, but for us to have invited President Najibullah on a State visit to Delhi in April 1988 (President Gorbachev only met the Afghan President in Tashkent) was proof of a failure to comprehend the Soviet Union's priorities and policies. In Iran we, like the USSR, have been neutral to Islamic fundamentalism. It would have been prudent to have nurtured the same detachment in Afghanistan so that we could enlarge our options in an uncertain future which we could not fashion. It has been a sound tenet at non-alignment that outside interventions to shape internal regimes is wrong in principle and generally doomed in result.

Our errors of judgement could not have suited Pakistan better. Our public position enabled Pakistan to argue that it was threatened with further dismemberment by a pincer and India was abetting in a grand design to advance towards the oil-laden, warm waters of the Gulf. Our original vote facilitated the resumption of the US military aid to Pakistan, which had been terminated in 1965 and not even revived during the tilt of 1971. The resultant subcontinental arms race has been a bonanza to the arms exporting countries and a convenient argument for Cold War hawks, but the consequences for India and Pakistan have been horrendous deficits and economic distortions. On a conservative estimate, India and Pakistan must have acquired or ordered new weapons systems worth US $ 20-30 billion during these years.

There are persisting differences between the US and USSR on the Afghan problem but whether the hapless country burns or simmers, the developing bilateral relations between the superpowers will not be impaired. The terrible legacy, human and economic, will rest heavily and for long on the countries of the region. The Afghans will have to rehabilitate their devastated homeland. A million and a half Afghans are said to have died; some five million are refugees; some 10 million mines are strewn in pathways, in fields, and at random all over the country. The numbers of maimed will increase, even if the violence ends.

The political, diplomatic, and economic wages of misperceptions, both short-term and long-term, for Afghanistan for the region cannot be minimized. We could, no doubt, contribute to the UN rehabilitation operations under Prince Sadrudin Aga Khan, but our bilateral relations with a restructured central government or a factious Afghanistan will for some years be on the political defensive. The long resident Indian community in Afghanistan may have to suffer taunts from the returning Mujahidin in what will be looked upon by the Afghans as their struggle for liberation.

The irony for India is that by surrendering our principles and prophylactic diplomacy, an opportunity to serve our long-term interests of regional harmony was allowed to slip by. We are on the sidelines (or considered partisan) and so unable to assist in the non-ulterior search for a democratically responsive, responsibly moderate, non-aligned Afghanistan.

12

Afghanistan: Superpower Episode but its Regional Consequences

By the fall of 1989, when it is proposed to hold this conference, it may be over six months after the completion of the withdrawal of the Soviet forces from Afghanistan. When the Soviet Union invaded Afghanistan, President Carter reacted with alarm and called it the most serious threat since World War II. It caused a setback to the ongoing superpower dialogue, the ratification of SALT-II was jeopardized, and it culminated in a protracted conflict between the Kabul government and Soviet forces on one side and the Mujahidins who received arms and support from the US government on the other. Contrary to general expectations, however, in 1988 the USSR agreed to the Accords, under the auspices of the United Nations (UN), negotiated under which had a predetermined schedule for withdrawal of their forces from Afghanistan. The Soviet intervention was the first case of military violation of the demarcations agreed upon at Yalta (1945), but also, if completed, it will be the only example of the withdrawal of forces after being engaged militarily. What is more, unlike some other interventions like the Cuban troops in Angola and Ethiopia, it will all have taken place within a decade.

It is proposed to start the conference with an inaugural address, hopefully by somebody with policy insights in decision-making during the crisis and an overview paper which the undersigned will prepare for circulation to the participants. In the following day and a half the conference will have four working sessions concentrating on the following specific headings (a separate discussion paper will be circulated to the panelists in advance for each of these sessions):

a. Afghanistan 1978-88: A case study in Soviet foreign policy (from Brezhnev Doctrine to Gorbachev's Glasnost)

*Theme paper sent out in January 1988 when inviting participants to the conference proposed to be held in October 1989.

b. Afghanistan: as an example of superpower perceptions and crisis management
c. The regional fall-out from Afghanistan: the impact on South Asia and the Islamic World
d. The future in Afghanistan: rebuilding the political order and economic rehabilitation of the country
    At the concluding session there will be no papers, but all the panelists will jointly review the discussions and answer questions from the audience, and the senior academics presiding over the session in his address will distil lessons on great power interests and Third World crises.

This brief theme paper seeks to draw attention to possible questions which can be raised and discussed at the conference in examining the Afghanistan crisis. In a retrospective analysis comparisons could be made with other frustrating interventions like Vietnam. Afghanistan is, however, a rare case, where, even while actively embattled, a Communist power came to publicly acknowledge that its military adventure was a mistake. The challenge before governments and thoughtful minds everywhere is to assess whether the intervention was the last instance of the Brezhnev doctrine and the withdrawal, if completed as scheduled, signifies the proof of Gorbachev's Glasnost and the promise of a new turn in Soviet foreign policy. Would it represent the historic finale of 40 years of the Cold War and the opening chapter of a new era in great power relations? Or will it be only a tactical retreat, under temporary economic compulsions, but such adventures may re-occur in the future because the expansionist purpose remains unchanged? It would obviously be important for the new administration in Washington to make a careful judgement as it could determine the thrust of future superpower relations and international politics generally.

Many questions could be raised in looking back on the events in Afghanistan starting from the Saur Revolution in April 1978 to the signing of the Geneva Accords in April 1988. Was there a Kremlin-planned conspiracy to undermine the Daud regime in 1978 as part of a grand strategic design or were the Soviets just agreeably surprised at the Khalq–Parcham seizure of power and gave recognition and support to the new 'candidate member' of the Socialist Commonwealth? Was the USSR party to, or powerless when the Khalq faction, led by Taraki and Amin, banished the Parcham faction of Babrak Karmal within weeks of the revolution? At least until the late spring of 1979, Amin seemed to have been allowed by the Soviets to concentrate power in his hand and given support and personnel for his Leninist decrees, which incidentally reduced Taraki to a figurehead. Did the Soviets switch their preferences to Taraki because the Kremlin discovered Amin's ideological fidelity was actually alienating the Afghan people and making the Soviet Union unpopular, as it had never been under the monarchy or the oligarchic presidency of Daud? Was then, the Soviet invasion and the brutal removal of Amin because of the inability to control an ideological votary who was indifferent to the fact that promoting communism was actually creating disaffection and that too in a country contiguous to the sensitive Central Asian republics? Can one relate the timing of the invasion to the fall of the Shah, the oil crisis, the taking of the American hostages in Teheran, because it provided a tempting opportunity to realize Peter the Great's ambition to reach a warm water port? Or was it never the Soviet intention to go beyond the frontiers of Afghanistan? All these answers could help illuminate the interplay of the critical dichotomy between ideological compulsions and national security perceptions in the formulation and decision-making in Soviet foreign policy.

It has been argued by many that the USSR did not cross into Pakistan and reach the Gulf coast to sever the oil artery only because of sharp US counter-measures such as the imposition of the grain embargo, the withdrawal from the Moscow Olympics, and the concentration of the Rapid Deployment Force. In the light of what actually happened, were these US measures really necessary or did they lead to self-inflicted economic damage for the USA? The initial alarm died down long before the Carter administration went out of office. But, consistent with his election platform, President Reagan after assuming office revived the propaganda focus on Afghanistan as proof of the unrelenting militancy of Communism and Soviet expansionism. Afghanistan was played up to wring maximum political advantage when Russia seemed to be caught in its own 'Vietnam'. It was also used to justify the new US administration's thrust to re-establish overall military superiority over the USSR. The US military support to the insurgent groups was a sort of indirect attrition of Soviet military and economic power. Some commentators have taken the view that the improved military capability of the Mujahidin, supplied with sophisticated weapons like the Stinger missiles, was the critical factor leading to the Soviet withdrawal. Whether it was military frustration or Gorbachev's fundamental reappraisal and altered national priorities that led to the Soviet withdrawal, it would correspondingly determine the calculus of deterrence, response, and crisis management in similar future Third World problems. If the Soviet withdrawal suggests that the pursuit of new priorities—Perestroika and economic and technological modernization—are the indications of long-term policies, it would be important to evaluate whether the Soviet Union may well go on to reduce or even jettison other current commitments in the Third World.

Whatever the consensus on the rationale of the Soviet withdrawal, by the fall of 1989, Afghanistan may have only a residuary importance on the East/West agenda. However, the Soviet intervention and the US military aid policies will continue to cast a shadow over the politics and the security picture in South Asia. It will be recalled that relations between India and Pakistan were slowly improving in the 1970s. Pakistan was, however, able to exploit the Western alarm and India's non-critical attitude toward the USSR's intervention in Afghanistan. It repaired its relations with the US and obtained the resumption of massive commitments of military and economic aid on the hypothesis that Pakistan was defending the Gulf and the oil flow for the West and Japan. India did not *prima facie* accept that the military support for Pakistan could be effective enough to face the Soviet threat if it materialized, and hence perceived it as a repetition of the old US policy of deliberately building Pakistan's military capability against India. But in accepting, at face value, the Soviet justification for its intervention, India got out of step with her neighbours and most of the Non-aligned countries. As a consequence of these divergent national perceptions which were often erroneous, a mutually reinforcing subcontinental arms race started, which has added serious burdens on their respective economies and aggravated political problems in both countries. It may take a much longer time to unscramble the Afghanistan legacy in South Asia but an incisive analysis could help the process of decoupling the subcontinental security problems from the ups and downs of superpower relations.

In showing solidarity and support for Afghan resistance against the Soviet Union, there was a rare unanimity amongst the Islamic countries and a sort of confirmed revulsion against Communism and Socialism. The faith inspired the resistance, and the religious leadership of different tribes and areas have spearheaded most of the insurgent factions. Some commentators have argued that the Soviet intervention was to pre-empt the contagion of Islamic fundamentalism reaching the Central Asian republics of the USSR. What, if any, has been the impact inside the Soviet Central Asia of the Islamic call to Jehad against Soviet presence and policies in Afghanistan? The future of Afghanistan may depend on whether and how and to what extent the deeply cherished Islamic faith and resilient tribalism will adjust to the secular political ideas and demands of a modernizing state and society.

The most pernicious consequence of this decade-long bitter military conflict is the political confusion, the blighted economic landscape, and the human distress inside Afghanistan. As Sir Winston Churchill noted after service on the North-Western Frontier in 1897, every tribal in that gaunt landscape has multiple loyalties and everyone is both a warrior and a theologian. The national personality of Afghanistan had emerged in the last century only. The tribal feuds had become muted only when facing an intruding foreigner. To recreate even the old tenuous national political infrastructure will require rebuilding Afghanistan from above and below. Or will Afghanistan get divided, with the region north of the Hindu Kush becoming economically so dependent on the USSR that it could be politically manipulated from across the border? Or will King Zahir Shah, if restored to the throne, and carrying Moscow's blessing, be able to persuade the refugees to return, and the tribal or religious leaders to join a Loya Jirgah or a Shura (internal assembly) and succeed in fusing together the warring factions and establish a national government in Kabul that would command the allegiance of the entire country?

The conference can incidentally 'revisit' the Great Game and identify the penalties of ignoring history. In the twentieth century there are new features both in the exercise of coercive power and of defiance against its abuse. The Soviets, no doubt, had much greater military capacity than the Czarist or British imperialists. A helicopter gunship can all but overcome the tactical advantage of the impenetrable valleys and boulders which provided protection for the insurgents. But the Soviet experience in Afghanistan can also show that a great power's attempt to compel the militarily weak serves also to strengthen the capacity of political defiance. Time after time militant nationalism, fighting on homeground, has effectively harassed a mighty power. This has lessons for the great powers and even middle powers.

There are now approximately three million refugees from Afghanistan in Pakistan and more than one million in Iran. In addition, there may be two million internal refugees who have fled their homes but are still in Afghanistan. Some 10 million mines are embedded in the fields, mountain footpaths, and valleys of the country. The challenge of rehabilitation and reconstruction is awesome, and massive and sustained international aid and technical cooperation will be needed to rehabilitate the country and the uprooted millions. As has been seen in Vietnam, even after militarily defeating a powerful invader, an equally determined effort will have to be marshalled for sustained economic reconstruction. The heroic spirit seems to have flagged in Vietnam. Will it be adequately mustered in Afghanistan?

There may be a special political problem for Pakistan in the re-habilitation of the Afghan refugees. During the last four decades Afghan–Pakistan relations have deteriorated from time to time since the British delineated the frontier (the Durand Line) that had artificially divided the Pasthun tribes. Periodically the governments in Kabul have raised demands to unite the tribes in a Pashtun homeland or even to establish a Pakhtun state. At moments of heightened tensions, Pakistan even denied transit rights for Afghani-stan's seaborne trade which went mostly through Karachi. The Soviet intervention and the arrival of three million refugees has substantially increased the proportion of Pathans living in Pakistan. Smuggling, drug trafficking, and crime in the major cities of Pakistan have become a way of economic survival for many refugees. Pakistan has no doubt earned the gratitude of the Afghans for having given asylum to millions fleeing under harsh conditions, and so the memory of past Afghanistan–Pakistan tensions has no doubt receded. But, even so, will most of the Afghans be willing, or even be induced, to leave Pakistan and return to their homes, especially when their villages and the agricultural base are badly shattered and their fields are strewn with unexploded mines. Much would depend on the degree of confidence inspired by the new political set-up in Kabul and the economic recovery inside Afghanistan. But the voluntary repatriation of the Afghans could become a delicate challenge to Pakistan. Do we have here the embryo of an autonomous Pashtun homeland straddling the old Durand Line?

For six years the UN was involved in finding the modalities and framework for a solution to the Afghanistan problem. The UN could not effect a breakthrough because on the one side there was a superpower directly engaged, and on the other were nationalist insurgents, who were not able to coalesce into a united 'Liberation' movement and, in any case, were denied international recognition and a forum in the UN. It is noteworthy that the Soviets, having taken a decision to withdraw, have also decided to fund the UN to undertake the process of economic reconstruction of the country. If the UN could provide a common funnel for international aid for Afghanistan where the US and USSR both contribute, it could augur well for the UN and for international aid in other disaster situations. Going further, could the Afghanistan episode provide an opportunity to revive the idea of a UN peace-keeping force or at least contingents in different countries earmarked for assignments as a body of neutral international observers?

The future in Afghanistan, in any case, is grim. Lying as it does at the crossroad between the different parts of the Eurasian land mass, Afghanistan remains important. The challenge for the East, the West, the Non-aligned, the countries in South and South West Asia, the UN, and the international community in general is to help restore Afghanistan to political stability, economic viability, and effective independence. For the superpowers, Afghanistan may, in retrospect, become a finite episode albeit one which may lead to a reassessment of costs and benefits from military interventions in the Third World. For the region however the consequences may be longer lasting and more painful. After a quarter of a century, recently some Soviet and American adversary decision-makers and historians and analysts from both sides have been able to meet under academic auspices and frankly and review relive the Cuban Missile Crisis. An academic conference on Afghanistan so soon after the superpower intervention may have greater relevance in avoiding penalties of misperceptions in a non-nuclear international crisis, which, alas, may persist in the turbulent Third World. We must look at the past, but the focus of the conference should be on the lessons to be drawn for the future.

13

The Legacy and Lessons
of Afghanistan

Introduction and Summary

In trying to grasp the dimensions of the Afghanistan crisis, starting
from the overthrow of the Daud regime in April 1978 and persisting
today after 11 years, I found myself turning to the analysis by
Barbara Tuchman in *The March of Folly* of how governments,
regardless of place or period of history, pursue policies contrary to
their self-interests. She defines Folly where the decision taken could
have been seen as counter-productive in the lifetime of the decision
makers themselves, feasible alternatives were rejected, and the
consequences persisted beyond the political careers of the decision
makers. She illustrates her thesis by surveying four turning points in
history: the Trojan defeat after allowing the wooden horse across
the walls of Troy, the Renaissance Popes provoking the Protestant
secession, the British loss of America, and America betraying itself
in Vietnam. In the epilogue, entitled 'Lantern at the Stern', Barbara
Tuchman concludes that reason more often than not got over-
powered by 'ambition, anxiety, status seeking, face-saving illusions
and self-deluding fixed principles'. The policy makers predetermined
the boundaries of the political problem and then pursued policies to
uphold the ideas with which they started, and when they found
themselves to be failing and functions and dissensions began to
appear, their mindset only became more rigid and the damage was
compounded. Afghanistan has the features of a contemporary case
of *The March of Folly*: the diverse governments and political actors
on the Afghan stage pursued policies contrary to their best interests;
and even when the tragic consequences became plain, the pre-
conceived attitudes persisted in defiance of reason. When we, who

*Keynote address given by the author at a conference at the University of Texas,
Austin, 19 October 1989.

belong to the non-existent international guild of diplomats (and of course our respective policy makers in different capitals), look back on this decade, we may have to quietly confess that we have been guilty of gross errors of judgement at the expense of the Afghan people. Most scholars with their small library of books, articles, films, and television videotapes cannot claim to have had better insights. Vested interests in hypotheses, which have proved erroneous, may now well be the greatest inhibiting impediment to bringing the requisite sense of urgency in the search for a solution in the present destructive drift.

Afghanistan is a microcosmic tragedy of Cold War politics dominating international relations. As in Vietnam, a superpower propelled itself into a thoughtless intervention against nationalism and, thereafter, objective judgement sought to vindicate the predetermined goals by military means; the economic and political costs were obscured by self-generating propaganda and has left near irreparable damage in the Third World. The superpowers are now beginning to make a balance sheet of decades of mutually reinforcing fears and reorienting in general their priorities, but in Afghanistan the restoration of stability in the country is riddled with the legacy of an acknowledged disaster.

The present agony of Afghanistan started with the quest of modern socio-economic progress by native ideologues, overlooking the true character of their own national personality. Of all nations who faced the covetous advances of European imperialism, Afghanistan had the bravest record of defiant nationalism. The Soviet invasion overlooked the lessons of its own Czarist experience and in a misconceived involvement, invited frustration and failure. Both Vietnam and Afghanistan were cases of mutually reinforcing misperceptions; both illustrate the abuse and limitations of military power. The American involvement in Vietnam stemmed from false fears of both ideological and strategic dangers. Paradoxically, the Soviet intervention in Afghanistan was made to actually moderate counter-productive ideological militancy in order to pre-empt a perceived security threat near its border. The future of Afghanistan depends, in the final instance, upon whether the nationalism, which was so heroic in defiance, can rise to the responsibilities of independent statehood, shedding the diverse props of foreign dependency.

This conference at the University of Texas in Austin, should not shirk from introspective criticism, and from weighing the opportunity costs of the mistakes and the wages in human suffering. It should not be restricted to hindsight sagacity and accusatory criticism but, as an academic effort, seek to distil lessons to facilitate the search for a solution and caution against faltering similarly in the future.

The Afghanistan problem now looks very different from what it appeared for all these years after the Soviet invasion. The Soviet invasion of Afghanistan was projected at the time as the greatest threat to world peace since World War II. It aroused fears that the geo-strategic interests of the West in the vital oil exporting region were endangered, and the independence of the countries in South and South-West Asia was under threat. The Soviet intervention invited the moral condemnation of the international community and led to the suspension of the SALT-II agreement and the imposition of economic embargoes. It accelerated the embodiment of the Rapid Deployment Force and the Central Command to meet the expected Soviet military advance towards the warm waters of the Gulf. Even when the Soviet Union met with determined resistance from the Afghan Mujahidin, it was assumed that the Soviet Union would battle on until effective and permanent control was established—turning Afghanistan into a Mongolia. The USSR has now withdrawn its combat forces but the conflict has continued, and the compounding misery of the Afghan people is receding from international public attention.

Unforeseen Revolution: Impetuous Invasion and No Wider Conflagration

What follows is entirely an individual analysis, for which the Indian government is in no way responsible. But let me, as a starting point, recall some personal insights which came my way in 1978 and 1979 when I had the privilege to hold a post in the Government of India. Ambassador Yuri Vorontsov, then Soviet Ambassador to India, until recently Ambassador to Afghanistan, and now Deputy Foreign Minister, was sitting in my room in the Ministry of External Affairs in New Delhi on one of his periodic calls, when on 27 April 1978 I was informed on an internal telephone that President Daud had been dethroned and, along with the cabinet and his family, killed and Taraki had proclaimed the Democratic Republic of Afghanistan with himself as President. I conveyed this to Vorontsov and while I would not discount Vorontsov's diplomatic capability to feign and play-act, I got the distinct impression that he was surprised at the news.

From other related evidence, one could not but be convinced that the Saur Revolution was locally improvised. It was facilitated by the ineptitude of the Daud government, but was not externally engineered from Moscow. India was quick to recognize the new People's Democratic Party of Afghanistan (PDPA) government, as did the United States. Notwithstanding a sharp change in the ideological orientation, there was a shared hope that Afghanistan would stay non-aligned and there would be no wider fall-out. I went to Kabul in June 1978 and was, I believe, the first foreign representative to do so after the events of April 1978. I called on President Taraki, Hafizullah Amin (then only a senior member of the government), and other members of the government. The Parcham faction led by Babrak Karmal was already in disfavour. Taraki was looked upon by Amin and the rest of the coalition as the father of the new Afghanistan. There was clear proof of deference to him (Taraki had to tell Amin to sit down even after I had done so). There was no evidence of the rivalry between the two which developed later. The Soviet Union was, of course, satisfied with the unexpected extension of the domains of socialism and pledged financial military and advisory support in the hope that the new government in Afghanistan would serve as a security buffer along the southern reaches of the USSR. I went to Kabul again in October 1978, this time accompanying the Foreign Minister. One could sense that despite the induction of Soviet advisers and economic support, the government was far from self-confident in the exercise of its power.

In June 1979, after a visit to Moscow with the then Prime Minister of India, I stayed in Moscow and had an opportunity for a day-long discussion with Soviet officials on the deteriorating situation in Afghanistan. It was evident that the Soviet appraisal of Afghanistan had changed from quiet satisfaction to fermenting anxiety. In the previous year, Amin, with his ideological zest and administrative capability, had gathered much of the sinews of power, and Taraki had been reduced to a figurehead. The Soviet Union had acquiesced in Amin's policy initiatives in excluding the Parcham faction from the government and arresting important military commanders like Qadir, Watanjar, and nationalists who had helped to establish the People's Democratic Republic of Afghanistan. During the special UN Conference on Disarmament in 1978, soon after the Saur Revolution, Amin as representative of Afghanistan had demonstrated his unquestioning loyalty to the Soviet Union by outdoing the Soviet Union in criticizing the United States. Unlike the cautious Soviet approach, but consistent with Marxist–Leninist orthodoxy, he denounced the theocracy established by Ayatollah Khomeini in Iran in 1979. It was Amin who negotiated the new Treaty of Friendship with the USSR, although for protocol reasons it was Taraki, as the opposite number of Brezhnev, who signed the treaty in Moscow in December 1978. Taking an imitative cue from Lenin, Amin was the author of a succession of decrees on land reform, language, women's liberation, and a radical social restructuring to transform the deeply religious conservative tribal society into a Socialist State. However by the summer of 1979, the Kremlin seem to have realized that as a consequence of Amin's whipped gallop to a Socialist Utopia, the regime had become alienated from the people and the sporadic insurgency had spread and gathered in intensity. In the bargain, the Soviet Union and its advisers found themselves becoming unpopular as they had never been under the monarchy or the Daud regime.

The killing of Soviet advisers in Herat in March 1979 was an eye-opener and brought home to the Soviets, the possibility that the promise of gratuitous ideological and security advantages expected from the Saur Revolution seemed to be turning sour. Even so, there was no suspicion of Amin's disloyalty to the Soviet Union. Indeed in that very month, Amin had assumed the position of Prime Minister. (Those who subscribed to the theory of Kremlin control and direction would have to concede that it was with Moscow's approval.) In my conversations in Moscow, Amin was not directly criticized, but reading between the lines there were hints that the Soviets felt Amin was driving too impetuously towards Socialism. The dilemma which confronted the USSR was a painful one; it was the advent of Communism which was alienating a consistently neutral, friendly country and, in the process, turning a contiguous neighbour into a security liability. The point to note is that, notwithstanding the presence of Soviet aid and advisers and a dependency syndrome, the adverse developments were because decision-making was in Afghan hands. As has happened not infrequently in these decades, a Third World tail was wagging a superpower mastiff.

There is no reason to believe that the USSR was indulging in a conscious deception when Brezhnev assured President Carter at Vienna in June 1979 that there was no intention to militarily intervene in Afghanistan. Soviet policy had metamorphosed slowly and in stages: it started with acquiescence and support of Amin; when the insurgency increased, the Soviets cautioned moderation; but when this did not dilute Amin's ideological militancy, they conspired with Taraki on his way back from the Non-aligned Summit at Havana to effect a palace coup. Only when it failed, and Amin escaped, did they plan an invasion of Afghanistan and the installation of a puppet government iǹ Kabul. The old Russian paranoia about security was compounded by the rampant and unexpected hostility of the Afghan people to even an advisory presence in the country. The Soviet intervened because they feared a disillusioned Amin might switch sides, as did Sadat in Egypt, and invite the US to establish a presence in Afghanistan. There was no plausibility in the *post hoc* Soviet denunciation of Amin as an anti-Soviet and long-time CIA agent. The irony is that if the palace coup planned in Moscow against Amin had succeeded and the milder and more amenable Taraki had been restored to effective power, there might have been no invasion and, therefore, none of the international consequences which came in its wake would have occurred.

Amin had come to suspect, and was later shocked, that despite his steady loyalty to the Soviet Union and its ideology, he was to be politically, if not physically, eliminated. It was only then that he started trying to distance himself from the USSR and don nationalist colours. It was an Amin desperately striving to survive who, in a total reversal of earlier policies and postures, made overtures to the Mullahs, released the nationalists, dropped the mention of Pakhtunistan, and generally muted the propaganda against the United States imperialism. But Amin had already been branded in the eyes of the Afghan people as a Soviet quisling and his previous record was too brutal for him to carry credibility as a twice-born nationalist. Since his government was already so besieged by widespread disaffection, he had no prop except to rely on Russian support against the growing insurgency. Amin's last 100 days—as Bradsher[1] calls them—were a battle of wits of mutual deception between him and the Soviet Union, with both sides showing outward *bonhomie* which concealed distrust of the intention of the other.

The Soviet Union did not anticipate that in the situation of 1979 with the oil crisis and American hostages in Iran, the invasion would look provocative and bring about worldwide condemnation. It failed to foresee the economic embargoes and the heightened military reaction that it would generate. The intervention, at one stroke,

[1] Henry Bradsher, 'Soviet Afghanistan', Kennan Institute, Occasional Paper No. 153, Washington, DC, 1981

jeopardized the worldwide ideological appeal built up by Soviet Russia since the October Revolution.

But neither the tell-tale facts nor the chronology could be fitted into the theory of a masterminded grand design for strategic or ideological expansion planned by the Kremlin, of which the invasion of Afghanistan was the first step. The West reacted the way it did because it had become conditioned to see every move of the USSR as directed against Western interests. The United States failed to see that removing a former pro-Soviet ideological militant who had got disillusioned was an impetuous move but could not but be a defensive reaction. It was not to enforce ideological orthodoxy, as in Hungary (1956) and Czechoslovakia (1968), but to dilute the imposed Leninist doctrines which had alienated the people. The Cold War mindset triggered both Moscow's action and Washington's excessive reaction, and then by mutually reinforcing each other's fears, a local revolution was transformed into another East–West confrontation.

Similar sudden changes of government and violent coups with ideological overtones or rationalizations have, alas, happened all too frequently in the Third World but they have not led to any long-term jeopardy of superpower interests. No analogies are exact, but one can recall the change in Indonesia in 1965 (the pro-Chinese Leftist coup failed and vengeance was inflicted on the local Chinese), and in Peru, Ethiopia, and Nicaragua (where the Leftists evicted the non-Communists) without any impact on the equations in the great power relations. Amin himself was imbued with the Cold War mindset and his tragic end came about because in his ideological fidelity, he expected nothing less than unrelenting support from the Soviet Union.

The worst-case scenario—of the Soviet Union going beyond Afghanistan—did not come to pass. During nine years of civil conflict in Afghanistan, international attitudes and media comments went through various stages. The initial chorus of alarm underlined the geopolitical significance of the Soviet violation of the Yalta demarcations decided at the war time summit in February 1945. Later, when the Soviet forces met resistance there was *schadenfreude* satisfaction at the Soviet Union's own Vietnam. The heroic bravery of the Mujahidin commanded admiration and attracted adventurous journalists to report vividly on the guerrilla war. The 'migratory genocide' evoked widespread international sympathy. The Rapid Deployment Force under the Central Command held some exercises, but the proposal for a new strategic northern tier to be activated to face any further military move by the Soviet Union evoked no positive response from the region except from Israel. Every year the United Nations debated and passed resolutions, and the voting remained firm in its condemnation, but beyond starting the intermittent proximity talks, they could not be translated into any concrete progress. Within months of the invasion, it became clear that the military conflict was going to remain internal, but, for the region itself, it had more lasting adverse consequences.

The Shadow of Afghanistan over South Asia

The ideological reorientation in Kabul had taken place after the Saur Revolution (April 1978), but even though concern was aroused in Pakistan, it has not been sufficiently noted that Indo–Pakistan relations had remained relatively harmonious until the Soviet invasion. The atmospherics of the Cold War tensions localizing over South and South-West Asia provides the clue to India's indulgent attitude in accepting the Soviet explanation for its intervention. The substance of the speech of the Indian Ambassador during the UN debate in January 1980 put India out of step with the majority of the non-aligned countries. For the first time all of India's immediate neighbours voted differently from India in the UN. It was the initial reaction of India which facilitated the resumption of American arms supplies to Pakistan.

I have argued that a coincidence in the dynamics of internal democratic politics in India with the Soviet invasion provides an insight into the Indian approach. The Soviet intervention came just ten days before the Indian general elections which brought Mrs Gandhi back into power; the UN debate took place within a few days of her being sworn in as Prime Minister. In the competitive run-up to the elections, the Congress (I) pledged to take India back from Morarji Desai's 'genuine non-alignment' to approaches which were in closer proximity to the Soviet position, specifically promising the recognition of the Heng Samrin government in Kampuchea. The criticism was just part of electioneering as Indo–Soviet relations had remained unimpaired in spirit and substance when the Janata government was in power. I have expressed the view, admittedly only speculative, that had Mrs Gandhi been in office since 1977— when she lost the elections—or had Morarji Desai's government not disintegrated prematurely in July 1979, India's attitude to the Soviet invasion would have been different and the dire consequences for South Asia—and the recoupling of South Asia with the East–West Cold War—might have been averted. This was particularly unfortunate because there never was a more propitious moment for full Indo–Pakistan rapprochement than in the immediate wake of the Soviet intervention in Afghanistan. It slipped by because of the divergent reactions of Pakistan and India to the Soviet intervention. Needless to say, India was not honestly informed of the Soviet assessments leading to the invasion.

As stated earlier, within weeks, or at best months, the international alarm of a threat to the vital interests of the West and a wider conflagration had been dissipated. What continued for years was that the Soviet force got militarily bogged down and Afghanistan became a propaganda argument in the spirit of the Cold War. Even after the early fears stood falsified, the combination of domestic policies and the Cold War mindset, Afghanistan was used by the Reagan administration to justify the urgency of establishing military superiority over the 'Evil Empire'. This thrust of policy led to the pledge of over US $ 7.5 billion of military and economic aid to Pakistan. Military aid to Pakistan had been terminated during the India–Pakistan conflict in 1965 because the arms supplied for the containment of Communist expansion were used against India. Just before the aid bill was passed in the US in 1981, I made bold to write an article in the *New York Times* that it was a *déjà vu* situation.[2] As in 1954 a military aid relationship was being forged, where the rationalization of a shared threat perception only concealed a divergence of purposes. The United States was concerned primarily with the Soviet threat and Pakistan was more bent on improving its capability against India.

Aside from radar and aerial defence capability, the aid package included F-16s, battle tanks, heavy artillery, and even naval arms, which were unsuitable for operations in or near Afghanistan. Predictably, India launched on its own extravagant militarization, probably expending some US $ 20 billion on weapons acquisitions from diverse sources. It was never credible in India that even with the induction of US military aid, Pakistan could withstand a massive attack by Soviet forces, and consequently the suspicion grew that it was a deliberate American policy to encourage Pakistan's belligerence and impede India's rise to its economic potential and

[2] J.S. Mehta, 'Déjà vue in South Asia', *New York Times*, 24 April 1981.

international position. Indeed, in some minds the confidential hope was nurtured that it would be a lesser evil for India, if on the other side of Pakistan, the Soviet presence and effective control became permanent and Afghanistan was turned into another Mongolia. India never unconditionally disapproved the Soviet invasion of Afghanistan but, not too long after the Soviet intervention, the Indian Prime Minister, when asked, stated publicly that the Soviet Union should withdraw its forces from Afghanistan. This was also urged in confidential discussions with the Soviet authorities but year after year India abstained in the UN resolution which had over-whelming support of the Non-aligned nations. Later India officially expressed the hope that the proximity talks under UN auspices might achieve a breakthrough, but no direct Indian initiative was ever launched. The ironical fact is that the reluctance to embarrass the Soviet Union meant that when, after Brezhnev's death, the Soviet Union was looking for an honourable and safe exit, India had forfeited the standing necessary to prove helpful. As a consequence of a serious misjudgement, India found the military capability of Pakistan greatly strengthened, but was unable to play a political role to arrest and reverse the situation in Afghanistan.

My own fears from 1980 onwards have been that while the Afghanistan crisis did not pose serious international dangers, Afghanistan and South Asia would be the real direct victims of the tragedy. In a paper written[3] in 1981, I suggested that, through sequential steps starting with the 'Swedenizing' of the surrounding region (i.e. the voluntary reassertion of neutrality in the great power conflict) and involving the consensus of the Non-aligned nations, specially the regional and Islamic countries in South Asia and the Gulf, Soviet security anxieties could be assuaged and Afghanistan could be 'Finlandized', its independence restored, and as a final step all Soviet forces could be withdrawn. But the pervasive Cold War atmospherics and politics were too strong even when they were transparently removed from the realities of the 1980s. India, for its part, remained indifferent for too long to the agony and conflict in Afghanistan and now, regretfully, stands marginalized.[4, 5] The

[3] J.S. Mehta, 'Solution in Afghanistan: From Swedenisation to Finlandisation', Kennan Institute, Woodrow Wilson Centre, 1981. (A summary is also given in *Foreign Policy,* Summer 1982.)

[4] J.S. Mehta, 'The Prospect in Afghanistan: Can India Remain Indifferent?', *Foreign Policy Annual,* 1985.

[5] J.S. Mehta, 'Afghanistan: Why India Stands Marginalized', *Indian Express,* 13 February 1989.

vigorous official Indian commitment to the present Kabul government in 1988, after the Soviet Union announced its withdrawal,
could pay off only if the Najibullah government remains the centre-
piece in a government of national reconciliation. But the present
Kabul authorities have to go beyond survival and live down the
stigma of being installed by the Soviet Union and this would inhibit
establishing legitimacy with the bulk of the Afghan people, including
the refugees outside, and the afflicted within, the country.

Pakistan's position has, no doubt, been unenviably difficult with a
'live' western border and an unending stream of refugees straining
its administrative and social structure. Pakistan's diplomacy certainly
showed a shrewder grasp of the reality of the continuing hold of the
Cold War mindsets in Washington. With the Soviets at the Khyber
and the scholarly reminders of the Great Game of the nineteenth
century, the Carter and, even more so, the Reagan administrations
were at first in genuine, and later cosmetic, alarm and Pakistan
succeeded in projecting itself in the role of holding the frontline for
the defence of the West.

It is hard for me to tell whether Pakistan seriously anticipated an
onward march through Baluchistan to the Gulf or saw it merely as a
remote and unlikely contingency but one providing an appealing
argument in Washington. In retrospect, one may also ask whether
Pakistan truly feared or only asserted because of its plausibility, that
by virtue of the India's treaty with the USSR, there existed a conspiratorial strategy by which India would take advantage of the
Afghan crisis to dismember Pakistan again. (I needn't add that the
Indo–Soviet Treaty does not have any secret protocol like in the
Molotov–Ribbentrop Pact of 1939 for conspiratorial territorial
adjustment.)

The Soviet intervention earned Pakistan great international
dividends and enabled it to repair its relations with the US, which
were at a low ebb in 1979. Pakistan was also able to obtain an
indulgent US attitude on many counts, including a waiver of the
provisions of American enactments against suspected nuclear proli-
feration. Pakistan, as a proclaimed Islamic State, had a natural
advantage in commanding the sympathy and support of the Organization of Islamic States and received generous support from Saudi
Arabia and other Arab countries. It also earned admiration for
providing a haven to three million co-religionists and creating the
infrastructure for the distribution of a billion plus dollars worth of
American, Chinese, Saudi, and Egyptian arms and aid for the
Mujahidin.

As the prospect of a victory and Soviet withdrawal seemed round the corner, Pakistan developed the vision of an Islamic republic in Afghanistan, which would forever be beholden to and could be controlled by Pakistan and so lay to rest the ghost of Pakhtoonistan. There were even glib remarks that the 'Khyber' would move to the Oxus river. But this policy perspective, which emanated from the late President General Zia-ul-Haq, may also have overlooked the lessons of the Great Game of the nineteenth century, which demonstrated the Afghan tradition of sturdy independence. After nine years of fighting against the foreigner, the Afghans are unlikely to accept becoming a subordinate constituent even of an Islamic confederation. Pakistan's own experience shows that religion is an insufficient cement to hold together distinct cultural and ethnic national personalities. It could also learn from the Indian experience in Bangladesh (and from Americans with many aid recipients) that nationalistic independence does not remain subservient to a one-time benefactor. No doubt Pakistan has been in a position to influence the refugee tribal groups, but in making selective preferences from them, it may have only accentuated counter-productive friction. Not surprisingly, the so-called Afghan interim government promoted by Pakistan remains riddled with dissension and intra-group rivalries, sometimes resulting in factional violence. Drug trafficking and the sale of pilfered Kalashnikov rifles and other military weapons have become dangerously rampant across the length of Pakistan. The presence of Afghan refugees has strained the law and order situation and created enormous, possibly long-lasting, internal social and administrative problems for the country. In brief, the political, economic, and military benefits which flowed to Pakistan may well be outbalanced by the seeds of long-term internal instability for the country.

The fact is that the Soviet invasion of Afghanistan and ten years of strife have inflicted incalculable penalties on both India and Pakistan. Even with all the possible external support they may be able to muster, neither India nor Pakistan can sustain the respective burdens of enhanced militarization. The challenge of bringing about a regional détente and starting arms control talks in the subcontinent was always difficult but the legacy of Afghanistan has greatly complicated it. Statesmanship and skilful confidential diplomacy, combined with courageous public postures, will be required of the two countries for return to the promise of regional stability which was on the horizon before the Afghan crisis erupted.

Pre-Saur Revolution Background and
the Run-up to the 1978 Crisis

To put the present problem, its origin, the denouement, and the framework for the resolution in an historical perspective, it is worth looking back a little at the previous decades. Even at the height of the Cold War—in the 1950s and the 1960s—the West never attached great strategic and political importance to Afghanistan. There was obvious regret in the West that, unlike neighbouring Iran and Pakistan, Afghanistan did not respond positively to join the Baghdad Pact (1954), but there was understanding and not too great an alarm when Afghanistan adopted the policy of non-alignment, which was basically the continuation of the traditional policy of preserving independence between competing great powers. Indeed since Abdur Rahman's time (1880), Afghanistan had adopted a policy of voluntary 'Finlandization'; in other words, to resist encroaching rival powers but not to provoke its great neighbour to the north. Despite pressures from both sides, it was neutral in both World Wars. Even after the Russian Revolution next door, the country remained Islamic, conservative and oligarchic. The ideological pressure of Communism was never seriously subversive but such as it was, the succession of Afghan governments effectively resisted it. The State to State relations with the Soviet Union were correct without any serious friction. In fact, the Soviet Union was the first to recognize Afghanistan when, under Amanullah, it declared its full independence in 1919 after the Third Afghan War (the United States only established relations with the Afghan government in 1934). Afghanistan had acquired arms from Soviet Russia even in the 1920s, and when Daud did so in the 1950s, it was only after the United States had refused an Afghan request. When Bulganin and Khrushchev were in Kabul in 1955, the former had endorsed the Afghan claim to Pakhtoonistan. The idea of a Pakhtoon state to reunite the Pathan tribes which had been divided by the British delineated Durand Line in 1892 had been raised after the British withdrawal from the subcontinent and the creation of Pakistan. The proposed state would, in effect, have detached the old North West Frontier Province and so, not surprisingly, it was resisted to the point of interrupting the transit of Afghan trade through Pakistan. Afghanistan, being landlocked, suffered considerable hardship until the Soviet Union improvised a small land outlet through its own territory. The demand for Pakhtoonistan was looked upon with disfavour in the West as

Pakistan had become an important ally in the Baghdad Pact and SEATO. It should be noted, however, that although the call for Pakhtunistan was raised from time to time, frequently when a new government came to power in Kabul, the Soviet Union has never reiterated support for it, except for the Bulganin statement. The PDPA itself raised the demand vociferously when it was proclaimed in 1978, but Soviet support was not reaffirmed even after the Soviet intervention in 1979.

The Soviet aid to Afghanistan in the 1950s and 1960s was primarily for the development and supply of gas to the Soviet Union for the construction of minor industries like cement, etc. The Soviet aid was really rather small and most projects were earmarked for development north of the Hindu Kush. The American aid to Afghanistan was comparatively even less, and was primarily meant for education and the plans for the development of the Helmand river in the south. Both the superpowers helped in road construction and there seemed to have been a sort of unspoken agreement on the demarcation of areas of aid operations between them. Indeed, before 1978, Afghanistan was considered as an early example of co-operative coexistence, as opposed to vigorous competition, between the superpowers in aid relationships in a Third World country.

However, as part of the Cold War syndrome, intelligence agencies of both powers were ever vigilant in a country which had obvious strategic importance. As everywhere else, the KGB maintained steady contacts with the Leftist elements and potential influentials in Kabul. In 1973 the KGB had a role in bringing together the small Marxist-inclined Khalq and Parcham parties, which ended their factional competition. Military officers were sent for training to the Soviet Union as a by-product of the arms supplies and, according to the normal pattern, attempts must have been made to tutor them ideologically. Such trainings, exchanges, and facilities for travel for educated and not so well-educated professionals and political activists to the respective donor nations was part of the Cold War competition. Non-aligned countries permitted their officials and citizens to avail of such facilities with both blocs. Afghanistan, in fact, had an unusual tradition of fostering parallel diversified links with European powers even before the Cold War. The British, the French, and the Germans were all allowed to run schools or university departments but care was taken that none dominated even urban education or intruded too deeply into Afghan society (for theological education, the links were with Egypt). In recent years the

KGB (and other intelligence agencies), in their professional zeal, not infrequently have been known to develop a momentum of their own which went beyond their respective governmental policies. In retrospective analyses, such contacts, training, educational, and leader exchanges are cited to prove the Kremlin's conspiratorial intentions and the grand design behind the Soviet invasion. But it should be noted that neither the Khalq nor the Parcham, nor both together, had been accepted as 'Communist' parties up to 1978 as was the Tudeh Party in next-door Iran.

It is worth digressing that attempts at 'brainwashing' of Third World elites, including civil and military officers by combining professional training with ideological indoctrination has generally proved counterproductive or yielded no more than minimal success anywhere. The billions spent in official propaganda and supplemented by intelligence operations have not caused any great political turnabouts for either bloc. The present systemic repudiation of Communism in Eastern Europe and the rise of the appeal of democracy cannot be attributed to the success or failure of intelligence activities or propaganda persuasion. The tens of thousands of students who were taken to the Lumumba University in Moscow, as often as not, turned into anti-Communists.

African students after years in China came back anti-Chinese. Two generations of Tibetan youth who were taken to China and were given political orientation seemed to have remained defiantly Tibetan, rejecting the logic of Chinese Communism to facilitate Han domination. On the other side, most active Marxist leaders in the Third World (like Hafizullah Amin) developed their convictions by studying social science and literature emanating from the West. Many turned radical by opportunities provided by the United States Information and Cultural Services! The appeal of Socialism and Communism, in our times, and more particularly in the Third World, before and after independence, was primarily because of socio-economic conditions in their homelands and not because of the success of Soviet or Chinese indoctrination or subversion. The inspiration for the small leftist parties and intellectuals in Afghanistan, which seized the accidental opportunity to bring about the Saur Revolution, were motivated more by the protest against deteriorating economic conditions, corruption, and the oligarchic exploitative dispensation in urban Afghanistan. For the KGB to attribute the origin and success of the Saur Revolution to its exertions is mere self-flattery.

The *post hoc* explanation of a long and assiduous preparation towards a takeover or a Soviet invasion is as much a convenient distortion as the Third World arguments, advanced in many countries, of a 'foreign hand' responsible for internal disorders. Both arguments are two sides of the Cold War coin—of relentless competition by all means at the command of the State.

The fact of the matter is that the Saur Revolution was not expected either in Washington or in Moscow. Even after the oil crunch and the Ayatollah calling for the overthrow of the Shah in Iran, Afghanistan could rejoice in the continuation of benign neglect or comparatively minimal attention from the superpowers. If the contrary was the case, Ambassador Dubs, as Deputy Assistant Secretary, would not have testified just six weeks earlier in March 1978 before a Congressional Subcommittee, that the situation in Afghanistan was stable and constitution-making (under President Daud) was going on satisfactorily. The few scholars who followed Afghanistan closely saw no reason to upgrade vigilance or modify prevailing low-level attention to Afghanistan. The scholar emeritus on Afghanistan, the late Louis Dupree, was in Kabul at the time of the revolution.[6] He had a difficult experience in getting out of the country, but even so, he told me and wrote in 1978 that the Saur Revolution was an accident and it was the ineptitude of the Daud government which resulted in its violent overthrow. Even in the first half of 1979, he discounted the possibility of a direct Soviet intervention. Dupree's analysis was correct but he did not reckon with the march of events and of the ingrained fears which exaggerated the malevolent intentions and capabilities of the Soviet Union.

Neither the USSR nor the USA tested their respective assessments against what Barbara Tuchman calls the Socratic 'divine fire of reason'. The Brezhnev Politbureau could have seen in the period of September-December 1979 that Amin, as a renegade ideologue turned nationalist, could not have become a menace because he simply did not (like Tito in 1948 or Sadat in 1973) have domestic credibility. It was also not too far-fetched to see that the United States, having lost the Shah as the regional gendarme on their behalf, was too baffled on how to rescue the American diplomats taken hostage in Teheran and could not risk an adventure in Afghanistan. Under the Carter Presidency, US–Pakistan relations were so enfeebled that for Pakistan to provide a base for Western military

[6] Louis Dupree, 'Red Flag Over the Hindu Kush', *American Universities Field Staff Reports, 1978-79.*

action and more so, to coordinate an intervention with Amin inside Afghanistan was wholly unrealistic, at least in 1979-80. The adverse political consequences of intervention, and the resulting frustration of the military, were also predictable after the US experience in Vietnam. The impetuosity of the Soviet decision becomes obvious because even Cuba, which had only recently (September 1979) become Chairman of the Non-aligned Movement and was just embarking on trying to politically veer the bulk of the Third World to look upon Socialist countries as their natural allies, was not consulted. The Soviet invasion put Castro on the defensive for the entire period of his Chairmanship.

The misjudgement in the West was more surprising because so far it seemed to have had a fairly objective picture of the development in Afghanistan. The Saur Revolution was correctly perceived to be one of the many Third World violent unconstitutional changes, and hence low-level normalcy was maintained in the relations, at least until Adolphe Dubs, the American Ambassador, was taken hostage and killed in February 1979. Even then, it seems to have been recognized that his death occurred because of impetuous handling by the Afghan security units in trying to rescue him alive. Even in the public uproar in the United States which followed, there was no accusation of direct Soviet involvement in the kidnapping and the tragedy. The broad fact of the failed elimination of Amin in September 1979, the eventual death of Taraki, and subsequently Amin distancing himself from the Russians was well-known in the diplomatic circles in Kabul. Amin's insistence on the recall of the Soviet Ambassador, the release of nationalists, and the muting of propaganda against US imperialists and Pakistan were not secret. The fact that the US had an inkling of the ominous developments became obvious because Archer Blood, then Deputy Chief of the US Mission in Delhi, with previous experience of a posting in Afghanistan, was deputed and spent several weeks in Kabul in November-December 1979. He found a strikingly less hostile attitude in Amin towards the US. The invitation of Agha Shahi, the then Pakistan Foreign Minister, was also a tell-tale sign of Amin's metamorphosis. It is now confirmed that the Soviet build-up as a preliminary for the intervention had been detected in a satellite picture by the American intelligence establishment. It was not far-fetched to piece together that the Soviet Union was politically on edge and was trying to deceive and keep Amin off balance while simultaneously planning to intervene in the country. If subjective anxieties—the Cold War mindset on the one side and the domestic political climate within the United States on the other—could have been kept separate, it could have been seen that Soviet intervention was not a move on the strategic chessboard. The US could have given a stronger timely warning and international public opinion could have been built up and possibly the invasion might have been averted. The US could have defused, in advance, the Soviet fears that the US was planning aggressive moves into Afghanistan in collusion with Amin, the disillusioned Communist. The United States might have obtained even greater political mileage from the Soviet blunder if, while joining in the widespread condemnation, the strategic alarm had not been raised. Confidential, but vigorous, diplomacy in December 1979 might even have tilted the vote in the Kremlin against the intervention. The memoirs of the then Secretary of State, Cyrus Vance, reveals differences with the White House in the assessment of the fluid situation in Afghanistan. One cannot help speculating that the White House, which gave the clue for the alarmist post-intervention reaction, rejected the considered appraisal of the State Department.

In hindsight, one cannot but conclude that both in Moscow and in Washington the decision-making processes of weighing the premises and making anticipation and judgements were flawed. In the defensive anxieties of the two countries, a series of local events, were needlessly elevated into an East–West crisis. Both powers became prisoners of their self-deluding fixed principles and propaganda habits. The conflict continued for eight years in the Soviet quest for 'face-saving illusions' until Gorbachev showed the political courage of incisively examining the rationale and unilaterally declaring the intention to end the Soviet involvement. In unusual candour, in subsequent official statements the Soviet government have acknowledged that the intervention in Afghanistan was a mistake and a misadventure.

The Cold War Hypnosis as the Clue to an Avoidable Tragedy

The clue to the succession of misjudgements can be traced to the mindsets bequeathed by the Cold War. It provides insights into why the Soviet Union discounted the local dynamics and underestimated the resilient nationalism and feared that the United States would jump to take advantage of instability in the country. It also explains why the United States did not see that ideology had a negative relevance. Both suspected strategic dangers to which realistically appraised could have been seen did not exist. The divergent reactions of Pakistan and India to the Afghan developments, in turn, were derivatives of the superpower postures in which they grafted their own deep-seated national security preoccupations. Historical analogies like the old Russian quest for warm water ports were applied, ignoring the wholly novel modern situation and, above all, the total transformation of international politics and military restraints brought about by nuclear weapons.

This is not the place to discuss whether the Cold War in its comprehensive dimensions could have been averted, or could have been arrested and reversed earlier. But the backdrop of the parallel international developments are relevant to the analysis and the parameters for a solution. After four decades, Stalin's paranoia which imposed control and Communism as his permanent solution for the Soviet Union's security is only proving to be an agonizing liability. A Finlandized Eastern Europe might well have been less burdensome and ensured greater sensitivity to Russian interests and security if democratic coalitions had been allowed to function in the different countries. It is ironical that it is Communist Hungary which has triggered the haemorrhaging of the socialist system and made a mockery of the Berlin Wall. Starting with Yugoslavia (1948), the notions of Communist solidarity have suffered reverse after reverse, the biggest one being the Soviet 'loss of China' which ended all possibilities of political and strategic unity of purpose amongst the Communist States. Mozambique, Kampuchea, and Ethiopia are not success stories for Communism; nor has the victory of Vietnam or Castro's Cuba proved a militant menace or a contagious example in their adjoining regions to vindicate the domino theory. Military containment was either not necessary or was ineffective in the Third World. The inordinate fear invited frustrations not only in Vietnam but also in the Bay of Pigs and even in Nicaragua.

It was the 'fixed principles' of global competition which linked the Soviet intervention, not just as a regional danger but to widely separated developments in Angola, Ethiopia, Vietnam's invasion of Kampuchea, and the Russian brigade in Cuba. Taken together, they were adduced as proof of the abiding ideological militancy and expansionist designs which got defined as the Brezhnev doctrine. It was argued that the détente was only a brief interregnum, and these apprehensions became self-fulfilling. Each of these developments had separate dynamics and it was the intellectual conditioning which was behind the suspicions of 'linkages'. Other developments which did not confirm the analysis were ignored. For example, in the same period, the Soviet Union actually retreated without much resistance from strategic vantage points in Africa. In Somalia, the Soviet Union accepted without much protest its eviction even though it meant giving up the Barbara base; but one suspects the Soviets voluntarily withdrew from Mozambique (which had proclaimed itself as a Marxist State) because of its inability to furnish the necessary economic support. The prospective energy shortage in the Soviet Union was advanced as the ultimate rationale for the march into Afghanistan as a first step towards the Gulf, but later it was acknowledged as an incorrect assessment by the CIA. The suspicion that the Soviet Union would use Afghanistan as a base to play the Baluch card to destabilize Pakistan was also an extrapolation from the Cold War analysis.

In 1989, the vast military and political edifice which the Cold War built is crumbling. In adjusting to the new situation, the greatest problem may be the intellectual reconditioning which it will demand. In the process of historical rectification, many myths and falsehoods are being exposed. Even those who drew their legitimacy in power (such as the Communist rulers in Eastern Europe) and those with material, political, or intellectual vested interests in the falsified past are beginning to acknowledge that the Cold War syndrome had long ceased to correspond to prevailing realities. The trade embargoes, the boycott of the Olympics, and not ratifying the SALT-II Treaty amounted to policies against self-interests.

The Soviet Union also precipitated unforeseen domestic reactions from their military misadventure. The units drawn from the Central Asian Republic, instead of winning over their ethnic co-religionists, started fraternizing and becoming sympathetic to the Afghan insurgents and had to be replaced. The morale of even the White Russian soldiers was known to be adversely affected. The justification for the expeditionary force that Russia's security was endangered proved transparently unconvincing to them. Instead of Imperialists, the Soviet soldier found himself to be facing native bearded Afghans and teenagers, fired by religious zeal and patriotism, who, disregarding sacrifices, kept harrying the well-equipped Soviet formations. They also found that even after killing tens of thousands of Afghans, destroying countless villages, uprooting millions, and inflicting every kind of retaliation, there was no weakening of the morale and fighting determination of the Mujahidin. Many eminent citizens like Andrei Sakharov had started questioning the rationale of the intervention even while the conflict was continuing, and when failure was obvious, the reason for persisting at the expense of so much blood and resources in a brutalizing involvement. Not surprisingly, large numbers of Russian soldiers took to drugs. It was the first experience for the Red army to be asked to fight a war which was transparently non-patriotic. It may well have introduced the virus of political disaffection even amongst units which were not deployed in Afghanistan. There are apparently Afghanski clubs in Russia because veterans found callousness instead of sympathy towards them on their return.[7] (This recalls the attitude towards GIs returning from the 'dirty war' in Vietnam.)

It would be intellectually honest to surmise that to a future historian, the Cold War era may appear as a period of self-inflicted economic enfeeblement for both superpowers. In Afghanistan it should have been apparent that any Soviet attempt, directly or indirectly, to get control of the oil-exporting Gulf—so clearly a vital interest for the West and Japan—carried the same risks as an attempt to overwhelm West Berlin. Both the risk of provocation and the reaction were misjudgements.

Against the notion that there never was any extended military danger, the intellectual riposte would recall the negative lessons of Munich and Pearl Harbor and the positive ones of determined reaction instead of acquiescence to the Berlin blockade (1948), Korea (1950), and missiles in Cuba (1962). In the same rationale, it would be argued that it was the arming and support of the Mujahidin and the unambiguous reactions in the West which made the Soviet Union retreat from the original expansive design. The military argument to explain Soviet withdrawal, in effect, amounts to isolating Afghanistan and the regional problem from the broader international landscape. If, in fact, the goals were for wider expansion and the prize as important as suspected, then disregarding economic costs, the Soviet Union could have doubled the military effort. Abandoning unilaterally the conditions which had gridlocked negotiations for five years was not because of military frustration but as an earnest

[7] BBC Report, 18 September 1989.

of the decisive reorientation as a national goal in Soviet priorities in pursuing detente in world politics. The purposeful effort at détente with the West, underway since 1985-6, the unilateral steps initiated by Gorbachev to catalyze nuclear and conventional disarmament, the scaling down of commitments to Cuba, Nicaragua, Vietnam, and other parts of the Third World, the permitting of plurality and democratic innovations in Eastern Europe, the toleration within limits of nationalist assertion in the Soviet Republics, and behind it all, Glasnost and Perestroika—all these factors combined, help to illuminate the timing of the Soviet withdrawal from Afghanistan. It was equally fallacious to argue—as was done at the time—that the Soviet Union did not smother Solidarity in Poland because the Soviet Union was bogged down by the military resistance in Afghanistan. Common sense would point to the conclusion that the withdrawal came from a belated but overriding recognition that there were no vital interests at stake, and persisting with the intervention only jeopardized urgent national and larger contemporary goals.

It could be argued that in the situation in Afghanistan, as it is in October 1989, the Soviets may have withdrawn its own troops, but the original ambition to control Afghanistan has not been abandoned. In fact the arms supplies to the Mujahidin on the one side and the Kabul government on the other is a residual involvement for political prestige of non-defeat and for retaining negotiating bargaining counters for the endgame. The supply of surplus-obsolescent arms involves limited real economic costs of transportation only. Superficially, the present situation has the features of a proxy war, where the US and the Soviet Union continue to arm and bolster their respective clients. But all the other collateral evidence suggests that both superpowers implicitly recognize that Afghanistan is of marginal importance for them. It seems to me that in the final instance both superpowers' will be reconciled to whatever emerges and establishes stable authority over the country; be it a victory for the Kabul government or for the anti-Communist insurgents or even a fundamentalist ascendancy. If the country continues in the present divisions and it becomes as an Afghan variant of Lebanon, there might be exasperation, rather than a re-escalation of their military commitments. To claim Soviet withdrawal as a victory for military aid would only protract the ongoing fratricidal conflict; indeed if in retrospective analysis the military or strategic aspect were overdrawn, it would distort the lessons for the future.

The Lessons from the Afghanistan Experience

Before exploring the approach to a solution it is worth distilling lessons from the past. As Barbara Tuchman says in the concluding chapter 'the light that shines on the waves behind us, can help to infer the nature of the waves ahead' and these may have wider application.

Firstly, that the nature of power, which provided the sanction behind diplomacy and the pursuit of national goals in peace, has changed. We face the anomaly that military capability which has been immeasurably enhanced with modern weaponry and technology, can no longer be translated into political compulsion even against the weak, the poor, and the backward. In the post-war situation the two superpowers with their nuclear and conventional armouries outclassed other States even against any hypothetical balance-of-power coalition, but their domineering position has suffered erosion all around, including the distancing of their protected allies. But more significant is that political awareness and the capacity for nationalistic mobilization has also developed the unforeseen strength of 'people's power' which frustrates organized military power by guerrilla war. The political 'conscientisation' of the post-war world started with decolonization, but has been strengthened by the Information Revolution. This capacity sometimes turns into national chauvinism ('rogue nationalism') and may even become suicidal (e.g. Iran–Iraq war) but comes into its own in defiance of external military coercion. On their home-ground of ravines, boulders, and mountain hideouts (or paddy fields in Vietnam and tropical jungles in Sri Lanka), a few thousand fearless and motivated locals are able to frustrate an organized military force with modern weapons, including the mobility of helicopters with search-and-destroy capabilities.

Afghanistan may signify that the era of coercive pressure of 'sending the marines' even in the limitrophe neighbourbood against nationalism to establish preferred internal dispensation is politically doomed. (Operations against islands with small populations like Grenada only prove exceptions, perhaps that too temporarily, but do not negate the validity of the generalization.) The Soviet Union has now all but lost Afghanistan politically at least for some years to come, but this loss does not necessarily mean the United States or any other power will be welcomed as a substitute political overlord.

Secondly it also becomes patent that socio-economic progress and the modernization of traditional societies have to evolve and find their own pattern. Foreign models, even if promoted by native leadership, produce reaction and invite reversals. The Soviet Union, in a sense, got hoisted by its ideological petard in providing support to its dutiful surrogate who was wanting to imitate Lenin. After the invasion, when Karmal was enthroned and the Soviet Union was more in control, the pace to socialism was deliberately slowed down, and indeed, in many respects, reversed. The socialist model, however moderated, remains alien to the country; it has failed in impact even when it was backed with diverse inducements and propaganda from the government in Kabul. An outsider cannot even bring about a Prague Spring. The hold of tribal Jirgahs (assemblies) and of Khans (landlords or local leaders) must have been somewhat diluted as a result of the massive upheavals of the decade, but what grips most Afghans, particularly from rural areas is still Islam, and often that too the particular sectarian variant to which a particular tribe belongs. Be it socialism, democracy, secularism, or their eclectic mix, the attempts to plant it in the Afghan soil, even by native leadership, will require comprehension of the social structure and great political skill in grafting it to the process of modernization. Development and social change have to be domesticated, foreign ideas and ideologies, imposed do not take root in foreign mud.

Thirdly the Afghanistan story also illustrates the difficulties which beset the Third World countries in relation to the major powers. The Cold War led to an oscillation between the assertion of nationalism against the great powers on the one hand and, often simultaneously, an expectation or support from one or both power blocs on the other. It came to be assumed that a partisan commitment could be obtained from one or the other superpower in an internal, wholly bilateral or a purely regional conflict. It is conceivable that the present Kabul government wanted the Soviet Union to go beyond warnings and limited transborder raids to take more punitive action against Pakistan. It certainly must have been surprised and disappointed when Gorbachev conveyed the decision at Tashkent to withdraw the Soviet combatant forces. The Mujahidin groups still bank on continuing support from the United States, even to advance fundamentalist goals, notwithstanding known American reservations, in principle, towards Iran, Libya, etc. Pakistan was skilful in its diplomacy in Washington but by assuming the role of the guardian of anti-Communism in South-West Asia, it cannot for long square with native nationalism, democratic aspirations with civil supremacy, and domestic economic priorities. Though anti-Americanism is muted in official statements, it is more rampant than is sometimes recognized.

Notwithstanding their declared postures, and some costly exceptions, the superpowers have been reluctant to get directly involved in regional problems and conflicts. In 1965 Pakistan expected more sympathy than it got, once the conflict against India started. The Soviet withdrawal from Afghanistan may be the end of the era of partisan military backing in regional conflicts. The Third World will not now be able to frighten one or the other superpowers into friendship in the future. Alternating or combining the approaches of dependency and independence may no longer be effective in the post-Cold War world.

The Future in Afghanistan

As one writes, there is no end in sight to the agony of Afghanistan. Earlier too, the country was one of the poorest; the cataclysmic events of the decade have destroyed its economy, and its social fabric. Upwards of a million have been killed or maimed. Although Afghanistan did not suffer the commanded genocide of Kampuchea under the Khmer Rouge, and the absolute numbers of refugees do not equal the ten million who came to India from East Pakistan (Bangladesh) in 1971, but with two million refugees who fled the country and perhaps two million obliged to leave their hamlets, in proportional magnitude, it exceeds any another brutal uprooting.

The Afghan tribes have, once again, lived up to the traditional reputation of temporarily forgetting their old vendettas and uniting in a militant Jehad (religious war) against the foreigner. But it would seem that the ethno-linguistic tribal rivalries were only suspended but not subsumed by this ordeal of invasion and defiance. The impressive insurgent military effort consisted of many parallel operations with limited coordination, and no united command and direction was forged. (It was not like the 13 colonies who in the common struggle for independence got welded into the future American union.)

The key to the future in Afghanistan hinges on whether and how soon a new cohesion, between the proud tribal identities, can be pooled for a restored nationhood which commands sufficient legitimacy to end the war and prepare for the constructive challenges that will have to be faced thereafter. International observers and regional specialists who have visited the camps have described at length, if not exhaustively, the divergent motivations of the groups in the camps in Pakistan. Fewer details are available about the more dispersed Afghan refugees in Iran. The major and minor factions amongst the refugees in Pakistan, the warlord autonomy of the field commanders, the unbridged chasm with the two million-odd Shiite refugees in Iran, the sectarian religious and political differences, and not the least, the myopia and ambitions of many of the leaders presents a distressing picture. They all battled the Soviets and still oppose the Kabul government but they cannot join together around the immediate goal to regain stability and independence for their country. It would seem that even in the face of well-meaning counsel and insistent persuasion by aid-givers, no united front of the anti-Kabul factions has been welded. Even after the *émigré* interim government of the seven principal groups in Pakistan was finally constituted, there has been no indication of immediate military co-ordination or common negotiating positions. The Shura held in February 1989 was managed by Pakistan. It was not fully representative even of the Pakistan-based factions and failed to bridge the historic animosity with the Shia group which is largely in Iran. In the lip-smacking at the prospect of the collapse in Kabul after the Soviet withdrawal, the debilitating dissensions seem to have got intensified. The ambushed killing of officers of Masud's force (considered the most effective in military operations) by the followers of the Hekmatyar faction (favoured specially by the intelligence organization in Pakistan) has dramatically exposed the fractured state of Mujahidin politics. The mutual distrust and rivalries were in part the reason for the failure to capture Jalalabad. The reports of tentative confidential contacts by some factions with the Kabul government mocks at the sacrifices and the affirmation of no truck with the 'puppets' foisted by the foreigner.

The Kabul government, on the other hand, presents a more confident face. It is better organized, and well-stocked with arms which are being regularly replenished. In the absence of insurgent unity and coordinated sagacity, the government troops have become more firmly loyal to the Kabul government. But the Najibullah government remains besieged in the towns and politically at Bay. As the winter approaches, the military stalemate would also be frozen, but the problem of logistics to feed the bloated populations of the towns could become more difficult.

The Parameters for a Solution

In this background how can Afghanistan be restored to meaningful independence? No solution to a complex situation, can be detailed in advance or should even be attempted. At this stage only conditions should be created to start the process of thinking constructively and responsibly. Even at the risk of some repetition, let me recapitulate some points which, if intellectually recognized, could push towards improving conditions for a solution.

First, the superpowers are not now in the mood to obstruct independence and non-alignment; they are both half-way into the withdrawal syndrome. At this stage, local clients of differing hues are appealing to their benefactors for continuing support with resurrected ideological and military arguments, which were earlier voiced by the superpowers and have now been virtually disowned in practice though not in pronouncements. In the USSR there is a mounting domestic challenge to Perestroika; the US faces deficits, formidable demands on its own social and economic agenda, and for all its wealth there is resistance to tax increases. Sooner rather than later, there will be superpower agreement to a negative symmetry to slow down and mutually cut off support for their respective recipients. Afghanistan, which initially gave credibility to Glasnost, will not be allowed to impede détente in East–West relations.

It is not certain whether the Afghan factions have become aware of this handwriting on the wall and the implications of the withdrawal syndrome. In passing it should be noted that there has been no serious contagion of Islamic fundamentalism in Soviet Central Asia as a result of Iran under the Ayatollah. The rise of subnationalism in the Soviet Union is an old problem which was in the womb of time and predates the developments in Iran and Afghanistan. It must therefore prudently be understood that neither superpower will pay any price, or carry any burden, to stay the course to deliver a political solution for their respective clients. Now, and more so in the future, the burden of choice between the present stalemated violence and a political settlement will rest on the multiplicity of Afghan leadership. The reluctance at this stage for the superpowers to unambiguously express their ultimate attitudes must not raise hopes of sustained competitive backing.

Second, India and Pakistan can also help create conditions which would facilitate and support an Afghan settlement by grasping the inevitability of the superpower withdrawal syndrome. The present economic distortions, social strains, and federal/provincial/state tensions in both countries are being indirectly fuelled by the burdens of their post-Afghanistan militarization. Even so, neither country, in a comparative balance sheet is either more or less secure than it was in the 1970s before the induction of costly modern weapons systems. The South Asian nuclear weapons guessing game has gotten worse because the United States abandoned the earlier yardstick of non-proliferation. The deterioration in the climate of relations in South Asia as a whole, with alarms about India's hegemonistic designs, is also to some extent a by-product of the Afghanistan-induced military build-up.

An Afghan settlement and South Asian rapprochement must, in fact, go hand in hand; both are contingent on the harmonizing of regional approaches. The present attempts at influence-building and shaping non-national politics, even using arguments of religion or ideology, have been and are likely to be almost as frustrating as military interventions. Pakistan must abandon the temptation that the shared faith and the Sunni majority could be used to make Afghanistan into a docile, dependent, Islamic state. India could hamper the prospects of a significant improvement of relations with Pakistan if the suspicion persists that the identification with the Najibullah government is to secure a Soviet controlled secular Afghanistan in order to keep Pakistan under threat of a pincer. Pakistan should understand that the present US aid and strategic policies, conceived in the wake of the Soviet invasion and the likelihood of Soviet mischief or intrusion in the Gulf, are bound to be moderated as perceptions of the threat gets diluted by the pace of the current détente and defence allocations are pruned to meet domestic priorities.

It would be a telling contribution to a solution in Afghanistan when all the outside world—the superpowers and the regional and Islamic countries—makes known confidentially, if not publicly, their restraint and detachment from counselling on the future dispensation for the country. Some countries like the USA, USSR, and Pakistan wield influence and leverage but it is negative not a capacity to impose a lasting solution. Ideally all outside well-wishers should end their arms supplies commitments to their respective dependents/clients. Benign detachment by outsiders, parodying Dr Johnson could help to concentrate the minds of the multiplicity of factional Afghan leaders on the threatened destruction of their homeland as a state, and the deteriorating plight of their countrymen. This might dramatically change the present climate of sluggish political mobility and make a telling push for deliberations amongst all the representative Afghan leaders.

Finally, this brings me to the heart of the matter—whether the will to nationhood has been irreparably damaged because of the nature of Afghan society and the ordeal of the last decade. The scholarly work of Olivier Roy on Islam and the resistance in Afghanistan is relevant and instructive.[8] We have been reminded by him and by other scholars that Afghanistan, as we think of it, was born only in the mid-eighteenth century when under the Durrani leadership the tribal conclave rejected the Persian overlordship, and chose Ahmad Shah as the hereditary Emir of the Afghan confederation. This new Afghan entity got the paraphernalia of a state with a central authority when the confederacy had to face the parallel and competing external pressures and intrigues of the British and the Czarist Empires. Paradoxically, the Western quest for and concept of a 'buffer' state seems to have strengthened Kabul's raison d'être and the domination of the Pathan tribes over the minorities. The central bureaucracy became more powerful when the country had to manage its external trade. The post-World War II period with aid flows and modern communications inevitably led to greater centralism and gave it power of economic patronage but still only limited capacity to overwhelm the traditional tribal autonomies. But while social historians and anthropologists help to illuminate the resilient divisions and rivalries, there is need to guard against the incipient half-expressed ideas that the Humpty-Dumpty of the Afghan state cannot be put together again. The revitalization of sub-identities with centrifugal pulls is a feature of many new states in the flush of recent independence, including in Pakistan and India. Afghanistan, like the rest of the newly independent nations, has to move towards modern statehood. Out of the country's own societal past, new political and economic structure has to be evolved. The old tribal society could not have remained embalmed in medievalism even if the decade's upheaval had not enveloped it. If conservatives want to revert wholesale to the past pattern, they would be pleading for confusion, not peace or stability for their country.

It has been suggested that to obtain economic progress the country could, or even regretfully might, end up in a *de facto* three-way partition, with the Soviet Union controlling the area north of the

---

[8]Olivier Roy, *Islam and Resistance in Afghanistan*, 1986.

Hindu Kush, Pakistan dominating the south and the east, and Iran extending its influence in the west. Such a partitioned dispensation would be economically retrograde and would invite the political peril of different kinds of 'neo-colonialisms'. The threat and, in any case, the likelihood of the removal of outside props (not to mention the weariness of the major outside supporters) may be the necessary spur to the Afghan leaders to rise above parochialism and competitive sectarian ambitions for power.

Preliminary Steps to a New Loya Jirgah

President Najibullah, in comparison with his predecessors (Taraki, Amin, Karmal), has shown remarkable capabilities as an administrator, politician, and military tactician. But his passport to power has a Soviet stamp and has a biodata entry about being the former head of the Khad (the Afghan intelligence organization). He is seeking to refurbish his Afghan personality including identifying himself as a devout Muslim, but having been branded as the instrument of a foreign power will remain a continuing handicap in becoming the nucleus for national reconciliation. A well-timed offer of withdrawal from the political scene by Najibullah (which is different from the USSR suggesting that he is a disposable bargaining counter) would be a demonstration of patriotism and a step towards bringing the insurgents and the Kabul group together. There should be a corresponding pressure on some non-representative sectarian leaders, now in exile, to urge willingness for similar self-denying renunciations from power ambition. This is not entirely wishful because many have come to rely on outside encouragement which probably will dry up in the foreseeable future.

To bring about the removal of impediments to the reconciliation process requires stronger national and international collective pressures and also a neutral but national focal point. Even a partial clearing of the political stage might make it possible for somebody like King Zahir Shah to play a coordinating role to get the traditional Afghan consultative process underway. The former king has not been identified with any outside power, and despite some controversy about his past, he provides the nucleus of a rallying point for a national consensus. No other Afghan is more suited to preside over a national Loya Jirgah. The heredity principle does not have to be re-established, but the old king can play his role as a fatherly figure and former first citizen of the country. His call for a ceasefire would not evoke suspicions. If he presides over a Shura or Loya Jirgah, it could move towards a consensus on the future constitution for the country.

It has been suggested that, since there is not full acceptance of ex-King Zahir Shah, the Secretary-General of the UN should play the catalytic role of bringing together an assembly of the diverse Afghan groups which could be called in Geneva. The UN and its Secretary-General can never be wholly immune from the play of international politics. Diplomacy on the East river in New York would be un-realistic deflection of attention from where the burden of res-ponsibilities squarely rests—the Afghan people and their leaders. Decision making must be seen to emerge from the cauldron of Afghanistan. The impact of any offer of 'incentives and disincentives' for a settlement will be ineffective if the Afghans remain rigid and recalcitrant. The UN Secretary-General, however, has a role in promoting non-political modalities, as he did in the run-up to the Geneva Accords. He can offer conference facilities but he must not run the risk of being perceived as an arbitrator or even as a mediator, because he has even less capacity of enforcement within Afghanistan.

However, as a parallel to throwing the problem back to the Afghans and concentrating their minds, there is scope, indeed necessity, to extrapolate and publicize the economic and social consequences of the present drift and to highlight for world attention the dismal future for the country. While the impasse and civil war continue, the opportunity costs of delay in settlement are being overlooked. With the great powers privately recognizing that Afghanistan is no more a threat to international peace and dramatic developments in Europe, a world amnesia for Afghanistan's agony is underway. The Secretary-General of the UN, at his own discretion, could take a hand in having an impartial non-partisan group of economists and social scientists compile and extrapolate into the future the magnitude of the mounting and needless suffering of the Afghan people. Such a short publication, simple enough for wide comprehension, could create the international opinion for the resources which will be required for rehabilitation and recon-struction of Afghanistan, but more urgently, it could have an impact on loosening the present rigidities of the Afghan leaders.

Pakistan should take note that the continuing economic plight of refugees from Vietnam is of little and only of spasmodic international concern. Even the initial human sympathy for the refugees who fled has evaporated, and now the boat people are actually being rejected and even forcibly evicted. No modalities or resources are available for their rehabilitation even inside Vietnam, much less in safe havens elsewhere in our crowded planet. Pakistan's problem of millions of Afghans on its border could be compounded by delay in finding a solution. The problems arising from their long-term presence may prove to be graver than the earlier imagined threats to its security. As time goes by, more and more refugees will resist repatriation; indeed they will get settled in their honourable or not so honourable ways of livelihood (drug trafficking and arms sales, etc.) or get accustomed to refugee status dole-outs.

There is every logic and, in my view, no alternative to putting the ball back where it all began—in Afghanistan. There is no one with the charisma to become a supreme Ayatollah who has behind him the institutional cohesion characteristic of Shiism; amongst the Afghan leaders, there is no one of the stature of a de Gaulle in sight and not much hope of a national Bonaparte emerging from amongst the field commanders. In any case, Afghanistan would need a representative coalition and a sort of collective leadership which has built-in checks and balances against the individual lust for overriding power. Similarly no one tribe, not even the Pathans, can now easily re-establish domination over the others. The only certainty is a negative one: that the blueprint for the future must not have a foreign label to it. The solution in Afghanistan, in sum, must get in step with the global phenomenon evident everywhere; that is the domestication of responsibilities and the burden of independence for nations resting on their own collective wisdom. They have the challenge and the ordeal to determine their priorities and to shape their external relations on the basis of ideological agnosticism. The simplest lesson from the Afghanistan story is that it should have been left alone by the Soviet Union. It follows that nothing can finally rescue a country except the wisdom and call to nationhood of its own citizens.

Finally, although it is premature, sometime soon in the future, after the guns have stopped, will come the gigantic task of refugee return, the defusing of anti-personnel mines, and the economic rehabilitation and reconstruction of the country. With both the USSR and the USA now wanting to reinvigorate the world body, the UN is now in a position to create the funnel for financial, technical, and economic assistance in what could be one of the biggest operations for the international organization. Both superpowers, after an initial political stand-off, will, one hopes, exemplify their new relationship by not programming their aid bilaterally but by generously contributing to bolster the international funnel. Europe, Japan, Saudi Arabia, Kuwait, and the other rich nations should donate resources for the UN controlled rehabilitation operations. It would be prudent that the peace-keeping observer functions of providing for the technical and administrative infrastructure be entrusted to nationals of neutral, regional, and non-aligned countries. Reconstruction and aid giving must be insulated from the old ideological and great power rivalries and leave the role and balance of diverse religious sects to be internally determined.

Conclusion

Afghanistan was one of the worst tragedies of the Cold War; it could, however, become a demonstration model for the transition to the post-détente twenty-first century international politics. It may well have been the last nervous gasp of the Brezhnev doctrine. The Soviet Union's unilateral withdrawal which has no real parallel, could be the earnest of a new kind of world politics of political non-intervention and a reminder of the futility of doing so. If the final settlement ends in restoring Afghanistan to independence and non-alignment, it could be a giant step to erase the entrenched hold of the Cold War mindsets. If the story of Afghanistan brings home that Third World countries have to resolve their own national and regional problems, it could become a spur and positive example to the healthy process of the domestication of international politics. This, in due course, could accelerate the process of restoring and reconciling nationalistic diversity to the international system.

The Afghanistan story also demonstrates that the economic rationale is now overtaking the paranoia of the strategic and military calculus. The UN role in Afghanistan was useful in providing the umbrella to work out the modalities for the Geneva Accords but marginal to the dramatic political change which came in 1988; however, the UN role in starting the political process and, following an accord under Afghan auspices, superintending an international rehabilitation programme could be an unprecedented opportunity for the international organization. In Afghanistan, exported or imposed ideology has been exposed as a false God or an irrelevant bugbear, but the legacy and lessons from the experience could revitalize faith in reasoned idealism and enlightened internationalism in a world facing the prospects of ecological doom. If all this can be distilled and demonstrated, Afghanistan will have been less than an uncompensated 'March of Folly'.

14

The Afghan Conflict: Where India and Others Blundered

The world is littered with the debris of the Cold War: a disintegrated Soviet Union, an enfeebled United States, Eastern Europe groping in adjustment and scores of overmilitarized, economically stagnant, and internally destabilized Third World countries. No nation has been left more ravaged than Afghanistan and none suffered as much from direct and migratory genocide.

This destruction of a brave nation was throughout pointless. The compounding folly can be traced to the direct or derivative hypnosis from the Cold War. The Saur Revolution (April 1978) was triggered by internal disaffection and not masterminded by the Kremlin; Brezhnev authorized direct intervention in December 1979 because the whipped gallop to socialism by a pro-Soviet ideologue (Hafizullah Amin) alienated the Afghans, as had never happened under the monarchy or the Daud oligarchy. The action was fatally conceived but defensive, not strategically or ideologically expansionist. However, instead of an honest explanation, the ritual Cold War line—that it was to pre-empt a CIA takeover—was trumpeted. Some even in India swallowed the rationalization but many in Socialist countries were unconvinced and Cuba, made Chairman of NAM barely three months earlier, was obviously embarrassed.

The Carter White House, with near universal academic endorsement summarily concluded that the purpose was to sever the Gulf oil artery, fulfil Peter the Great's quest for a warm water port, and thus posed 'the greatest threat to peace since World War II'. SALT-II was abandoned, strategic consensus sought, the Rapid Deployment Force constituted, and détente reversed.

Soon the United States realized that MAD (Mutual-Assured Destruction) was never challenged but the Reagan administration,

Statesman, New Delhi, 28 May 1992.

committed to military superiority and the attrition of the 'Evil Empire', decided to provide military aid to Pakistan (suspended since 1965) and through its agencies to the Mujahidin. It was Gorbachev's statesmanship which in 1986 acknowledged that the Soviet involvement was without reason and announced a unilateral withdrawal. Now, when the G-7 countries are desperately mustering resources to rehabilitate the Russian economy, there must be agonizing regrets that the vindictive policies were needlessly protracted, accelerating the economic emasculation of both the USA and the USSR.

For India and Pakistan 1980-1 was a re-enactment of 1954-65. Both were a quadrilateral of misperceptions: Pakistan and India in their regional security anxieties got hooked into the superpower paranoia and a vicious subcontinental arms race followed. In 1991 as in 1965, Pakistan realized that an alliance relationship with a superpower does not ensure sustained partisanship and India discovered that superpowers can have common conflict resolution approaches and negative symmetry interests.

Tragically India compromised its own cherished principles of non-intervention to the calculus of not displeasing the Soviets. Had we joined the Non-aligned—many of them equally friendly to the Soviet Union—in condemning the intervention in 1980, we could have exposed the American alarm, sought to keep the superpower competition from South Asia, and ensured better standing in helping to extricate the USSR. With sensitive prophylactic diplomacy we might have prevented the resumption of military aid to Pakistan. With Pakistan concerned for the first time with a non-Indian threat, it was the most propitious moment to rationalize India–Pakistan relations. I was no longer Foreign Secretary but in January 1980 I made urgent specific suggestions to this effect through influential officials and non-officials. I warned that our indifference to the Afghan liberation struggle risked marginalization and alienating the Afghan people. We may have invited the hazard of revanchist hostility of militant Mujahidin against India.

New Delhi did not anticipate the Soviet Union jettisoning the Kabul government. India continued to look upon Najibullah as a dependable bastion of secularism against Islamic fundamentalism. For all his remarkable survival capability, Najibullah was bound to remain branded as a foreign implant. Three years ago at an academic conference involving several nationalities, I urged that Najibullah could facilitate a coalition of reconciliation if he voluntarily stepped down and the Soviets present concurred with me. When the old tribal, ethnic, and religious factions appeared irreconcilably rampant, it would have been principled and prudent for India to remain non-partisan. Whether the new dispensation in Kabul will be militantly Islamic or moderate will be decided by the Afghan cauldron and not by Pakistan, Iran, or any other outside combination.

Pakistan too is the victim of a decade of costly wishful reflexes. Pakistan pleaded and no doubt got militarily and economically rewarded by the United States as a 'frontline' State. India's indulgent attitude towards the Soviet intervention was used to spread the canard that the two countries conspired to dismember Pakistan again. Pakistan won sympathy and support for sheltering the refugees but did not foresee that refugees and arms induction would raise the Frankenstein of kalashinikov and narco-terrorist culture. President Zia-ul-Haq's vision of a confederation with Islamic Afghanistan under Hekmatyar as junior partner and the Khyber moving to the Oxus was as much of a fantasy as the hope of some Indian officials and non-officials of Afghanistan being 'pacified' into a Sovietized Mongolia. Both Pakistan and India overlooked the fact that the Afghans who had defeated Czarist and British imperialism would not acquiesce in foreign domination or be coerced even by helicopter gunships on 'search and destroy' missions. Pakistan belatedly switched support to the UN efforts for a broad-based coalition. But ultimately, the billions of dollars in aid and arms, Islamic sympathy, last-minute diplomatic agility, etc., cannot obscure the dire legacy of crime, economic burdens and political tensions which are by-products of gamesmanship in Afghanistan.

It was intellectual paralysis which allowed the Cold War to become such a destructive multiplier for both rich and poor nations. Afghanistan illustrates the swing from paranoic, strategic, and ideological globalism to a withdrawal syndrome, where except on nuclear militarism, foreign policies of Great Powers were being domesticated to economic compulsions. Restoring the fractured personality of Afghanistan will depend overwhelmingly on the disciplined sagacity of the Afghans. Islam can be a rallying point but fundamentalism has finally to adjust to internal national challenges of modernization and socio-economic fulfilment.

The resolution of the derivative parallel calamities facing India and Pakistan (debts, deficits, poverty, ecology, strident sub-nationalism in Kashmir, Sindh, Punjab, Baluchistan, and Assam, abysmal social indicators, etc.) also requires serious introspective reconditioning. We must accept biting austerity at home but also recognize that neither can master their separate destiny if beggaring the neighbour remains the litmus to foreign policy. The distancing of partisan godfathers, however, means less hindrance to bilateral diplomacy and enlightened regionalism, which must also include harmonized commitment to the rehabilitation of Afghanistan. India and Pakistan came to their present impasse because they got tempted or succumbed to linkages with the Cold War. Now for the future they must shed decades of intellectual dependance and excercise their independent judgement in determining their own long term priorities.

15

Afghan Tragedy: Needless Tribal Conflict

The bloodletting still going on in Afghanistan is about the worst tragedy of these post-war decades. Like Vietnam, the brave nation of Afghanistan was defiant of Imperialism—for over a century—but unlike Vietnam, it has disintegrated into bitter internecine tribal conflict. Put into perspective, this catastrophic end can be traced back to monstrous misperceptions, initially by the two superpowers but compounded by misinterpretations and wishfulness by the regional actors—Pakistan and India.

In December 1979 the Soviet Union intervened to try to damage-control the disaffection which paradoxically had developed with Hafizullah Amin's impetuous imposition of Socialism on a conservative Islamic society and in the process, he alienated the people who were friendly towards the Soviet Union under the monarchy of Zahir Shah or the oligarchy of Daud. Soviet motives were not vicious but the USSR leadership overlooked that in the face of the competitive Great Game play between Czarist Russia and British Imperial Forward Policy, the Afghans had inflicted the most humiliating defeat on the British Indian Army when it invaded the country in 1839.

This time it took eight to nine years for the Afghans to drive away the invading force and when finally the Soviet forces withdrew, the experience of coping with the fearless Mujahidins had damaged the morale of the Red Army, somewhat akin to the USA after Vietnam.

Intervention

In reacting to the Soviet intervention, in a reflex conditioned by the Cold War the US jumped to the conclusion that the Soviet action could only be directed against US strategic interests—specially to

Statesman, New Delhi, 28 November 1996.

cut off the oil flows from the Gulf, so vital for the US, Europe, and Japan. Almost every non-official American analyst echoed the Carter administration's alarm and many were persuaded that the USSR was out to fulfil the three 'century' old ambition of Peter the Great to reach a warm water port. There was in fact never any danger of the Soviet forces crossing into Pakistan and capturing the Gulf and no reason to constitute a Rapid Republic force. Once again a local problem had been misinterpreted and magnified to take on global dimensions.

These alarms and misperceptions were to Pakistan's advantage. Pakistan held out to Brzezenski the dreaded prospect of Russians at the Khyber, seized the opportunity to repair the frayed relations with the US, and revived the pre-1965 pretension of being in the frontline against Soviet expansionism. However, the aid that was offered by the Carter administration was dismissed as peanuts but no concerted independent initiative emanated from the subcontinent. No one even paid attention to the fact that Babrak Karmal's government, installed by the Russians, moderated socialist decrees, reopened the mosques, and sought to assuage Afghan opinion. When Reagan became the US President in 1981, Pakistan was embraced as the bastion of democracy against the expansionist Evil Empire. A first instalment of US $ 3.6 billion worth of military aid was pledged and, in addition, Pakistan became the conduit for military hardware for the Mujahidin. Pakistan, in turn, developed grandiose illusions of Afghanistan as an Islamic satellite with effective Pakistani influence right up to the Oxus.

India, by its own misjudgement, actually facilitated the remilitarization of Pakistan when it became out of step with the overwhelming Non-aligned and international consensus. We took an indulgent attitude in the United Nations (UN) towards the Soviet invasion and thereby compromised our cherished principle of non-aggression, non-interference, and respect for independence of a non-aligned nation. Our own Cold War-derived mindset was one of not displeasing the Soviets. In the process, since January 1980, we lost our standing as a reliable friend of the Afghan people and became marginalized.

No doubt, privately we advised the USSR to find ways to withdraw from Afghanistan, but in the UN, year after year we kept on voting against the international consensus which condemned the Soviet action. Some in India even hoped for a military triumph for the Soviet army.

I am persuaded that the Soviet Union would not have taken it amiss if we had joined the Non-aligned attitude critical of the invasion. In the years 1981-9 we would then have been in a better position to help rescue the Soviet Union by working for a negotiated Finlandization of the country enabling a dignified exit. Our misjudgements continued. Our support for Najibullah even after Gorbachev had distanced himself was in the hope that he would succeed in turning Afghanistan into a secular nation—in other words distanced from Pakistan. We overlooked the fact that in Afghan eyes, Najibullah was tainted with the suspicion of being in the pay of Russian intelligence. Our wishfulness had got the better of our professional objectivity when we discounted the abiding hold of Islam and tribal loyalties. Of all the important international actors Iran alone was prudently detached: Iran gave refuge to the Shias from Herat and western Afghanistan but it neither condoned Soviet intervention nor joined the American policy of indirect attrition of the Evil Empire.

Misjudgement

What was common in all these misjudgements, including our own, was the discounting of Afghan nationalism, which has always been fiercely tribal and divisive at home but militant and united against the non-Afghan intruders. The notion of an anti-Taliban coalition of Iran, India, the Central Asian republics, etc., as an immediate pacifier seems as wishful as the nation of the Taliban itself being able to capture the whole of the country with the support of Pakistan and thereby turning Afghanistan into a Pushto-dominated Islamic state.

Neither India nor Pakistan anticipated the end of the Cold War or the unilateral withdrawal of Soviet troops or the summary termination of US aid. It was pathetic to find Mujahidin leaders lecturing the State Department in Washington on the menace of Soviet Communism. Pakistan has now squandered the sense of gratitude which different Mujahidin groups felt after Pakistan provided them refuge and in different measures gave them arms and support for 10 years. Pakistan is awash with American small arms and has invited upon itself the rampant narco-terrorism which is plaguing the country. It has deflected some fundamentalist zest eastwards into Kashmir. The temptation to seize and to rejoice in outside aid and arms has left behind the legacy of near un-governability in three out of four provinces.

By our policy of balancing remilitarization, with the purchase of arms with scarce foreign exchange and surrendering our independent judgement, we too have become, indirectly, the victim of the strife and false alarms in Afghanistan. Our economic situation has suffered greatly compared to our potential ever since 1980.

The tragedy for the subcontinent is that January 1980, when Pakistan was deeply worried about Soviet intentions, was perhaps the best moment to rationalize India–Pakistan problems. It was a more propitious time than Simla 1972 or even post India–China war talks in 1962-3. All we had to do was to join the Non-aligned in openly urging Soviet withdrawal, and make measured unilateral gestures to show that India will not take advantage of Pakistan's problems.

Assurance

In 1978, after the Saur Revolution, the Janata government gave such unilateral, unsolicited assurance of not using the moment to dismember Pakistan by an Indo–Soviet pincer, and relations with Pakistan did not deteriorate for the next 20 months. In 1982, Kashmir was quiescent with no Pakistan support for the disaffected in the valley. I was no longer Foreign Secretary but I might as well reveal that in January 1980, I volunteered advice on the above lines to the External Affairs Ministry and also made sure it reached the higher echelons through influential interlocutors. I warned in writing that if we did not take timely steps to safeguard regional non-alignment, it would lead to massive remilitarization of the sub-continent. Alas, we were paralyzed from any initiative because of our own entrenched misperceptions. Narsimha Rao did strike the right note in Karachi in June 1981 by showing understanding for Pakistan's predicament but by that time Pakistan had been lured by the promise of massive US military aid and assurance of Islamic and international sympathy.

India and Pakistan are basically now on their own, left to husband their commerce and economy and to decide on the strategy to develop or damage their respective national futures. Sooner or later the realization must also come to the Afghans that constructive nationalism must resume command, tribal feuds must end, and the Afghan people must be given peace to rehabilitate their homeland.

The UN can keep on trying to play a catalyst role, but outside powers who in different ways became partisan in the previous decade and half may have to be content with benign detachment, at least until there is collateral exhaustion from the unrelenting quest of a brave nation for self-destruction.

16

Afghanistan: A Tragedy Born of Cold War Mindsets

Everyone agrees that Afghanistan must go back to the beginning—that is, be a non-aligned independent state—but no one quite knows the way back. Ambassador Vorontsov came to Delhi to share with India the Soviet assessment and possibly its anxieties. This was a courtesy, consistent with Indo-Soviet friendship. From our capital, he reiterated confidence in the military capability of the Kabul government and voiced warnings to Pakistan and United States. But the Soviet media had already publicized the relief and rejoicing of the Soviet contingent and its commander when Afghanistan was behind their backs. After the withdrawal in strict accordance with an internationally determined schedule, it is only through skill of persuasion and indirect assistance to the Kabul government that the USSR can ensure a say in the future dispensation of the country. Indeed following the withdrawal, the USSR has moved quickly to re-establish its position in the Middle East and its image in the Islamic world and even effect a rapprochement with fundamentalist Iran. One cannot but conclude that for the Soviet Union, Afghanistan is now secondary and subordinate to its new global politics and domestic economic priorities. Pakistan, with geographical proximity and having given refuge to 3 million Afghans and having acted as a conduit for aid, is somewhat better placed to influence at least the Sunni insurgent groups. It must have played a behind-the-scene role in the recent Shura and would now try to manage the search for an understanding with the Iran-based Shia groups. But for all the leverage of a shared faith and physical conduit of arms, Afghans are no more likely to become a province of Pakistan than acquiesce to be a Soviet republic.

Our own future standing in Afghanistan has got very narrowly

Statesman, New Delhi.

identified with a government which the overwhelming majority of Afghan people distrust and which the Soviet Union is seen to have, abandoned, if not at least left to its own devices, and which is considered by much of the international community as militarily besieged and politically at bay. Whether the country staggers in chaos or warlordism or inches towards stability under Zahir Shah or a working coalition, future historians with no vested interest in present politics, are likely to be critical at the jeopardy of our interests, and obvious damage to the traditional regard of the Afghan people for India.

It is often overlooked that the insurgency and defiance of the People's Democratic Party of Afghanistan (PDPA) government in Kabul started soon after the Saur Revolution in 1978 and that was before Soviet intervention (1979) and the massive American aid to the Mujahidin (1981). Historians of the British-Indian Empire recalled the debacles of the First and Second Afghan Wars in the nineteenth century, but obviously the Brezhnev Politbureau forgot that the Czarist experience was also one of frustration and defeat at the hands of the Afghan tribals. It was not the lack of Soviet military capacity or the American aided military capability of the Mujahidin but Gorbachev's statesmanship which recognized the folly of Soviet intervention and announced the virtual unconditional withdrawal of its forces. This dramatic decision was crucial in winning credit and credibility for the historic transformation brought about by Gorbachev in Soviet foreign policy and world politics.

For us, the opportunity costs of policy towards Afghanistan, both positive and negative, have little to show on the credit side. In the wake of the Soviet intervention in 1979, there was a more promising opportunity to normalize on all Indo–Pakistan problems than at any time in the past, including at Simla in 1972. Superficially, it looked as if the old British Imperial nightmare was being enacted—the Russians at the Khyber! Pakistan was truly worried about its security and, for the first time, recognized that the primary threat to its future did not emanate from India. India was in the best position to assure Pakistan that the Soviet intervention, no doubt disastrously misconceived, was defensive in intent and did not pose any aggressive threat to Pakistan. The Western alarm that Soviet forces would cross into Baluchistan, rush to control the Gulf and throttle the oil flows to Japan and the West was wholly fallacious. (I am not indulging in hindsight wisdom, because even though I was no longer officially concerned, within a fortnight of the intervention I made bold to suggest this in private representations to our decision makers. I also shared my assessment that there was no threat of a wider con- flagration with Emily Macfarquahar who anonymously summarized it in the *Economist*.) It was wholly implausible for us to echo that Soviet intervention was at the invitation of Hafizullah Amin's government, and therefore, in accordance with the Afghan–Soviet Treaty of 1978. What we needed to do was to show prompt understanding and sympathy, in word and concrete gesture, to Pakistan and then lead South and South-West Asia in a collective effort to ask for Soviet withdrawal on the one hand and warn the West against counter-intervention on the other. We may or may not have succeeded with the White House, which was turning hawkish after American hostages had been taken in Iran, but it could have gone someway to insulate the region for non-alignment and preserve out international credibility. I made bold to suggest a step by step sequential plan for a 'solution' in Afghanistan (From Swedenization to Finlandization) which would have enabled us, along with other non-aligned to play a constructive role and might have saved some of the fruitless bloodletting over these years.

Though not in so many words but in actual implication, our statement in the UN acquiesced in the paradigm that Soviet inter- vention was indeed a move in the Cold War albeit to pre-empt a CIA takeover. We sided with the Soviet Union not because of Non-aligned principles (which have been fundamentally on the side of national- ism, liberation struggles, and against great power interventions) but because of the superimposition of the Cold War on the subcontinent, the USSR had been a well-tested friend of India. The irony is that had we taken the same position as the Non–aligned majority, far from damage to Indo–Soviet relations, we would have been better placed to safeguard our national interests and also to rescue the Soviet Union from a no-win situation and, in the present dilemma, in the search for a broad-based government.

The vote on Afghanistan in the United Nations (UN) in January 1980 was one of the first occasions when all our neighbours voted differently from India. Our position allowed itself to be misconstrued as creating a precedent for intervention by a big country in disregard of the sovereignty of small neighbours. It reversed the developing promise of improved bilateral relations with China. It is true that in subsequent months we showed qualified disapproval of Soviet intervention. Had we, in January 1980, taken the same position promptly and publicly as we took later, and had we shown the same understanding for Pakistan as reflected in the speech of our Foreign Minister in Karachi in June 1981 (which conceded Pakistan's right to somewhat improve its defence capability), we might have reduced if not averted the massive military aid programme launched by the Reagan administration. The Carter administration even in its alarm offered what General Zia-ul-Haq dismissed as 'peanuts'. We did not read the handwriting on the wall that Reagan in his election campaign in 1980 had taken the position that if elected, he would seek to re-establish military superiority over the Soviet Empire and aid countries in the 'frontline' against USSR. We also made no effort to show sympathy or extend humanitarian help to the Mujahidin when the Afghan people claimed that, as in Vietnam, they were only fighting the 'foreigner' in their homeland.

It has been obvious to thoughtful observers for some time that the Soviet Union has come to recognize that its intervention in Afghanistan was militarily frustrating and politically a mistake. But too many in India have quietly assumed that the Soviet Union was bound to marshal the resources necessary to succeed even if it took some years to do so as this would dilute for ever the threat to India from Pakistan. We failed to anticipate and understand that the Soviet Union policies transcended ideology and that it no longer felt the old nervous apprehension of Western threats to its security. Beyond occasional statements of sympathy we seemed not to have agonized with impatience at the tragic violence in Afghanistan. (In the *Annual Foreign Policy Review* for 1985, brought out by Professor Satish Kumar of the Jawaharlal Nehru University, I made bold to urge that India should, in its own interest, not remain indifferent to the Afghanistan problem.) We woke up to active diplomatic interest in the Afghanistan crisis only in 1988 and that was after the Soviet Union announced its withdrawal.

The objective of our policy after the Geneva Accords has been that the present government in Afghanistan should remain a dominant partner in a future coalition. It is understandable that we would prefer a moderate secular dispensation in the country. But for us to have invited President Najibullah on a state visit to Delhi in April 1988 (President Gorbachev only met the Afghan President in Tashkent) was proof of a failure to comprehend the Soviet Union's priorities and policies. While the retiring commander of Soviet forces stated that the government of Kabul would collapse after Soviet withdrawal, some of our analysts argued that with the support of an efficient and dependable military, the government could hold Kabul and save Afghanistan from a fundamentalist takeover. This reminds one of the American hopes in the longevity of the Kuomintang government and in preventing a Communist takeover in China in 1947-9. Our wishfulness may well have compounded the alienation of the bulk of the Afghan people from India. In Iran, like the USSR, we have been neutral to Islamic fundamentalism; it would have been prudent to have nurtured the same detachment in Afghanistan so that there could be wider options to adjust to a future which we cannot mould. The distilled essence of Non-alignment is that intervention to shape an internal regime is wrong in principle and doomed in practice.

Our errors of judgement could not have suited Pakistan better. It was our public position—a pointedly minority view in the UN—which enabled Pakistan to take advantage of the Western alarm and privately argue that India was abetting in a grand design of the USSR to advance towards the oil-laden warm waters of the gulf. Our original vote facilitated the resumption of the US military aid to Pakistan, which had been terminated in 1965 and not even revived during the tilt of 1971. In the voting in the subsequent 8 years, we won no additional adherents to our position. The resultant sub-continental arms race has been a bonanza to the arms exporting countries and a convenient argument for cold war hawks but the consequences for India and Pakistan have been greater economic distortions and horrendous deficits, grossly aggravating the political and social tensions besetting both countries. On a conservative estimate, India and Pakistan must have acquired new weapons systems worth US $ 20 billion during these years. With better prophylactic diplomacy, what could have been an opportunity for improved relations has resulted in the re-enactment of the post-1954 syndrome: India and Pakistan once again becoming surrogates of superpower misperceptions. Whatever may presently be stated from Washington and Moscow, following the Soviet withdrawal, the two superpowers are bound in due course to reduce their commitments to their respective clients in Pakistan and Kabul. In fact, the differences between USA and USSR on the complexion of the eventual solution are less important than their shared hope that a stable non-aligned Afghanistan might somehow emerge out of the Afghan cauldron. Both are uncertain and powerless on how exactly to bring this about. What is absolutely plain is that whether the country continues to burn or not, Afghanistan will not be allowed to affect the developing bilateral relations of the superpowers.

The legacy of devastation and complications in national and international relations will rest heavily and for long on the countries of the region. The Afghan nation will have to rehabilitate their devastated homeland. A million and a half Afghans are said to have died; some 5 million are refugees; some 10 million mines are strewn in the pathways, the fields, and in random over the country. The numbers of maimed will increase, even if the violence ends.

The political, diplomatic, and economic wages of misperceptions, both short-term and long-term, of Afghanistan of the region cannot be minimized. India, which had helped liberation and reconstruction in many countries, may find itself at a disadvantage. We would be able to contribute for the rehabilitation of Afghanistan through the UN operations under Prince Sadrudin Aga Khan. But the future of our bilateral relations with a restructured central government or a factious Afghanistan will for some years be on the political defensive. The Indian community long resident in Kabul, Jalalabad, Kandahar, and in other places may have to suffer taunts of callousness from the returning Mujahidin in what the Afghans will look upon as their struggle for liberation.

Afghanistan in many respects is an encapsulated microcosm of the tragedy of post-war international politics. It was a needless conflict made more destructive by modern weapons; it was in a Third World country; it happened because local developments through misperceptions were turned into a Cold War confrontation, which disregarded the regional fall-out. The military frustration of a superpower was symbolic of the strength in defence of Third World nationalism. Eventually the superpowers, after incisive re-examination of their relations, came to recognize that a Third World conflict was inconsequential to their own security, and in slow detachment, began exploring the improvement of their own relations. But the concerned Third World countries remained trapped in the Cold War hypnosis which was originally propagated by the great powers and was subsequently modified. The developing countries thus find themselves left to defuse, figuratively and literally, the mines left behind by the great power interventions. They have also to muscle up to rebuild their countries largely with their own exertions. Even while professing and pleading for Non-alignment, too often the mistake in the Third World was to have taken the superpowers too seriously on essentially local or regional problems. The lesson is patent: the primary responsibility and not inconsequential power to control their destinies rest on the people of every nation; interference, subversion, domination can be self-defeating and cause tragic violence.

The irony for India is that by surrendering sound principles we let pass an opportunity to serve our long-term interests of regional harmony, and in the bargain, became spectators to a needlessly bloody and destructive conflict and also suffered a loss of standing which might have helped in the non-ulterior search for a stable democratic non-aligned Afghanistan.

17

Why Not an Indian Initiative?
Removing Landmines

India and Pakistan could join in helping war-ravaged Afghanistan sweep the minefields and earn international goodwill.

Some five or six years ago, soon after the needless alarm of an India–Pakistan war raised by the Gates Mission from the US the issue of how to break the paranoiac gridlock of India–Pakistan relations became paramount. The moot question then is how to catalyze some way by which South Asia does not keep losing ground in economic progress and human development. In 1989 the Berlin Wall had come down and Gorbachev had ordered the summary withdrawal of Soviet forces from Afghanistan. The USA followed by terminating the ill-advised military aid to the Pakistan government and the CIA turned off the arms supply pipeline to the Afghan Mujahidin. But having become greatly flushed with sophisticated arms, the Afghan refugees spread all over the Pakistan provinces, undermining law and order enforcement. Some authorities in Pakistan purposely deflected the fundamentalist zest of Jehad eastwards and fuelled the insurgency in the valley of Kashmir.

But the triumph of Afghan factions against Soviet forces, instead of reunifying the country, only exacerbated the fragmentation. With continuing aid flows from Pakistan, Saudi Arabia, Iran, and the newly independent Uzbekistan earmarked for their preferred faction, the civil and ethnic turmoil worsened. In a country which in the nineteenth century had been uniquely effective in warding off the then Great Power Game, Afghanistan approached to near disintegration. It was a tragedy, the more so as it was avoidable. It could be traced to a quadrilateral of misperceptions in which the former USSR, USA, Pakistan, and even India (looked at from their respective national interests) were all guilty of gross misjudgements.

Statesman, New Delhi, 26 October 1997.

One of the informal propositions floated against this background was to leave aside the bilateral problems of India and Pakistan, and make a humanitarian gesture to ameliorate the terrible suffering of the innocent Afghan people. The idea was to constitute a dozen or so unarmed joint teams of trained sappers from the Indian and Pakistan armies, with or without UN approval, and approach the Afghan authority or authorities with an offer to sweep the land free from the mines which the Soviet forces had left embedded in the mountain pathways of Afghanistan. The Afghans would have to assume some responsibility for the deployment and protection of the teams. Such an offer would be the demonstration of our shared concern at the destruction of Afghanistan where the people of India and Pakistan have had age old stakes.

Many summers have passed since then and more blood has diluted the waters of the Kabul river. The Taliban displaced Rabbani but the civil war continues. What is relevant is that since the Saur Revolution of 1978, it is suspected that 1 million Afghans have been killed, 5 to 7 million (between a third and half of the population) displaced, and most built houses all over the country have been damaged or destroyed. Some claim that 10 million uncharted mines still remain concealed in the ground turning the whole country into killing fields.

Every year 25,000 Afghans become new victims—either in death or injuries and permanent disabilities from accidentally triggered explosions. The victims are not combatants but civilians and mostly women on their daily chores or unwary children at play or going to school.

The magnitude of the special problem of landmines has since been publicized internationally. It is estimated that about 100 million mines are embedded around the world. The biggest uncharted minefields are in Angola, Kampuchea, and Afghanistan. In Korea and in Bosnia the locations of these mines are known and can be systematically swept when the concerned governments authorize such operations but in Afghanistan, unlike in Angola and Kampuchea, there is still no end to the fighting and hence the civilians are in double jeopardy of the ongoing conflict and unintended hidden deaths. If the operations for mines clearance are further delayed, infants yet unborn may be the victims of one of the most vicious legacies of our times.

In the last year or so, an international crusade to abolish anti-personnel mines has gathered momentum. It is supported by the International Red Cross and highly respected non-governmental organizations (NGOs). Whereas the prohibition of chemical and biological weapons depends on the governmental decisions, the horrific consequences of landmines befall civilians and the casualties are haphazard, unforeseeable, and in the womb of the future.

It is accepted by most governments that the security rationale of landmines is not so significant as compared to the horrific human losses involved. During the last year, international conferences to ban the deployment and manufacture of landmines have been held in Brussels and Vienna (where a treaty was drafted), and more recently to finalize it in Oslo. The draft of the treaty has now been approved. The Canadians have been in the forefront in mobilizing international support and the process will culminate in the treaty being opened for signature in Ottawa from December 1997 onwards.

President Clinton, while stating that he was sympathetic to the objectives, expressed reservations because of the alleged special military threat in Korea and wanted US adherence deferred. However, over one hundred countries, many with their own particular security anxieties, have acclaimed the new treaty even in defiance of the American reservations. Alas India and Pakistan, like Russia and China, did not participate in the conference to ban the landmines. Once again we may find ourselves out of step with an enlightened international consensus. Exceptionalism has never reinforced India's international standing as a morally sensitive country pledged to principled politics.

But regardless of whether we sign the treaty in Ottawa or not, for our regional concern, India and Pakistan could cooperate to defuse landmines in Afghanistan. The climate for such a tripartite operation with Pakistan and Afghanistan as partners may well be considered premature and dangerous. Pakistan may be rigidly inhibited at joining hands with India. Afghanistan remains in turmoil and there may be no authority in a position to give minimal cooperation even in the comparatively stable southern half of the country. Risks to the life and limbs no doubt, exist but they are not too different from those in Somalia, Bosnia, or wherever else the UN has got involved in peacekeeping.

Notwithstanding all these negative reasons, India's offer, initially to be made diplomatically and not publicly pressed to embarrass our proposed partners, can be a non-controversial earnest of our concern and goodwill.

On balance, the positive fall-out from such an offer far outweighs the hazards and difficulties. It would evoke worldwide admiration.

It could come in the wake of the feeling of millions who have come forth with what an Indian paper described as 'Princess Diana's special tryst with landmines'. India extended a special honour of a state funeral to Mother Teresa, her adopted country, because she had come to be seen as a symbol of compassion for the dying and the helpless. We could recapture something of our lost moral standing by volunteering to work on a mission, which carries serious hazards but is targeted to help peaceful inhabitants of a neighbouring country. It could be a step to Indo–Pakistan cooperation and, rather optimistically speaking, catalyse the beginning of the end of the mutual paranoia.

For both India and Pakistan, helping Afghanistan should be independent of international politics. This may scale down narco-terrorism in Pakistan. For India it would restore the belief that our attitude to disarmament would serve the ends of social justice and find resources for national and regional development implicit in the Gujral doctrine. Such an international humanitarian mission would be like peacekeeping in the Congo in 1960, and would have been seized by Nehru. Even Gandhiji might have blessed an initiative where our trained military personnel were to be employed to save innocent lives.

18

Human Bombs Attack America: The World After 9/11

The Self-image of US Democracy Shaken by Terror

The Sherlock Holmes Society in its quarterly named appropriately the *Baker Street Journal* chose for its Christmas card of 1979 a reproduction of an etching, that had first appeared in the *FUN* magazine in 1878. The original caption was reproduced 'Afghanistan: Christmas Eve-Thoughts of Home'. The year 1978 marked the hundredth anniversary of the Second Afghan War when as in the First Afghan War (1839-42) the British Imperial forces suffered a humiliating defeat. In 1979 on Christmas day the Soviet Union embarked on what also proved to be an ill-fated intervention in Afghanistan. A Reuter despatch from Moscow in February 1989 carried a comment by Karen Katchaturov, the deputy head of Novosti Agency: 'Brezhnev [who had died in 1982] had plenty of time to seek opinions of historians before he authorized the invasion of Afghanistan in 1979. If he had, they could have told him that British colonialists after swallowing half of Afro-Asia only choked on the Afghan bone'. The Russian commentator seemed to be steeped in Sherlockiana and went on to confirm that Dr Watson had, indeed, got his leg wound in Herat (western Afghanistan). The British know how to laugh at the blunders in their history. They recall Guy Fawkes every year on 5 November with bonfires even though it is the anniversary of the attempt by Catholic revivalists to burn down the House of Lords in 1605. It is only the media in the United States which now recalls 7 December when Pearl Harbour was attacked as the day of Infamy as Japan has been a treaty friend of America since 1951. 9/11, however, will remain etched as the day when a handfull of men acting as human bombs, fired by the faith that they were doing God's will, crashed into the World Trade Center and the Pentagon. We are led to suspect that the fourth Boeing was heading for the White House or the Capitol. In India, we are likely to recall 13/12 every year as the day when a similar suicidal but fortunately failed attack was made on our Parliament, the symbol of India's democracy. 9/11 and 13/12 together may mark the autumn of 2001 as the advent of a new era in international politics and security: hereafter terror and desperation will be seen as the gravest threat to democracy and to all civil societies, which cherish plurality and consistentally permit dissent. India had long been familiar with the menace of terror but it came as a shock to the developing confidence in the invulnerability of the United States of America.

The Economist of 23 October 1999, in a cover story entitled 'America's World' showed the North American continent spread over the whole page with captions of alleged American pre-occupations; 'Surfin in Hawai'; 'huntin in the Rockies'; 'fishin in the Atlantic', 'exploitin in Central America'; and 'fightin only in some distant places' in the world which was shown in a corner shrunken to the size of a postage stamp. This was a sarcastic distortion of the perceived introverted arrogance of United States on the one hand and its limited concern for the problems of the rest of the world on the other. There were reasons enough for this gloating confidence. America had won the Cold War; the Soviet Union, the enemy of 40 years, had disintegrated and the residuary Russia looked to the United States itself for economic rescue; Iraq had been defeated with precision-guided weapons with practically no loss of GI lives; America's wealth was so enormous that the whole world looked to Washington for aid or access to its vast markets for trading opportunities; the best scientific and professional brains, not just from the poor nations but even from the richest countries, were queuing to become part of the American dream; the globalization of finance and technology was reinforcing America's established lead. The United States could plausibly feel that its pre-eminence gave it hegemony over the Earth, the Oceans, and even Space. It could understandably rejoice with an inner glow of being not just the sole superpower but the 'indispensable' power for the solution of any or the entire world's political and economic problems. In this confidence, Washington could choose whether to consult, accept, or arbitrarily reject the consensus of the United Nations or even the confirmed tenets of international law by judging them solely from the test of America's narrow and immediate interests. The American people could be forgiven if they thought that their homeland was immune to enmity and malevolence from any individual or nation. After 9/11, however, there never again will be the same confidence or complacency; America was shocked to find it was flattered not just by envy but by hate.

'Rigidified' Mindsets in a Changing International Landscape

What transpired on 11 September 2001 was a tragedy but the irony implicit in the attack should not be slurred over. A frail bearded man, sitting somewhere in the caves of Afghanistan's barren mountains had shaken America's self-image; he first came to the country and so did tens of thousands of foreign Islamic fundamentalists encouraged, facilitated, and possibly financed as part of the deliberate policy of the United States itself to fight the Communist 'infidels'. The decision makers had not registered that the Communist monolith had already splintered (China, Yugoslavia, Romania, etc.) and there was no heart or real vigour left in the crusading zest of Communist regimes in office. (The ideological fire continued to burn but only in the minds of men aspiring to power.) The Soviet Union was already bestirring with centripetal nationalism and, in fact, was concerned at the reviving religious orthodoxy and in comparison, the loyalty to Sunni Islam was growing, as it had in Shiite Iran in 1979. It is ironical that in the eyes of the Islamic militants, transported under US policy auspices to join in the anti-Soviet struggle, it is the US which now is perceived as the arch criminal, which must be humbled and destroyed. The momentum of the old fear in the minds of anti-Communists has still not lost its grip. As late as 1998, somebody like Brzezenski,[1] who was the National Security Adviser in 1980, justified the American policy to help the Taliban as calculated to bring about the collapse of the Soviet Empire. Such *ex post facto* rationalization glosses over the fact, that at the beginning of 1980, the White House was fired with a wholly unfounded but genuine alarm at Soviet expansionist intentions. There are other examples of contemporaneous misjudgements. Bill Gates, at one time Director of the CIA, boasted of the planned 'Bear Trap'[2] to bog down and bleed the Soviet Union.

---

[1] Interview with Le Nouvel Observateur in January 1998, quoted by Pankaj Mishra, New York. Review of Books, 25 November 2001.

[2] Yousuf and Mark Adkin, in *Bear Trap*, 1992.

With Casey, the Director of the CIA under President Reagan, President Zia-ul-Haq connived to make the ISI the conduit for arms including Stinger missiles for the Mujahidin of which many were pilfered and sold openly in Pakistan. Supporting Islamic fundamentalism was looked upon as the instrument for advancing American interests against Soviet Union. Thousands of copies of the Koran were smuggled through Pakistan into Tajikistan, Turkmenistan, and Uzbekistan with the deliberate object of inflaming Muslim militancy in the Soviet Central Asia.[3] With United States now hunting Osama-bin-Laden, bombing the Al-Queda and the Talibans, there could not be a stronger example of dialectical reversal.

The Soviet Union disintegrated because of inner contradictions within the bloc; Eastern Europe repudiated the Soviet connection with the revival of historic nationalisms after decades of economic inefficiency; the ideological cement of Cominform and the military cohesion of the Warsaw Pact never gathered intrinsic strength. At all events in the 1980s, no one spared any thought to the possible blowback from encouraging Islamic fundamentalism much less that it would enthuse Islamic opinion round the world against the United States.

The acts of terror, the 'romancing' of Talibanization in Afghanistan, the affirmation of the overriding relevance of the Sharia law in its most conservative interpretation; the banning of women's education and outlawing them from participation in public life; the prohibiting of all forms of entertainment and relaxation relished by the people were all outrages against the accepted modern notions for a civil society. The destruction of the world heritage monuments like the Bamiyan Buddhas was a cultural abomination. To understand such religious militancy, even in educated minds, must be politically, teleologically, sociologically and psychologically analysed. The aberrations amounted to systemic failure and must be seen as a setback to the entire process of modernization and the values of a world wanting to advance towards individual rights of choice and freedom and collective hopes of greater social justice. Terrorism also flies in the face of people's political fulfilment, urbanization, plurality and civilizational diversity. It should become a matter of global concern when religion reverts to medievalism.

[3] Woodword: 'The Secret Wars of CIA 1981-87'.

In the essays collected in this volume the penalties of misperceptions runs like a *leit-motif* as in a Beethoven symphony but the
Afghan story ends not in an 'Ode to Joy' but in the unorchestrated
wails of millions of bereaved families, and the cries of orphaned
children with amputated limbs. It led to the displacement of almost
half the Afghan population many of whom for more than a decade
have been in refugee camps; indeed the tragic spectacle of a country
utterly destroyed after two decades of an ill-conceived conflict.
Unprovoked intervention was followed by summary withdrawal as
the tribal factions in their ambitions could never muster the will to
restore the old political unity. The whole world should share in the
guilt at years of unconcern. (The saga of callous brutality seems to
be continuing as one gathered from the reports that the US backed
Northern Alliance engaged in a factional fight to the point of
merciless extermination of the Taliban prisoners in the Mazar-e-
Sharif fort on 24-5 November 2001.)

In this concluding chapter, there are only stray reference to the
origin of the crisis. My own role and the ideas which I had for the
resolution of the problem run through the compilation and will be
recalled in one section in this chapter. The bulk will however seek to
concentrate on the far-reaching implications of 9/11 and how
internationalized terror could pose a challenge to governments
specially democracies in the new century. It will call for great
statesmanship and a new internationalism, supported by sustained
diplomatic sagacity, to contain terrorism in South Asia and to meet
the threat of disaffection turning into callous destruction around
the world as we move inexorably towards interdependence and
enmeshed modernization. As President Bush put it, it will be a
challenge to 'translate anger into a mission'.

In India we have been alive to sporadic terrorism in Kashmir and
random incidents for over a decade but going by published
information, even within the US, there were telltale incidents whose
full significance was ignored or underestimated. In 1993 the World
Trade Center itself suffered an attack, which apparently was not
fully investigated. The bombing of Oklahoma may have been the
action of a demented individual but it could have been taken as a
warning that high-rise buildings, with many corporate offices and,
therefore an economic hub, stand out as inviting perverse attention
of a sadistic mind. The attack on the US embassies in Nairobi and
Dar-e-Salaam, killing hundreds, was correctly traced to the malevolent mastermind of Osama-bin-Laden but the response with cruise

missiles aimed randomly in Afghanistan (and falsely at Sudan) was more symbolic than purposeful. Apparently the attack on the warship USS 'Cole' was also planned from Al-Queda bases in Afghanistan. These attacks on American diplomatic missions and warship were still outside the American homeland and did not apparently shake the embedded conviction that America, with two mighty oceans both several thousand miles in expanse on either side, made the country safe against all but inter-continental missiles: the old illusion of isolationism was creeping back into the American consciousness. It was confidently believed that with the technological capability of intelligence, remote sensing, etc., as commanded by the Pentagon, the FBI, and the CIA and a broadly contented and loyal citizenry, in a land of freedom and opportunity, United States could consider its homeland safe against desperate or demented violence from distant conspirators.

Terrorism: The Features and the
Problems of Combating it

One encounters a preliminary problem in defining terrorism. Obviously, it cannot be precise or comprehensive. Individual acts of senseless violence, including political assassinations, must be considered as crimes under the ordinary laws of the land but desperate conspiratorial action reflecting political, religious, or social grievances, which disregard collateral societal damage or the loss of human lives, amount to terror. In established democracies the use of terror is less justified although such open societies often give greater opportunity (as for example, in Northern Ireland and India) to perpetrate senseless outrages. Highjacking and hostage taking are forms of vicious public relations on behalf of a cherished cause but they can lead to indiscriminate loss of life and thus amounts to terrorism. In reacting to terror in established democracies, the temptation is growing inevitably to curtail the fundamental constitutional rights, including that of peaceful protest and dissent. In the heat of anxiety, the nature of the threat is often deliberately exaggerated; indeed, as often as not, it is used to justify the continuation in power of an individual or a clique. Even democratic governments are tempted to impose needlessly stringent restrictions on citizens', unreasonably curb the right of advocacy and obtain authorization for protracted detentions without trial. The suspicion of terror even becomes an excuse for brutalities and in effect to establish a regime of State terror. The rationale for the declaration of the Emergency in India in 1975 was an unwarranted fear of the loss of power. The proposed Prevention of Terrorism Act (POTA), under consideration by the Indian Parliament, is suspected of seeking far greater discretion than is necessary for executive functioning. The United States has enacted a 'Patriots Act' which authorizes special measures to detain, question, and investigate non-citizens on the basis of suspicions and denying them normal rights of defence. There is also the suggestion that civil law procedures be suspended in trying suspects belonging to the Al-Queda so that they could be dealt with summarily by military tribunals. Other countries are also contemplating special enactments to combat terror. However, countries in Western and Northern Europe have sought assurances from the United States that before agreeing to extradite suspects, the normal procedure for defence will not be shelved, and in any case, death sentence (which has been abolished in Europe) will not be imposed even if convicted in trials. The consensus is that in functioning democracies, anti-terrorism must be on guard not to undermine the accepted principles of dissent and individual rights, which are the backbone of the rule of law and democratic governance.

The truth, however, is that the rationale of suppressing civic and human rights in modern times has had a shameful international record. Great indulgence was shown by democracies towards non-democratic regimes because they pledged to fight against the then perceived bigger enemy—'Communism' and hence suppression of legitimate protest was permitted even going to the extreme of blatant domestic state terror. During the Cold War, too many tyrants and dictators were tolerated and helped to hold on to power even though they were transparently against Western ideas and democratic values (as for example Mobuto). The profession of anti-Communism and allowing bases for the NATO was accepted as justification for tolerating colonialism by Portugal when other European Empires had retreated. The bargain of ensuring the vital oil flow from the Gulf has led to the US turning of the Nelson's eye towards absolutist monarchies and emirates and even tolerating the financing of fundamentalism and religious militancy by Saudi Arabia. In hindsight, it is recognized that these compromises were horrible mistakes and made democratic United States appear like the guardian angel of repression and an obstruction to the broadening of freedom and justice demanded by political activists round the world. With the end of the Cold War and the nemesis we have seen brought about by

188   THE MARCH OF FOLLY IN AFGHANISTAN

terrorism, these residuary linkages of unprincipled *realpolitik* should be reviewed, and slowly reversed. Democracy by definition must remain committed to plurality and contrary-wise dictatorships, military or civil, are almost bound to suppress dissent and resort to violence in diverse ways. The apotheosis of smothering political opposition readily culimates in terror.

Professor Haykel,[4] a scholar on Islamic Law at New York University, has argued that 'Radical Salafism' provided Osama-bin Laden the theological justification for fighting the 'infidels' with every means possible. According to that dogma, even oppressive Muslim governments are to be destroyed and large sections of Muslims forfeit the right of belonging to the faith. The strength of Osama's wide appeal as a crusader of Islam is, however, because he articulates the protest at the stationing of US troops in the Holy Land of the Prophet. Osama has won respect with much of the Islamic laity including with many moderate followers at having humiliated the mighty 'Satan'. For all the American and British effort not to condemn Muslims in general, many of them, though finding terrorist actions abhorrent, secretly take satisfaction at Osama's 'achievement'. The feeling of smouldering anger and complaint at the West is re-echoing the notion of the clash of civilizations with Islam, seen in principled conflict with the Christian West.

Let it however be acknowledged that most religions are exclusivist or have gone through an 'intolerant' phase. Christianity certainly had its period of militant fidelity to its theology, which sanctioned utmost zeal in propagating the gospel. For centuries the crusaders were applauded; and the church was encouraged to follow the flag of conquest; wholesale conversion with violence was considered service to the particular Almighty. Protestantism was resisted by the Catholic church: Calvinist austerity spurned the Catholic rituals and the Inquisition rejoiced in the persecution of the Huguenots. The Jews were suspected and hounded long before Hitler. The alternation in the destruction of mosques, churches, synagogues and temples is part of the history of religion. Only orthodox Hinduism discouraged changing deities, but Brahminical faith made caste rigid in the belief that faith and caste at birth were not to be rejected during this life as it was part of the cycle of rebirth. But over the millennia Hinduism had a philosophic basis for toleration and co-existence of the diversity of faiths; however since the nineteenth century militancy

[4] Bernard Haykel, 'Radical Salafism', *The Hindu*, 1 December 2001.

and conversions had started creeping into the practice of Hinduism. At all events the challenge for every religion including Hinduism, is to adjust to the imperatives of social integration which is unavoidable in the modern urban, industrial and technological world. Emancipated societies do not forbid conversion but militant solidarity based on religion has problems in reconciling with economic progress. When the benefits of modernization do not reach the multitude then begins insidious alienation and when the social system is transparently iniquitous, even religion loses its hold and terror finds volunteers.

Violence for Self-determination

Terror thus always points to moral dilemmas of ends and means. Mahatma Gandhi was exceptional in his commitment that non-violence was as important as the goal of independence: for him hate was always demeaning. This gave India's freedom struggle a unique quality, but for most other countries, the aspiration for liberation, national self-determination, and the acceleration of de-colonization justified incidental violence even if it caused damage and disruption to civil society. The longest running terrorist campaign is in Northern Island where Protestants and Catholics have been locked in conflict on the geographical definition of self-determination. The IRA has received sustained non-official support from sympathizers in democratic United States. The struggle for pressuring or seizing political power has justified seeking and receiving foreign military support. The Spanish Civil War had an international brigade which had non-mercenary volunteers to fight the Franco dictatorship. In the successor republics of Yugoslavia, ethnic cleansing of minorities led to a cycle of brutalities. In post-colonial period, there were many ugly instances of terror. In the protracted Algerian war of independence there were thousands of deaths with brutalities. The Pol Pot regime literally rusticated millions from the towns and then ordered the indiscriminate killing of fellow Kampucheans to make a new communistic egalitarian society. The genocidal extermination of the Hutus was horrendous tribal violence, amounting to terror the worst of many in Africa. Even now some contemporary rulers in Africa in order to stay in power are restricting democratic functioning and squeezing out ethnic aliens by 'terror' tactics. Many liberation struggles condoned and even encouraged violence against class 'enemies' or suspected collaborators. After the 3-way split of the

Communist Party in India (CPI), the CPI(ML), sometimes referred to as Naxalites, were not ashamed to kill oppressive landlords; they had rejected the path chosen by the CPI and CPI(M) of using available constitutional means to change the established order. The current Peoples War Group (PWG) is not apologetic at the violence inflicted on innocent lives as they see no alternative to effecting their desired political change. The recent Maoist killings in Nepal have the declared aim of the overthrow of the Monarchy and this has led to hundreds of deaths including in the law and order forces. The Muslim Abu Sayaf movement in the Philippines, which has habitually taken foreign tourists as hostages to draw attention to their grievances, has the features of terrorism. It is alleged that in one incident they obtained as ransom $ 18 million, which then was used to bribe the anti-terrorist forces themselves! The Shining Path has a strong appeal for armed struggle among the disaffected youth in Peru. Che Guevera was a much-admired crusader against the iniquitous regimes in Latin America and attracted revolutionaries from many countries. He will remain a hero who sought to reshape society but the incidental killings of class enemies bordered on terrorism.

It is not easy to make a distinction between violence for a worthy crusade against oppression and callous terrorism. The litmus test must be whether legal options exist which give the right to seek relief to the grievances but without endangering the basic state structure. The violent struggle of the Muslim minority for independence of Chechnya is deemed to be a challenge to the integrity of Russia and so is considered terroristic, especially after foreign volunteers from other parts of Central Asia and the Talibans from Afghanistan and Pakistan were found aiding the struggle. This in turn justified the use of State power in fighting the insurgents. The flaw, however, is the absence of an established democratic infrastructure in Russia. In Kashmir, however, even though the exercise of civil and human rights is alleged to be frequently ignored by the security forces (and the National Human Rights Commission has not hesitated to point to such instances), firm provisions do exist for legal redress and democratic change of government. Some aberrations do not justify the armed infiltration across the Line of Control, assisted by non-nationals and this repudiates the claim for the insurgency in Kashmir to be considered as an indigenous freedom struggle. The two-nation theory has to be resisted by India to uphold our Constitution based on secularism. On the other hand, in Pakistan, democracy has been periodically overthrown and has never been allowed in occupied Kashmir beyond the Line of Control. The legality of the accession of Kashmir to India goes back to the Indian Independence Act of the British Parliament in 1947 which is not superceded by the conditional offer of a plebiscite. Cross border infiltration based and aided officially or non-officially cannot be legitimized as steps in the fulfilment of political aspirations.

There are no doubt cases of justified outside help but the question is whether democratic avenues have been explored and respected. India was involved in Bangladesh but the demand for independence was articulated when the results of the nation-wide elections in Pakistan in 1970 were set aside. Millions of refugees crossed into India after military operations were mounted in East Pakistan to suppress the clear demand of the people in support of independence. Indian military operations were authorized only after military provocations by Pakistan forces. Anyway the Indian army's presence was wound up within 100 days of the ceasefire. Bangladesh cannot be used to justify either Kargil or the sustained export and abetting of terrorism from Pakistan. Bangladesh was really a proof of the inherently flawed theory of nationhood based on religion.

UN and Terror

After the attack on the World Trade Center, the UN came to recognize that the menace of terrorism poses a new international threat, which required a collective international response. The UN Charter begins with the pledge to free succeeding generations from the scourge of war but terror is in some ways worse; the chapter could well be supplemented to save the world from the callous violence of non-official terror. Just as the original commitment to peace began with the pledge by the peoples and then left the implementation to sovereign nations, tackling terror first and foremost rests with independent countries but it would demand a new awareness that fighting terror cannot be compartmentalized nationally. As with the issue of environment, success depends on all nations cooperating in vigilance and taking prophylactic steps. The Security Council resolutions passed in September and October 2001, notably Resolution 1373 of 28 September, asks for detailed commitments under Chapter VII of the UN Charter to smother the manifestations of terror; it has operational implications for all countries of a kind never made before by the world body. Under the resolution, a Counter Terrorist Committee was appointed and all countries and even UN bodies were required to address terrorism operationally and comprehensively and report on measures taken. In effect just as we were getting used to the idea that internal and inter-State affairs would be governed more and more by secular factors, functional economics and technological advances, terror brought religion back into politics. For the first time, international religious extremism is seen as incompatible with the principles embodied in the Charter.

The UN Secretary-General, after asserting a new urgency on all the issues addressed by the world body up to 10 September, added that 11 September marked a new phase of responsibility for the United Nations. There was a clash between what he called two civilizations: on the one side 'were diverse religious and cultural issues and, on the other a global community respecting diversity, rooted in universal values and tolerant of plurality. The latter must be our choice.'

The dramatic attack of 9/11 brought an end to the complacency of national isolationism. Francis Fukuyama, in an article in the *Financial Times*, pointed out that it was the end of the feeling of American exceptionalism and the temptation to unilateralism. It is now widely recognized that the United States must again get engaged in the world and see the UN as an ally and not as a convenience to be used occasionally and ignored periodically. Terror has, in fact to be fought as a long-term enemy of all that the UN stands for and defeating it would require international political cooperation going beyond marshalling of the military for specific peacekeeping operations. Notwithstanding this advice, it remains a matter of regret that the USA did not seek the approval of the Security Council for its counter-terror measures against Osama-bin-Laden. It would have been readily endorsed in principle but by-passing of the international body shows that the old hesitation still persists in relying on the UN. This conservatism will weaken the prospect of 'uniting for peace' against terror.

Before addressing myself to the scaffolding of progress in Afghanistan and its important bearing for India–USA–Pakistan, let me speculate further on other general international aspects of terror as affected by the ongoing process of globalization, which was, in any case insidiously perforating sovereignty both in positive and negative way.

The New Emerging Horizonal Bipolarity:
Governments versus Internationalized Disaffection

Because terror can be suicidally motivated it is very nearly beyond direct punishment. And until it strikes, the virus of terror is invisible, but we know it is pervasive and yet it is most difficult to detect. The governments of the world—the superpowers, the great powers, the rulers of the Third World, even of Muslim countries—have only come alive to the menace and are now trying to join in a grand combination to identify and contain terrorism. However, with known diverse interests, it will be difficult to hold together this vast heterogeneous coalition in what President Bush has declared is 'War'—nothing less, against this malevolent long term international threat. However, it will not be easy for governments to erase from their minds, bequeathed from history, that conflicts are always of limited duration, which end in victory, defeat, or surrender. Strategies based on deterrence of the nuclear capability, space and ballistic defence, organized surface battles, or even subversion and promoted insurrection belong to a world of national level territorial conflicts where the enemy had a local habitation and a name. The provocation, in origin, may be local but, as we saw with Islamic fundamentalism, it could evoke spontaneous support beyond frontiers and that too sometimes in secret conspiratorial groups. It has its on non-official tentacles and (for a period Libyan government acknowledged official support) beyond borders, which makes it almost immune to conventional condign power.

In order that the international war on terror succeeds or atleast registers progress, it has to subsume or supercede existing political rivalries, historical antagonisms, and solve atleast some of the festering problems of power politics. Tactical compromises can be made, but in the final instance, only democracies can uphold faith in dissent and plurality. Meanwhile, we have to recognize the growing awareness, around the world, that the conditions for a few fortunate continue to improve within their own country and internationally while it gets worse for more and more of the people who are not amongst the elite and do not belong to the connectivity web. There is a rising sense of dissatisfaction that the poor and the unemployed all over the Third World are denied international social justice; the freedom and facilities to improve their lot in a prospering world is getting more restricted. Many countries are only too obviously case studies in failures of de-colonization with little or no improvement in the living standards of the majority. The reasons are of course many but the malaise is now more internationally transparent. The UN and other world institutions have for long been groping in diverse ways to urge strategies for the amelioration in the host of problems of the poor but what is new is the progressive internationalization of protest. It now surfaces more frequently—as recently as on the WTO in Seattle, on Environment in Kyoto, on aspects of Racism in Durban, on the dangers from nuclear radiation, and on gender issues many times. At these gatherings, the NGO protesters were agreeably surprised to find sensitive fellow activists from different parts of the world, including from the developed countries were engaged on parallel crusades.

Oppression and degradation persists and expectations get more sharpened and so frustration tends to turns to violence. Meanwhile notions of Universal Rights and Human Development have permeated the consciousness of millions round the world. While governments seek to forge a coalition of common interests against explosive grievances, they are generally unprepared to face this emerging unity of discontent. Islamic extremism may mark a new step in the internationalization of protest because Islam is now a world religion of a billion people with significant presence in Asia, Africa, Europe and North America. Desperate poverty is the tinder for terrorism; it is very much the agony of the poor Muslims who have generally been denied institutional democracy and good governance. It still remains to be seen if such religion-based indignation will make even tactical common cause with the foci of subsisting secular dissatisfaction rampant in the world. Regardless of the response, the plain fact is that the gallop of technology and communication has proved to be double-edged: it has increased the polarization of the rich and poor, advanced and backward, opulent and starvation divide. Economic globalization of trade, investment, technology and growth faces this developing globalization of disaffection.

The resolution of the globalization of disaffection cannot be left only to internationally sensitive development economists, especially when governments all too often are seen to be manipulating only to stay in power and to improve their access to perquisites at the expense of the taxpayer. The lip-service to democracy, political liberalism, broadened social welfare, and peoples' participation sounds hollow and meets more and more cynicism and only spurs the effort to establish stronger non-official linkages beyond established national frontiers. The attempt at suppression of dissent has intensified but it has not correspondingly weakened the protest: indeed it causes more international protest. The Tien-en-men revolt became instant world news because some Chinese had learnt the use of computers even before the Chinese government had become aware of its instant reach or how to obstruct it. The embedded image, which will be remembered by millions in the US, and which, within moments captured the attention of the whole world, was of Boeings, crashing into the twin towers; then the inferno of fire and thick smoke darkening the New York skyline—all on their television screens in their own offices or living rooms. They actually witnessed the collapsing of the twin towers of the World Trade Center in New York. The world also instantly guessed that amongst the victims were not only innocent American sons and daughters but also foreign nationals. 9/11 was a dramatic event, not only one of shock of deaths and damage to the world economy but also in the internationalism of awareness of the pernicious reach of terrorism. While it quickened the determination for governments to combine into a broader transnational challenge but it also heightened sensitivity amongst thoughtful persons that to scotch terror effectively would call for pooled sagacity and, to defeat it may eventually need nothing short of the promise of faster progress towards a new world order.

The world—developed and developing—must take note of this emerging bipolarity: on the one hand governments, with vested interest in stability, using national resources to enforce order, discharging administrative and development responsibilities, alas at times to a minimum extent, and on the other, a growing transnational grouping of discontent and impatience, glued by a sense of complaint, injustice, and deprivation and to react equally to non-national prepared grievances as to a national problem. This is not like the vertical bipolarity of the NATO (or the defunct Warsaw Pact or regional groupings), which brought only governments together but of the discovered common interest of peoples, united in disaffection. The irony is that both sides of the bipolarity are results of the same modernized communications. The horizontal confrontation, of course, is loose and not easily identifiable; but the world has come to realize now, as a side effect of 9/11 that this discontent was smouldering, though in different degrees of incendiary intensity over a long period. The deeper meaning of 9/11 is that no national government can now remain complacent at being immune to aroused anger, raw courage and unreasoned hatred. 9/11 has emboldened the powerless dramatically and hastened a new internationalism.

Commercial Motivation in Terror

In the attack on the twin towers of the World Trade Center, and the Pentagon there was suicidal determination of course but also there was high motivation with no trace of personal gain. Terror and violence have ugly faces too, where crime is not just callous to the loss of life but the motive is profit. There is an element of thoughtless terror, for example, in the international 'trade' in human cargo where huge sums of money are made by transnational gangs by exploiting intending migrants—and total number runs into millions—and pushing them into overcrowded old boats or dispatched in refrigerated containers. Narco-terrorism thrives on smuggling and disseminating harmful drugs in affluent countries, adversely affecting the health of millions. The mafia spreads its tentacles in the international underworld and leads to death and murder. Because the profit margins are so enormous, it does not stop at individual 'terror killing'. Alas, Afghanistan and the golden triangle of Myanmar, Thailand, and Laos have been involved for decades in such nefarious trade, which equals in value the drug operations in Colombia and other parts of Latin America. Some earnings, no doubt, percolate to the poor cultivators of poppy but the vast share goes only to a handful of intermediaries. What is worse, narco-terrorism facilitates arms purchases, smuggling, and the spread of 'guns'.

In a conference which I organized in 1984 when I was 'Tom Slick Professor' of World Peace at Austin, the theme I chose was 'Third World Militarization: A Challenge to Third World Diplomacy'. Some thirty scholarly participants—ex-diplomats and specialists on Asia, Africa, and Latin America—participated in a three-day meeting. I prepared the keynote address and the results came out in a book.[5] One of the conclusions, which emerged was that Third World militarization had led to the reinforcing of non-representative governments and intensified the frustration at the denial of democratic aspirations, and all this could be traced atleast in part to the

[5] J.S. Mehta (ed.), *Third World Militarization: A Challenge to Third World Diplomacy*, LBJ School, University of Texas, Austin, 1985.

vested interest of arm manufacturers, who manage to get the support of their governments including democratic ones in facilitating arms exports. The superpowers are, ofcourse, spectacularly in the lead— for some years valued at $ 25 billion—but other industrialized countries and some developing countries are also engaged in increasing their share of sophisticated weapons trade, disregarding the consequential destabilization and civil conflicts. The volume and value of arms trade but also the share of Third World countries is steadily rising. Moreover, the pressures are not only from the suppliers but also from the demand side, especially from the non-democratic countries. While the attack on the World Trade Center was free from militarism, the prevalence of terror as a phenomenon in the destruction of Afghanistan cannot be divorced from arms smuggled by the rival militant factions. Many countries including Pakistan, are today awash with illegal arms and this was no small part of the contributory factor to internal instability and failing governance. The military measures to suppress terrorism and factional conflict will have limited success if it is not combined with international political solutions, which must include restraint in arms trade at both the supply and the demand end. The graver implication of militarization is that it leads to more and more diversion of scarce resources from social expenditure, like on education and health and thus giving greater strength and muscle to the global fraternity of the frustrated and the desperate.

The Backlash on Immigration

There are other incidental consequences of dramatized terrorism from 9/11. The United States had come to perceive itself as having a manifest destiny as the land of opportunity for all, regardless of religion and origin, and as a guardian of freedom and democracy. As a consequence of the attack on the World Trade Center, the confidence of keeping an open society will have been jolted, but to what extent remains to be seen. However, one must anticipate aggravated conservatism and stricter regulations in the policy on immigration. Ethnicity was already emerging as one of the most intractable problems of the twenty-first century. I sought to address it in a recent pamphlet[6] drawing attention to its implications for the

---

[6] J.S. Mehta, 'Ethnicity and International Relations at the Turn of the Century', Centre for Policy Research, New Delhi, 2001.

developed and developing countries, particularly China and India who have the biggest diasporas abroad. During the process of decolonization, overseas ethnic connections were politically disowned, but after the non-resident communities proved a success in the West, many developing countries have come to look upon the diaspora as a supplementary source of investment for economic development. The events of 9/11 may result in a significant change of psychological attitudes towards non-Caucasian immigrants. From a traditional welcoming attitude towards newcomers, even if they were culturally different, but potentially economic assets, mainstream America is likely to harbour a nervous apprehension towards aliens as possible terrorists. It will be a more hesitant patriotic boast of the United States to claim being a melting pot for the poor and the persecuted from all parts of the world. There will be a quiet plea for more discriminating scrutiny of those who are different in racial or religious terms. This may lead to strangers being unpleasantly questioned and even result in witch-hunts against Arabs and Muslims.

During the Cold War years, all countries felt like David facing the American Goliath; the United States became the foil for small country nationalisms. After the end of the Cold War, the US took note but its response was calibrated according to its own interests and perceptions. Suspicion and prejudice against the benefactor is a familiar old instinct in individual and political relationships. I have always felt that in a miniscule way in the relationship with our contiguous neighbours, India faced a similar mix of presumed dependence on the one hand and unreasoned dislike on the other. But I also found that the adverse political reactions could be minimized by better anticipation and showing extra sensitivity towards the smaller countries. America likes to play the ideal neighbour to the whole world and, like India with her neighbours, it has to be more sagacious and restrained if only in order not to be seen as overbearing or compromising its ideals and international appeal. But the fact remains that the United States has all too often been considered arrogant and politically nonchalant and uncaring. The post 9/11 mood has not changed the governmental level reactions; on the contrary, while there will be more willingness of coming together towards other governments, and carrying similar burdens of countering terrorism, but there is bound to be far greater skeptical individual attitudes towards foreigners.

The United States has so far been unmatched as a spontaneous

and generally non-discriminating fountain of generosity, volunteering relief and help in all international disasters. The world has got
accustomed to the expectation of positive response and has looked
to the United States for succour—as we did when the earthquake
struck Gujarat on 26 January 2001. There is now a risk of American
sensitivity getting wounded. The world will now have to be careful
not to rejoice too openly at the spectacle of Gulliver being wounded
and humiliated by anonymous Lilliputians from distant 'shores'. It
could very well snowball into rightist polarization and strengthen
the perception of a conflict of civilizations in the making. One must
hope that this sympathy and spontaneity at the individual level (as
distinct from governmental aid) will not get shriveled, just when the
world needs a new internationalism of compassion.

While decision-makers in United States and in the West have
shown a determined pledge to hunt down Osama-bin-Laden, the
associated Al-Queda and the militant Talibans, they have repeatedly
tried to diffuse and dilute prejudice developing against Arabs in
general and the moderate Muslims. Osama focused on the removal
of American troops from Arabia but for most Muslims the disenchantment against United States is over other issues, specially the
Middle East question. By and large, all Arabs, many others in the
Third World and quite a few Europeans disapprove of United States
acting as the partisan godfather to Israel. This partiality in the Arab–
Israel dispute is of course because of domestic electoral compulsions,
marring objectivity in foreign policy. Colin Powell's recent initiative
was calculated to correct the impression that the Bush administration
was indifferent to the Palestine problem and to get broader international support to combat terror and not jeopardize oil flows from
the Gulf. Alas Arab–Israeli incidents have continued even after
Powell's speech. The cycle of suicidal attacks by Arabs against Israeli
civilians in turn provokes punitive reprisals by Israel. For the Arabs,
suicide bombers protesting against Israeli settlements are heroes; and
the bloody over-reaction by Israel is wholly unjustified. Similarly, as
the US maintains sanctions, preventing even milk and food for
children in Iraq, forfeits the claim that there is no prejudice against
the Arabs. Fortunately, in Europe there is greater sympathy for
Palestine and hence, at least slightly less antagonism in foreign policy
but even in Europe after 9/11, there is distinctly less tolerance for
Muslims, including North African Arabs in France and Turks in
Germany. These complications are illustrative of the problem of

maintaining a lasting broad-based coalition against terror.

In general, terror can only be contained if there is a greater commitment and worldwide progress towards equity, equality, non-discrimination, greater compassion, and at-least reduction of the many seeds of cynical desperation. 9/11, will, one hopes, start a process of empathic introspection and recognition that this invisible enemy, impeding enlightened governance of countries, could very well distort the constructive thrust of positive elements of inter-dependence. This should continuously nag at our conscience and spur us to greater sensitivity in distributional justice and toleration of diversity. The benefit of globalization of economic growth must ease, and not solidify, disaffection; it must not inflame the propensity for desperation.

The Scaffolding for a Stable Restructuring in Afghanistan

Let me now revert specifically to the problem of Afghanistan and its resolution. Many of the foregoing papers written in the 1980s carry the outline of what I thought could be the framework for a solution. Section VIII of the paper[7] written at the Kennan Institute of the Woodrow Wilson Center in 1981 under the deliberately intriguing title 'Solution in Afghanistan: From Swedenization to Finlandization' has six sequential steps for the resolution of the imbroglio. In the 1980s, the goal of course, was to persuade Soviet Union to withdraw its forces and forsake a meaningless adventure but at the same time assuage the apprehensions about Russia's own security. But the ultimate purpose was the same as at present, viz., to restore Afghanistan to stability, which would allow for the traditional tribal plurality and respect for the country's fierce identity. In the paper written for the annual review of India's foreign policy brought out by Professor Satish Kumar, in 1986.[8] I argued for an Indian initiative as a way to insulate South and South-West Asia for Non-alignment. I elaborated the process in ten sequential steps. The theme paper[9] circulated in January 1989, inviting participants for the conference in Austin scheduled for October 1989, was meaningfully subtitled 'A Superpower "Episode" and its Regional Impact'. The keynote address for the conference was called 'The Legacy and Lessons from

[7] See Chapter 3.
[8] See Chapter 10.
[9] See Chapter 12.

Afghanistan'.[10] I was able to attract a large number of American and foreign specialists on the area, a few Afghan residents in USA, some ex-diplomats including Ambassador Marker from Pakistan, and also from the Soviet Union. I corresponded with Ambassador Safronchuk who was with the Soviet Embassy in Kabul in 1979, at the time of the intervention and who I believe opposed it. In 1989 when he was an Under Secretary General in the UN. Safronchuk had agreed to come but at the last minute was prevented from doing so. The theme paper elicited interest and comments from Professors Stanley Hoffmann, Paul Doty, Joe Nye, and Ben Brown from Harvard; McGeorge Bundy and Selig Harrison from New York; and James Bill, Barnett Rubin, and others from different universities. Several Faculty members from the Centres of Asia, Middle East and East European Studies at the University of Texas took part in the discussions. Professor Sheila Fitzpatrick, a social historian of the Soviet Union, gave me sustained support. It was one of the very few conferences at the time which discussed Afghanistan and hence was extremely received well in American academia. Olivier Roy, one of the great experts on Islam, had promised to come from Paris but at the last minute could not do so. It was hoped that a book summarizing the discussions would come out as a follow-up to the conference. I came back to India, after one semester's teaching, and Barnett Rubin agreed to edit the manuscript, but later due to a new appointment regretted his ability to complete the summary.

On the recommendation of some participants, my keynote address was sent to William Bundy who was then the editor of *Foreign Affairs*. I had known him in 1969-70 when I was at Harvard for a sabbatical fellowship and he was teaching at MIT. He invited me to discuss the theme in New York and was initially inclined to carry an article based on the address in the prestigious quarterly. However, later he confessed on advice that the subject was no longer of great interest and that my thinking was a little too far from the thinking of experts in the area. With the benefit of hindsight, it should perhaps not have been dismissed as lacking in contemporary relevance for the US. Had an article been published it might conceivably have evoked wider curiosity and pre-empted the West from turning totally indifferent to the continued strife in Afghanistan once the Soviet forces had left. Had active US interest in Afghanistan continued in the 1990s, and atleast the CIA contacts left over from the strong

---

[10] See Chapter 13.

presence in Pakistan during 1980s maintained, the surreptitious plans of Osama-bin-Laden and Al-Queda and the Talibans could have been thwarted in good time. (The interest of diplomacy and the CIA remained focused on Russia and Communism.) There was mention in my paper of the possible ascendancy of fundamentalism but obviously for the US then no interest continued in the danger from Afghanistan much less from Islamic fundamentalism.

There had been of course, a radical change in the world situation at the end of the 1980s. Eastern Europe was repudiating Soviet Control and Communism. The United States and Russia at long last were discovering that, with their balanced mutually assured destructive capacity, they had an overriding community of interest. Extrapolating from the principles of Non-alignment, I had anticipated this kind of denouement in a monograph written at the Centre for International Affairs at Harvard in 1970 under the title 'The Reluctant Coalition for Stability'. However, when it happened in the 1990s, it totally diverted political concern away from the Third World, except where economic interests were at stake. The beginning of the new anti-Americanism was drowned in the earlier notion that religion was only an enemy of Socialism! If some little objective curiosity had persisted—dare one speculate wishfully—9/11 might have been averted.

Some lessons drawn out in the conference paper, remain valid to this day. In the twentieth century, the capacity of nationalist guerrilla defiance as exemplified in Vietnam—and in Afghanistan by the Mujahidin—could match overwhelming military power atleast in ground combat. Secondly modernization and socio-economic change of traditional societies can be shaped best only domestically. Even in 1989 I had argued that a stable solution could emerge from a Loya Jirgah presided over by ex-king, Zahir Shah who had remained above the factional fray, but the Jirga should, I argued, exclude all foreigners. The framework proposed envisaged a belt of surrounding neighbours, all with Islamic populations, who could collectively guarantee the neutrality and security from foreign interventions in Afghanistan and by-pass the vetoes in the United Nations. Later at a bigger meet of the Non-aligned, five or seven countries could be selected to help in peacekeeping and the holding of elections. The recommended step-by-step solutions might have worked—and the rise of Al-Queda and Talibans pre-empted—if only the United States and the West had not turned away in callous indifference with regard to the ongoing crisis in Afghanistan.

After Najibullah was overthrown in 1992 Rabbani became the President and right up to 2001 his nominees represented Afghanistan in the UN. However, the bitter ethnic fratricidal blood-letting between different tribal groups continued: Hekmatyar (with Pushtun backing), Dostum (with Tajik support) and Masud (with Uzbek and Hazara support) manoeuvered and fought instead of uniting to bring stability to the troubled country. It was in this confused situation that Pakistan using the ISI started the recruitment, training and operationalizing of the Talibans from the madarsas for the 'conquest' of Afghanistan. Starting in Kandahar in 1992, they took Kabul in 1996, which was followed by terrible violence and destruction. In 1997 there were similar massacres in Mazar-e-Sharif. The Talibans were unable to complete the conquest largely because of the determined and skilful resistance of Masud. However, in the vast areas, which came under Taliban control with Pakistan's backing, obscurantist medieval policies allegedly based on the Sharia were imposed, denying education and all rights to women and forbidding all entertainment. Pakistan only abandoned backing this pernicious interpretation of Islam following 9/11 when the anti-terror crusade was launched and the US President declared that those not with the US will be presumed to be against the US. How effective is Musharraf in his change of policy towards the Taliban, only the future will reveal.

For the present it is greatly to be welcomed that United States while deliberately keeping a low profile militarily is generously inclined economically. The US has affirmed that Afghanistan will not be abandoned, not just till the search of Al-Queda operations are over and the distribution of humanitarian aid is launched but until the political process of restoring normalcy is fully underway. However, one must be mentally prepared that factional violence and, ugly anti-foreigner incidents could recur which in turn could trigger populist pressures in the US demanding summary withdrawal as from Somalia and the international coalition itself could disintegrate. Even the establishment of minimal infrastructural and administrative restoration could get subverted by moral and mental fatigue.

It therefore needs to be emphasized that the threat of terror is far more insidious and longer lasting than even the old perceptions of Communism. The Communist expansionism was contained only partly by military defense (in Korea) but it was the 'Marshall' plan with its vision of sustained non-ulterior economic aid to rebuild the devastated nations, which restored Europe to stability and prosperity. The American taxpayer accepted that it would serve US interest to help in the reconstruction of Europe. Afghanistan is now in the stone age compared to Europe in 1947. The deeper origin of terror requires a similar imaginative approach beginning in Afghanistan but continuing beyond to other failing or stagnant states which are seething with discontent and might fuel the globalization of disaffection. A 'Marshall' plan for Afghanistan can only be led by the USA but it should be broad based carrying Europe including Russia, Japan and even some large Asian developing countries like China and India as contributory participants. Not competitive bilateralism but a common funnel, for integrated aid flows must be created. At all events corruption should be minimized. Only some such plan and structure would translate into Tony Blair's vision of an alliance of Compassion as the appropriate answer to the menace of international terror.

India–US–Pakistan

Now for the problems in the neighbourhood which has and will cast their shadow on the future of Afghanistan. Philosophically, historically and politically, United States and India have similar national ideologies but long ago I had argued that during the Cold War, US and India got divided by the very fact of being democracies as they came under pressure of conflicting populisms. Afghanistan has again highlighted the common approaches of USA and India but also their divergent priorities.[11] It was not surprising that with their established traditions of plurality and toleration, United States and India are both high on the hit list of Islamic terrorists. In fact India got earlier manifestations than the United Sates of cross-frontier militant violence but India's complaints against such Jehadi outrages were dismissed as residuary problems of decolonization and not symptomatic of a non-democratic political method of agitation where religion was being abused to destabilize established civil governance.

Over the last four years, after decades of intermittent ups and downs in relations, India–US relations held hopes of steady multipurpose harmonized cooperation and then, after 9/11, they plummeted reviving old suspicions of discriminatory prejudice. As a side

[11] J.S. Mehta, *India & the U.S., United or Divided by their Democracies* (ed. S. Cohen), University of Illinois, 1984.

effect of Afghanistan, both these facets came to the surface. In 1999 the United States looked on Pakistan's military dictatorship and involvement with Taliban and linkage with Osama-bin-Laden with pointed disdain and President Clinton showed only nominal courtesy of a five-hour halt after a five-day stay in India. The United States categorically condemned the Kargil cross-frontier intrusions by Islamic Jehadis and the militant Pakistanis. Notwithstanding Pakistan disowning direct responsibility and attributing the intrusions to grassroot 'freedom-fighters' with the support of foreign volunteers who were veterans of the anti-Soviet Afghan conflict, President Clinton unambiguously called for a withdrawal of all intruders behind the Line of Control. The Agreement was accepted by the Pakistan Prime Minister Nawaz Sharif but it was enforced by the Pakistan army under the command of General Musharraf. India showed diplomatic maturity in not authorizing hot pursuit of the intruders and this brought overwhelming international admiration for Prime Minister Vajpayee.

However, after the attack on the World Trade Center, there was a striking and unprincipled reversal. In the judgement of United States Pakistan looked crucially more important for the operations against Osama-bin-Laden, Al-Queda and the Taliban. In its dire economic straits, the military government of Pakistan readily reversed its past commitment, and pledged full cooperation in the anti-terrorist crusade. India suffered a significant loss of importance in Washington. The tactical convergence of United States and Pakistan, however, cannot obscure the deep-down conflict between Pakistan's domestic ethos, which was a derivative of the two-nation theory and many years of political support for fundamentalism on the one hand and the ready condemnation under duress and financial inducements of the militant insurgents on the other. General Musharraf himself cannot be fully certain that his own broad constituency has wholeheartedly accepted this dramatic turn about. The Taliban which was conceived and sustained by Pakistan's ISI may or may not peacefully go home; they could regroup with raging vindictiveness for having been undeservedly let down by their one time mentor and commander. General Musharraf was, in fact, trying to ride two horses at the same time: on the one hand, looking West, he courageously denounced terror and the Taliban and on the other, looking East, he continued to connive, condone or at least refused to rein in (or was unable to do so) those who were going across the Line of Control in Kashmir and launching terror attacks in different parts of India in the name of Islam. Musharraf's dilemma was an unenviable one: it became more acute as he was unable to articulate it publicly without risk of being considered a renegade at home or suspected as a mercenary abroad. To understand him correctly one should remember Musharraf was a child in India when Pakistan was born; the mantle he now carries mirrors the unresolved national schizophrenia of re-affirming periodically the sanctity of the Sharia and nationhood based on Islam and the ambitions for modernization cherished by the professionals and the elite like him in the country.

Musharraf might have found it politically feasible to continue to straddle the two horses but he found himself suddenly over-stretched in political gymnastics by the 13/12 terrorist attack on the Indian Parliament. My own guess is that he was ignorant of it and had not authorized this acutely embarrassing attack on the Indian Parliament, but even so in response to India's accusatory evidence and the strong international suspicion at Pakistan's involvement, he faced a difficult problem in categorically disowning the outrage. The Government of India demanded the delegitimization of the named terrorist outfits which were operating openly from Pakistan and the extraditing of listed Indian nationals long wanted for serious crimes committed in India who were known to be living in the neighbouring country. International sympathy, though showing a understanding for Musharraf's political dilemma, reverted back, atleast to some extent, to India. Initially Pakistan implied the attackers were only Kashmiris and prevaricated by asking for an impartial international enquiry. There was definitive proof about the national identities of the terrorists who were, in fact, registered with the Interpol. (Incidentally in the attending features, the actions in Delhi were similar to one of 11 September but no one in Pakistan asked for an international enquiry to trace the perpetrators of the attack on the World Trade Center and the Pentagon.) With the possibility of losing the advantages gained from cooperation in the anti-terrorist measures, Musharraf finally yielded. He proscribed Lashker-e-Toiba and Jaish-e-Mohammed and ordered the arrest of some prominent leaders. Whether the many sympathizers will continue to be tolerated in their anti-Indian activities in Pakistan remains a question mark but the steps ordered were bold and unprecedented. The latitude for not being considered anti-Islamic is severely limited. One cannot help speculating at the possibility that Al-Queda or unreconciled elements in the Taliban might have planned the attack on the Indian Parliament to kill two birds with one sling shot: on the one hand demonstrating that India remains a primary target of the Jehadis and their capacity matches their zeal, and on the other, deliberately embarrassing Musharraf in his relations with the hated new benefactors. The claim of no prior knowledge even by the ISI amounted to an unconvincing confession of incompetence but, in my view, there was no falsehood on the part of the General himself.

It is perhaps just as well for General Musharraf that the attack on the Indian Parliament failed. Had the terrorists entered Parliament, war could scarcely have been averted. Vajpayee could like Churchill during the Battle of Britain in 1940, by his famed oratory in Hindi aroused the passion of patriotism and led public opinion in India. Even in the failure of the terrorist attack, India could not but react with anger but, in fact, the retaliatory steps have been diplomatic show of military muscle which is serious but not provocative. The verbal belligerence underlined the gravity but it was calibrated to be short of impetuosity. However, it might have brought home that Musharraf's own survival does not depend only on material largesse and arms support from the United States but also on decision-making in India in response to incidents of terror. New Delhi could very well negate US diplomacy in Pakistan by simply imitating what US did after 9/11 or Israel does habitually; military reprisal disregarding political and economic consequences but gratifying domestic public opinion. India does not possess comparable military superiority or immunity from brisk even suicidal retaliation disregarding future consequences.

The incident drives home that for India, the scenarios of danger are no longer hypothetical: they border on grim dilemmas for decision makers. Such provocations of terror might recur any time from motivated Islamic kamikazes who are sufficiently supplied not necessarily dependant on specific Pakistani government authorization and yet probably think they would not face categorical disavowal or political repudiation. What this crisis, like others in the past, show that India and Pakistan have a vested interest in correctly understanding the political realities of the other country; paradoxically both are hostage to the exercise of restraint from impetuous action or reaction of the other. Peace may hang on somebody blinking first and consequently ignition of war on the failure of one set of nerves. Considering the long history of subjective interpretations and layers of prestige, backing down under pressure will never be easy. It now has the hazard of crossing the nuclear threshold; neither country can be fully certain of preventing escalation, avoiding retaliation and be confident of managing the consequences. There is the possibility that one or the other or both might suffer nuclear castration from outside like Israel inflicted on Iraq. Even setting aside the uncertain scenarios of a subcontinental nuclear war, in any projection for an enlightened modernizing future, both these under-developed countries face horrible choices. It is certain that the optimum fulfilment only points to functional co-operation based on the economic logic of a shared monsoon, and all that it has signified over the millennia in common rivers and culture. The very fact that non-official trade is four times the official trade, is an indication of the complimentarily between the two countries. The rush to travel by the Samjhauta Express was another proof of the unbroken emotional linkages. It would be a mistake for India and Pakistan to try to imitate the Cold War where the victory came to the West by economic attrition of the Soviet Union. Between the two countries, India has more staying power, but both are poor and have limited war-making capacity or the ability to recover from a serious debilitative conflict. Since 1971 not surprisingly neither has wanted an official war but Pakistan decided that by waging or fuelling guerrilla insurgency, India could be softened and its hold on Kashmir eroded and slackened into surrender. Extrapolating from 9/11 and 13/12, the lesson is that non-official terror now invites official reaction. Governments have to respond to democratic public opinion and in democracies the margin is narrow; acts of terror are now deemed as acts of war and therefore, if the tea leaves are read correctly, non-official provocations cannot guarantee immunity from governmental reaction. This is the essence of the problem for Musharraf but the consequences of escalation are also the problem of Vajpayee.

The real long-term answer is what the present Prime Minster of India has reiterated many times—before the Lahore bus journey in 1999, the Agra Summit in 2001—and what ran through in thoughtful reflections of Jawaharlal Nehru since 1947 'We in India cannot and Pakistan cannot choose our respective geography'. The quiet lesson to be learnt from the long story of Afghanistan is that except in a burst of frenzied activity, the attention span of distant powers specially of military engagement towards this region (and most others) is narrow and cannot be depended upon to be lasting in time or space. India must show respect for Islamic ethos of Pakistan but, in turn, Pakistan must see that it has a vested interest in India not giving up its secularism. When the fallacy and fears of the Cold War

stand exposed, we in the subcontinent—Pakistan, India, Bangladesh, Nepal, Bhutan and Sri Lanka—must all recognize that we
cannot run away from where we are located or the differential
equations of size and strength. Unless it happens to coincide with the
temporary interest of an 'outsider', no one will provide an umbrella
against sudden political storms at our request. Prudence, therefore,
dictates that we appropriate much greater responsibility for our own
destiny and be much less dependent on rescue, security-wise or economically from elsewhere. In the final instance, we in the region are
all our brothers' keeper.

*India's Rhetorical Belligerence
coupled with Wise Restraint*

In this context, India must be engaged on the calculus and weigh
carefully its own capacity and the long-term consequences of its
responses. After the attack on our Parliament, so far (until the end of
December 2001 when this is being written) India has managed the
tight rope act of strong righteous diplomatic protest without inviting
loss of international sympathy. Indian leadership has expressed
outrage but controlled public opinion almost better than Bush could
do after 9/11. It seems to me that the government has been quietly
more sagacious compared to public opinion consensus and rejected
impetuous suggestions made by a few commentators. As a retaliatory
measure, for example, it was urged that India should repudiate the
Indus Treaty signed in 1960. It is true India controls the upper
reaches of five tributaries of the Indus which flow into Pakistan but
what the commentators overlook, is that India is a middle riparian
on the main Indus and the Brahmputra and that the tributaries from
Nepal provide almost half the flow of downstream Ganges. The huge
dams at Mangla on the Jhelum and Tarbela on the Indus, completed
with the funds committed under the Indus Treaty, are outside our
territorial jurisdiction and so the extensive West Punjab canal system
could not be adversely affected by repudiating obligations under the
treaty which assigns the water of the Indus, Jhelum and Chenab for
consumptive use only to Pakistan. (It seems to have been incidentally
overlooked that effective diversion of the huge flow of rivers can
take decades.) Any way what is sauce for the goose—the diversion
of waters flowing from the Indian Himalayas—can provide sauce
for the gander—where other countries are upper riparians to India.
The Indus Treaty took twelve years to negotiate and was eventually

signed by President Ayub and Prime Minister Nehru; and while it is true that from the Indian point of view, the benefits were not equitable, the treaty has nevertheless worked unimpaired through the two Indo–Pak wars. For India to volunteer giving legitimacy to upper riparian neighbours interfering arbitrarily or even mentioning the idea, suggests a nefarious intent which could provide arguments for the scenario of the first Water War of this century or the desertification of vast areas of northern India. Instead of consolidating sympathy against acts of terrorism, it would make India an international pariah.

Incidentally since independence, in my view, the most monumental diplomatic failure has been in not succeeding in reaching cooperative arrangements for benefit both to Nepal and to India in harnessing hydro-electric power from the rivers flowing down from Nepal where the estimated potential is between 80,000 and 1,50,000 megawatts. A very substantial surplus could be available to India even after giving full right of economic benefit to Nepal. The failure has accelerated the deforestation and impoverishment of Nepal and aggravated the silt flow and consequently the floods in Bihar and UP (and Bangladesh) and also forfeited the availability of renewable sources of energy of which we are in dire need for our national development. The reason for this failure, it may be recalled, is that in the 1950s when the first flood control projects on the Gandak and the Kosi were developed, at the planning stage, the extensive benefit to Bihar overlooked the incidental submergence of land in Nepal. It was not deliberate but it planted the seeds of suspicion amongst the Nepalase that India always kept only its own interest in mind and was least concerned about the repercussions the decisions or actions would have on its neighbours. And such a feeling persists even 45 years later. Until the Pancheshwar Agreement of 1996, none of the other economically viable projects have matured because of political hesitation. The lesson is that even while pursuing national interest in case of national emergencies, like a terrorist attack, or the lure of economic benefit, like flood control in Bihar, the prospect of long term gain from these can be permanently or semi-permanently vitiated.

Pacifying Kashmir remains our greatest problem but it is a challenge to our internal democratic governance. Without making the restoration of democracy as a precondition—something we have not done in countless cases—we must never abandon the vision, however distant, that optimizing our own destiny indubitably requires facilitating the rise of responsive, responsible and stable government in Pakistan. Effective retaliatory measures against terror attacks and even military operations must be calibrated in a way not to damage the prospect of a future rationalization which, one day Pakistan too, in its own interest, must come to cherish. Only an enlightened perspective, blended with measured firmness and sensitive diplomacy can create the climate and conditions for optimum political rewards. As Talleyrand advised even under grave provocations *Surtout, Messieurs, point de zele* (above all, gentlemen, not excessive zeal).

If one may dare raise one's sight above the current dangerous build-up along the frontier, it seems to me, there is now, as never before, an unspoken convergence of interest in India–US relations and for both in relations to Pakistan. India remains firmly committed for direct dialogue with Pakistan but India now, like Pakistan in the past, in practice is banking that 'beneficial bilateralism' can be lubricated and facilitated by helpful nudging from the US and other benign powers. India–Russia relationship is no more the bug bear for the United States as it used to be; nor would India want to re-assert that Russia is the 'only time-tested friend' of India. What is pertinent is that from the crucible of aroused tensions, US and India, for different reasons, may have stronger parallel interest to see responsible and sober elements in Pakistan distant themselves permanently from the past political hypnosis when they relied on the support of religious orthodoxy. Musharraf seems to realize that, fuelling religious militancy impeded Pakistan's own development and resulted in the country squandering the outside development aid (even more than in India). Osama-bin-Laden gave Pakistan an unexpected bonanza by reviving US interest in the country but Pakistan cannot bank that incidents of terror will always come forth to provide justification for such largesse. Next time—and there could be a next time—terror incidents against the US may originate in a different part of the world. Neither the US (plus the West) nor India alone can successfully help Pakistan to wrench itself free from the legacy of its misguided patronage of the Taliban. India's help may be important, if only negatively, by not rejoicinging, distracting or aggravating Pakistan's problems but it will require highly sophisticated diplomacy and statesmanship to project that this is in the self-interest of India and not a gracious concession of a bigger country.

It should perhaps be clear that only democratic India can be a reliable ally of the US's broader crusade towards plurality all over South and South-West Asia. At a time when India is seething with deep indigration and the demand for punitive retaliation for the attack on our Parliament is being urged, my suggestion of a shared goal with the US may come across only as a pipe dream, but if we have no North Star of an ultimate solution to steer by, India will also be condemned to decades of enfeebling improvizations against a rudderless and compassless Pakistan still fired by a revived Taliban philosophy. A destabilized or distraught Pakistan is neither in US nor in India's interest. When the dust settles in Kabul and around Afghanistan, I can conceive, realistically not in starry eyed optimism, of a scenario when the triangular relationship may become much stabler and the propensity of suspecting the 'other' pair of relations as engaged in diabolical conspiracy inviting the familiar exertions for a competitive balance may be laid to rest.

To make real progress in this direction, both India and US must, of course get over the hypnotic hold of domestic populist parochialism and concessions. They must be seen to be living by their professed ideology of democracy and objectivity. The US must be more active in promoting accommodation between Israel and Palestine and India should not appear hesitant if the governing coalition in Kabul seeks a rational relationship between Pakistan and Afghanistan. Without such policy adjustments neither the USA nor India will regain the non-ulterior friendship and unqualified respect of the Arabs and the Muslim world. In both cases, there is a further common interest in resisting or disapproving of excessively violent reactions to counter terrorism even in the face of provocations. The cycle of consequences can be controlled only by statesmanship and not by the man-in-the street, simply because he has a vote.

Harmonizing Approaches is the Pre-condition to the Resolution in Afghanistan

Leaving bilateral and trilateral relations indirectly connected to Afghanistan aside, let me focus to the prospects in the country itself. In the keynote paper delivered in Austin in 1989 I had stated that a lasting solution will only come about if it is followed or is combined with a rapprochement between India and Pakistan and both countries see a common stake in regional stability. What was achieved in the year 1978 when the crisis in Afghanistan first erupted was a small beginning of preserving friendliness by prophylactic diplomacy between India and Pakistan even when the threat perceptions were widely divergent. India sought to prevent the *déjà vu* situation of the 1950s when India and Pakistan got hooked into the strategic rivalry of the superpowers and the resultant arms race. By 1962 in India and 1965 in Pakistan both realized that the fear, the damage and the benefit were less than what had been glibly expected. That was, however, before superpower détente: now, as mentioned earlier, the era when godfathers could be called upon for protection is transparently over. (It was, in my view, a delusion even in those halcyon days of the Cold War.) We have learnt by experience that Big Brothers can try to mediate (Kosygin's role in Tashkent in 1966), frighten (USS *Enterprise* sent in 1971 during Bangladesh liberation) and placate in self-interest (USA and Pakistan 2001) but big powers only bestir themselves in direct involvement when their own interests are perceived as under threat.

India and Pakistan both had cultural and historical affinities with Afghanistan which were stronger than that of any non-regional country; 1980 onwards, alas both departed from the traditional respect and understanding owed to Afghanistan's personality. Pakistan has a permanent advantage of geographical contiguity and the ability to provide or deny the preferred access to the sea through Karachi. Further it has unique religious and ethnic linkages with the Pathans who straddle the Durand Line frontier. India also has some advantage. Before independence it was the traditional beat of small itinerant traders on bicycles and even after the creation of Pakistan, it was a bigger market for dry fruit than present Pakistan. India can more readily rise above antagonistic tribal and warlord loyalties and so the geographical detachment may well, in some respects, be a positive factor. As far as Muslim theological links are concerned, India is home to Deobandis (the rivals of Wahhabis), larger number of Sunnis, Sufi eclectics and other Islamic sects like Bohras and Ismailis but it is not identified with any one of them and has no problem like with Qadianis in Pakistan. India now has as good if not better relations with Iran. Though India cannot claim credit for having given succor to millions of Afghan refugees as did Pakistan (like what India did for the Bangladeshis in 1971), it has other assets, which Pakistan cannot match. It has greater industrial, medical, technical, educational, professional and reconstructional capacity; all of them with more relevant experience than from the West and which will be in dire demand in Afghanistan. If both India and Pakistan could act together, they could accelerate the clearing of millions of anti-personnel mines and defuse the new ones, including non-exploded bombs from three months of aerial operations by United States. As stated, next to starvation, these lurking hazards are the greatest humanitarian imperative in the country. While the Europeans, even supplemented by the UN and international teams, may only stay for a short time and cover more limited ground. India and Pakistan together can sustain mine sweeping operations for years. The Afghan man-in-the-street would forever feel grateful for such a benign joint service, which they know only too well has its own hazards.

Most important, the eventual long-term economic viability and progress of Afghanistan may hinge on the country earning millions in transit dues for oil and gas pipelines linking the producers in Central Asia to the international markets running through Afghanistan. Ahmed Rashid in his scholarly work has described how over the last decade, murky political and economic competition has been under way to explore agreements for the energy export from these immense reserves which are ripe for commercial exploitation. Rashid calls it the Great Game of the twenty-first century. The leading players so far have been multinational corporations like Unocal (American) and Bridas (Argentinean).[12] The tentative negotiations were complicated by the prevailing conflicts but the corporations had their international political linkages. The negotiations oscillated with ups and downs depending on the ascendancy or otherwise of the Talibans in Kabul. Whether such export potential materializes, and what alignment gets chosen, will finally depend on the resolution of the diverse tensions and whether, in the minds of the investing corporations regional stability is receding or visibly on the horizon. What cannot be denied is that the shortest and most economically viable alignment would be pipelines going southward having outlets both in Afghanistan and Pakistan with the terminal in India which would enable easy distribution to the big market in the country and permit supply beyond through the Indian ocean. (Hypothetically a gas pipeline could go offshore from Iran to India and thus avoid Pakistan but this would be more expensive and cut out both Central Asia and Afghanistan.) Politically the US will now have a little more interest in American private investment in Afghanistan than when Taliban was in control. The optimal advantage would however only come if India and Pakistan jointly approached Afghanistan (and/or

[12] Ahmed Rashid, *Taliban, Islamic Oil and New Great Game in Central Asia*, I.B. Taurus, London and New York, 2000.

Iran) to facilitate the laying of pipeline to a South Asia terminal. If on the issue of the transit of energy, India and Pakistan do not agree to hang together and decide to do so quickly, both will be frustrated separately and the oil companies may explore the longer alignment to Turkey or even to China. Will Pakistan and India ever see that beggaring the neighbour is not sufficient enough ground to sacrifice the enormous potential in national economic advantage to both and which would incidentally help in the resurrection of Afghanistan? This is a challenge to the enlightened perspective of all three countries as well as to the producer nations. As with river flows, short-term prejudice or impetuosity can be the enemy of long-term gain. Or to put it differently, the question is whether India and Pakistan have confidence in their own constructive diplomacy or are they resigned to immediate and recurring conflicts and to unending confrontation. If the saga of India–Pakistan rivalry and cross frontier terrorism is not discontinued and muted in the foreseeable future, if both continue to support rival ethnic factions in Afghanistan, indeed if their respective perspectives remain that of hedgehogs, there will be little chance of Afghanistan settling down to reconstruction and economic viability.

Beyond external harmonization, after 20 years of aggressive splintering, it is a formidable challenge to restore a consensus and will to Afghan unity and recreate, what at the best of times was feeble and tenuous, a national administrative infrastructure. Modern Afghanistan, it may be recalled, has had a tortuous history. It only became an independent Emirate in the eighteenth century when Ahmed Shah Durrani rebelled against the Saffavids of Iran. After resisting the Czarist advances and defeating the British in two wars, the unity was consolidated by Amir Abdul Rahman in the 1880s. He did so by bloody suppression of numerous revolts in what resembled ruthless 'ethnic cleansing' of the non-Pashtun tribes. This is recalled because even after the Afghan state came into existence, intra-tribal and warlord loyalties did not abate. It got revived bitterly in the 1990s after the Soviet withdrawal and the rise of the Taliban. The point is that except for short spurts, the vicious struggle for power between the different tribal factions has never given institution building a chance. Democracy has never had a long spell of trial. But national unity, common institutions must now be high on the national agenda. With lingering suspicions and in the rubble of destruction, purposeful headway will only have a fighting chance if Afghanistan gets peace, indigenous purposefulness, sagacity of non-ulterior advice, steady generosity and the luck not be prone to political accidents and misperceptions but above all the tribal factionalism is moderated.

During our freedom struggle Abdul Gaffar Khan was known as the frontier Gandhi. He and his brother Dr. Khan Sahib were the leaders of the Pathans. In fact the Pashtun community has been the backbone of Afghan nationalism. Alas in the last 21 years, India got alienated from the Pathans. The US also gave military support to the Northern Alliance as it was sworn to oppose the Taliban and so interested in unearthing Osama and fighting the Al-Queda, disarming and dispersing the Talibans: most of whom were from the Pathan tribes. The United States and India in backing the Northern Alliance and Pakistan being identified with the Pashtuns (who had provided most of the Talibans) is a complication in restoring national cohesion. Real stability will depend critically on the cooperation of all important tribes and the moderation of aggravated tribal hatreds. In other words, 'outsiders' must be careful, not to remain over-identified with any one particular tribe or warlord. India and the US, I feel, must re-establish links with the Pathans and Pakistan with the Northern Alliance.

Twenty years ago I had encapsulated that the tragedy of Afghanistan was the consequence of a quadrilateral of misperceptions by USSR, USA, India and Pakistan. At present there is a vast host of nations with benign interest and goodwill towards the rehabilitation of Afghanistan. Russia (erstwhile Soviet Union) is now sympathetically inclined with no selfish stakes in the country. Most other countries of Europe specially United Kingdom, and all neighbours (Uzbekistan, Tajikistan, Turkmenistan, Iran, Saudi Arabia, United Arab Emirates, Qatar, Muscat, the Muslim world generally and others) want to contribute to the resurrection of Afghanistan. However, success in reaching and sustaining stability in Afghanistan will principally hinge on another quartet similar but not identical to the earlier 'gang of four'. Figuratively the primary mover (guiding and controlling the others) has to be the governing coalition in Kabul (or its successor) but the next in importance is the steady commitment of United States with its immense resources. The other two in the quartet—Pakistan and India—have their own special importance by their intention and ability to help or alternatively to delay, distract and deny progress. All four are going to play from different scores, but hopefully speaking, they would be able to orchestrate into a harmonized quartet. It is my firm conviction that to make amends and correctives of the mistakes of the 1980s and 1990s, it is only this quartet in Kabul, Washington, New Delhi and Islamabad which could put fractured Afghanistan figuratively back on the wall or to change the metaphor on the path to regained horizons. Success hangs by very thin threads of sagacity woven with other strands into a rope and firmly holding together for some decades. If any one of these strands snaps, 9/11 will fail to turn anger into a mission in its first big trial.

India Betrayed itself in Afghanistan

Before the final word, let me articulate something of my own *bon mot*, distilled by observing and being involved in achievements and failures in a career from 1947 to 1980 during which, by happenstance, eight negotiating responsibilities were entrusted to me, more than any other colleague. I have long believed that as in the Catholic faith so in politics and even in the conduct of foreign policy, honest confession in retrospect, is not dereliction from patriotism but the ingredient of true professionalism. Afghanistan, in my view, was the most serious avoidable mistake in 54 years of the foreign policy of India. We have paid a heavy price for having deflected from principled diplomatic indignation at the invasion of a small country and so exposed ourselves, needlessly, as departing from all that India had stood for in its own long quest for independence. As it happened, it proved a grave mistake, even from the point of view of narrow national self-interest, as it led—and this was not hard to foresee—to the remilitarization of Pakistan. On Afghanistan India got out of step not just with the US under the Carter and Reagan administration (and so remained under the elder Bush and Clinton), but we alienated all the Muslim countries, the vast majority of the independent countries of different political hues and for the first time ever *all* our contiguous neighbours voted differently from India. We provided grist to the suspicions that by condoning or atleast not joining in the condemnation of Soviet intervention, we were seeking to confirm our own right to *droit de limitrophe*—that a bigger country had the *right* to violate a small country's sovereignty to safeguard its own security. This contributed to the confirmation of the suspicion of hegemonism and provided the rationale for Bangladesh's initiative for the constitution of SAARC with the scarcely concealed purpose of Zia-ul-Rahman that the unity of the six neighbours could balance the size, the military and economic strength of India with which all had a separate common border. All this was of course, unwarranted conjecture about India's intentions but professionalism demands nothing less than sensitive anticipation of sovereign misperceptions. The supreme irony was that by getting and staying out of step with the Afghan determination to independence, we forfeited the chance to facilitate the Soviet exit between 1986-9 when Gorbachev turned to India for rescue from the Afghan morass.

With China, we normalized relations 14 years after the war in 1962 and since then we have re-established functional relations with the country. Between 1978-96, we had a succession of able envoys in Kabul and Secretaries in Delhi but after the 1980 abstaining vote in the General Assembly, the chasm of psychological estrangement and the disappointment of the Afghan people with India went largely unnoticed or atleast effectively uncorrected. It could have been the failure of political analysis or of intelligence or vested interest in the tactical rationale in Non-alignment or simply the hypnosis of wishful secularism, but brimming with the confidence after the triumph against the Soviet Union, all Afghan factions got sharpened in their religious fanaticism. Osama-bin-Laden returned after a sojourn from Sudan only in 1996, but religious militancy was brewing even before he came back to Afghanistan. India continued to be looked upon as the old ally of the invading 'infidels'. This reinforced the 'Jehadi' determination to fuel insurgency in Kashmir, which finally took shape in a conspiracy between the foreign militants, the ISI and the Pakistan army and in 1999 these militants surprised us along the high peaks of the LOC in Kargil. There were many who were Afghan veterans of the Mujahidin struggling against the Soviets. I cannot help feeling that had we taken a different attitude towards Afghan fight for independence, there would not have been foreign militants; Arabs and non-Afghans in the intrusions against India. We cannot be certain how long it will take to regain the psychological and emotional trust of the Afghan people, notably of the Pashtuns. Like the involvement of Indian Peace Keeping Force (IPKF) in Sri Lanka, our betrayal of Afghanistan may remain embedded like a landmine in the national memory of the country.

No doubt the insurgency in the valley which erupted in 1989, was compounded by several mistakes in domestic policy-making in Delhi during the 1980s. Later it got the support of the ISI and by volunteers who had fought in Afghanistan against USSR. I cannot help speculating that, had we in January 1980 not abstained from a moral position on the Afghan struggle to keep its independence, and alienated the Islamic World it is conceivable that India would not have been on the hit list of Osama-bin-Laden, the Al-Queda and the foreign-born militants: I would risk asserting that we might not be facing the cross-border infiltration and the terror attacks today. There was no infiltration whatsoever–not even of Pakistanis–up to 1980, either under the regimes of Z.A. Bhutto or General Zia-ul-Haq. These papers will, I hope, show such serious consequences were foreseeable.

There are lessons to be distilled which remain valid for the future. Professionalism demands volunteering unsought advice based on the long view and not succumbing to prevailing myopic short-term political attitudes all too likely in the prescribed punctuations of a democracy. Under our Constitution permanent civil servants can of course be overruled by political decision-makers but the professionals have life long tenures and have a duty to give objective timely counsel even if it has not been asked. We should have had greater confidence in the principles of Non-alignment and in not making tactical or wishful politically motivated compromises as against the prevailing ideological doctrines and strategic perceptions of the 1980s of the cold warriors; today economics, technological development and social progress along with democracy are on the ascendant. These principles of Non-alignment stand not only vindicated but universalized in practice. We should have anticipated and not been taken aback by the end of the Cold War and not relied on the approach as if it was only for tactical advantage. The US betrayed itself by needless involvement in Vietnam; it seems to me, by our moral detachment, India betrayed itself in Afghanistan. We today suffer the wages of that unprincipled betrayal.

Conclusion

Afghanistan 1978-2001 has been one long March of Folly. Only somebody like Barbara Tuchman could do justice to the full story as all major participants, at one time or another, acted against their own self-interest when better alternatives were available. It has left Afghanistan devastated and pushed it back a 100 year or more. The local Afghan leaders were initially to blame in overlooking their own national personality by trying to graft foreign ideological orthodoxy in their own conservative milieu, but thereafter the succession of mistakes were compounded by outsiders. The United States must be regretting the protracted crusade of fighting the Soviet Union till the last Afghan. Anyway both superpowers had no idea whatsoever of the crusading zeal of the Jehadis whom they left behind in 1989. The Russians got a blow back when a decade later Jehadis, some from Afghanistan appeared in Chechnya. It is just conceivable that the Wahhabis from Saudi Arabia who joined the struggle against the Soviets got inspired by the success of the Shias under the leadership of the Ayatollah in Iran in 1979 in their struggle against the USA. Iran is now modernizing slowly but surely and it would seem faster than Saudi Arabia. Anyway it was these 'imported' militants mostly Saudis in Afghanistan who planned 9/11. The big powers certainly looked away when Pakistan embarked on its own variant of the Great Game in operationalizing the Talibans. The vaulting ambition of Pakistan was initially whetted with the near conquest of Afghanistan but the cumulative result was rampant narco-terrorism, the Kalashnikov culture, the virtual collapse of the economy of the country. After 9/11 the USA generously rescued Pakistan because of its help in the counter-terrorist war. The fact, however, remains that America originally brought and Pakistan scattered the dragon seeds of terror. Counting from the time when the Reagan administration adopted the policy of remilitarizing Pakistan (and the deliberate induction of selected Islamic fanatics into Afghanistan), the 9/11 attack came just about 21 years later. Terror had attained adulthood and the world must now rise to the challenge of smothering it.

As I have recalled, the Duke of Wellington as Prime Minster when told of the First Afghan War (1839-42) perceptively remarked, 'After our military success will begin our political problems'. For over three months, the US pinpointed and carpet-bombed Afghanistan to give military support to the Northern Alliance faction. It has helped to achieve a spectacular military triumph but this will leave behind bitterness, which will impede the quest for a stable peace and the resurrection of Afghanistan. It will be a much longer problem than finding and punishing Osama-bin-Laden. However, the terrorist attacks masterminded from the caves of Tora Bora must not be seen as an isolated episode but as part of the worldwide malaise of global political and social disaffection, which seethes with the complaint that the 'entitled' share from the world economic and technological progress is not being justly distributed. Terror has now bared its teeth and also its artificial dentures. In the end civilization's fight for plurality can only be won with civilization's values, not by tactical compromises with dictatorships and unprincipled brutality. To banish terror from international politics and make the world safe for democracy, diversity and social justice will demand a sustained material and moral commitment. As it happens, the US and India have special responsibilities and capacities but we too will have to remain 'steady on the course' and keep faith in the combination of diplomacy with firmness and ensure continued support of the broad spectrum of enlightened internationalism. Those who abetted in terror—and Pakistan falls in that category—must be diplomatically helped including by India in a spirit of self-interest, to be shepherded back to the faith in modern values of toleration but the crucial and courageous decisions can only be by respective domestic governance. Kashmir is certainly one such problem for India but it is only a distraction for Pakistan. Mahatma Gandhi has abiding relevance: the cycle of violence only ends when individuals and institutions are wholly pledged to peace and non-violence. It is a formidable challenge to bring back hope and homes to the Afghan people. Though the era of care free 'surfin' in Hawai, 'huntin' in the Rockies, and 'fishin' in the Atlantic, in the confidence of invulnerability has perhaps ended, we must not overlook that only the US can provide the lead, the ideology and the resources to win the long war against world terror.

Select Bibliography

Arnold, A., *Afghanistan: Soviet Invasion in Perspective*, Stanford, 1981.

Afghanistan: Seven years of Soviet Occupation, United States Department of State, December 1986.

Afghanistan Tragedy, Report of the British Refugee Council, 1985.

Mohammed Amen Wakman, *Afghanistan: Non-alignment and the Super Powers*, Radiant, 1885.

Bradsher, Henry, 'Soviet Afghanistan', Kennan Institute, Occasional Paper No. 153, Washington, DC, 1981.

Caroe, Sir Olaf Kirkpatrick, *The Pathans*, London, 1965.

Chakravarty, Suhash, *From Khyber to Oxus: A Study in Imperial Expansion*, New Delhi, 1976.

Chari, P.R. and Pervez Iqbal Cheema, *The Simla Agreement 1972: Its Wasted Promise*, Colombo, New Delhi: RCSS and Manohar, 2001.

Current Digest of the Soviet Press, Columbus, 1978, 1979, 1980.

Cordovez, Diego and Selig Harrison, *Out of Afghanistan*, Oxford, 1995.

Dixit, J.N., *Afghan Diary*, Konarak, 2000.

Dupree, Louis, *Afghanistan*, Princeton, 1980.

————, *American Universities Field Staff Reports*, 'Toward Representative Government in Afghanistan', Hanover, 1978; 'The Democratic Republic of Afghanistan', Hanover, 1979; 'Militant Islam and Traditional Warfare in Islamic South Asia', Hanover, 1980.

————, 'Militant Islam and Traditional Warfare in Islamic South Asia', No. 21, *AUFS*, 1980.

————, 'Red Flag Over the Hindu Kush', Part III: Rhetoric and Reforms or Promises, *AUFS*, Part IV: Foreign Policy and the Economy, No. 27, *AUFS*, 1980.

Ewans, Sir Martin, *Afghanistan: A Short History*, Curzon, 2001.

Fraser-Tytler, Sir William Kerr, *Afghanistan*, London, 1967

Gregorian, Vartan, *The Emergence of Modern Afghanistan*, Stanford, 1969.

Harrison, Selig, 'Dateline Afghanistan: Exit through Finland?', *Foreign Policy*, Winter 1980.

Hidden War: The Strength for Afghanistan, A Staff Report for the Committee on Foreign Relations, US Senate.

Kakkar, M. Hasan, *Government and Society in Afghanistan*, Austin, 1979.

Meissner, Boris, 'Soviet Foreign Policy and Afghanistan', *Aussenpolitik*, Vol. 30, No. 3.

Misra, K.P. (ed.), *Afghanistan in Crisis*, New Delhi, 1981.

Monks, Alfred I, 'The Soviet Intervention in Afghanistan', American Enterprise Institute, Washington, 1980.

Moinudin, Kamal, *Taliban*, Oxford, 1999.

Nayyar, Kuldeep, *Report on Afghanistan*, New Delhi, 1981.

Newell, Richard S., *The Politics of Afghanistan*, Ithaca, 1972.

Newell, Richard and Nancy Peabody, *The Struggle for Afghanistan*, Ithaca, 1981.

Rashid, Ahmed, *Taliban, Islamic Oil and New Great Game in Central Asia*, I.B. Taurus, London and New York, 2000.

Red Flag over Afghanistan, Hammond, Westview, 1984.

Shrivastava, Mahavir Prasad, *Soviet Intervention in Afghanistan*, New Delhi, 1980.

Simes, Dimitri K., 'The Death of Détente?', *International Security*, Summer 1980.

Truth About Afghanistan: Documents, Facts, Eyewitness Reports, Moscow, Novosti Press, 1980.